The World-Literary System and the Atlantic

The World-Literary System and the Atlantic grapples with key questions about how American studies, and the Atlantic region in general, engages with new considerations of literary comparativism, international literary space and the world-literary system.

The edited collection furthers these discussions by placing them into a relationship with the theory of combined and uneven development – a theory that has a long pedigree in Marxist sociology and political economy and that continues to stimulate debate across the social sciences – but whose implications for culture have received less attention. Drawing on the comparative modes, concepts and methods being developed in the "new" world-literary studies, the essays cover a diverse range of topics, such as the periodization of world literature, racism and the world-system, singular modernity, critical "irrealism," commodity frontiers, semi-peripherality and world-ecology.

The chapters in this book were originally published in the journal *Atlantic Studies*.

Sorcha Gunne is Researcher at the Centre for Gender Research, University of Oslo, Norway. Her current project investigates the intersection of world literature and social reproduction feminism. Previous books include *Space, Place and Gender Violence in South African Writing* (2015) and *Feminism, Literature and Rape Narratives* (2010).

Neil Lazarus is Professor Emeritus at the University of Warwick, UK, where he taught in the Department of English and Comparative Literary Studies for over 20 years. Before that he was Professor of English and Modern Culture and Media at Brown University, USA. A new monograph, *Into Our Labours: Work in World-Literary Perspective*, is forthcoming.

The World-Literary System and the Atlantic

Edited by
Sorcha Gunne and Neil Lazarus

LONDON AND NEW YORK

First published 2021
by Routledge
2 Park Square, Milton Park, Abingdon, Oxon OX14 4RN

and by Routledge
52 Vanderbilt Avenue, New York, NY 10017

Routledge is an imprint of the Taylor & Francis Group, an informa business

© 2021 Taylor & Francis

All rights reserved. No part of this book may be reprinted or reproduced or
utilised in any form or by any electronic, mechanical, or other means, now known or hereafter
invented, including photocopying and recording, or in any information storage or retrieval
system, without permission in writing from the publishers.

Trademark notice: Product or corporate names may be trademarks or registered trademarks, and
are used only for identification and explanation without intent to infringe.

British Library Cataloguing in Publication Data
A catalogue record for this book is available from the British Library

ISBN 13: 978-0-367-64349-2

Typeset in MyriadPro
by Newgen Publishing UK

Publisher's Note
The publisher accepts responsibility for any inconsistencies that may have arisen during the
conversion of this book from journal articles to book chapters, namely the inclusion of journal
terminology.

Disclaimer
Every effort has been made to contact copyright holders for their permission to reprint
material in this book. The publishers would be grateful to hear from any copyright holder
who is not here acknowledged and will undertake to rectify any errors or omissions in future
editions of this book.

Contents

Citation Information   vii
Notes on Contributors   ix

Introduction: The world-literary system and the Atlantic   1
Neil Lazarus and Sorcha Gunne

1   The world-literary system and the Atlantic: Combined and uneven
development – an interview with Stephen Shapiro   7
Neil Lazarus

2   Three early modern genres: A microhistorical approach to "world literature"   21
William Boelhower

3   Contesting slavery in the global market: John Brown's *Slave Life in Georgia*   38
Michael J. Drexler and Stephanie Scherer

4   On transnational analogy: Thinking race and caste with W. E. B. Du Bois and
Rabindranath Tagore   54
Yogita Goyal

5   "Time's carcase": Waste, labour, and finance capital in the Atlantic world-ecology   72
Michael Niblett

6   From the *Novela de la Caña* to Junot Díaz's "cake-eater": World-literature, the
world-food-system and the Dominican Republic   90
Kerstin Oloff

7   Water shocks: Neoliberal hydrofiction and the crisis of "cheap water"   108
Sharae Deckard

8 From fishery limits to limits to capital: Gendered appropriation and spectres
   of North Atlantic fishery collapse in *The Silver Darlings* and *Sylvanus Now*   126
   Michael Paye

9 Feminist politics and semiperipheral poetics: Eavan Boland and Aislinn Hunter   142
   Sorcha Gunne

   Index   158

Citation Information

The chapters in this book, except Chapter 8, were originally published in *Atlantic Studies*, volume 16, issue 1 (March 2019). Chapter 8 was originally published in *Atlantic Studies*, volume 15, issue 4 (2018). When citing this material, please use the original page numbering for each article, as follows:

Introduction
The world-literary system and the Atlantic
Neil Lazarus and Sorcha Gunne
Atlantic Studies, volume 16, issue 1 (March 2019), pp. 1–6

Chapter 1
The world-literary system and the Atlantic: Combined and uneven development – an interview with Stephen Shapiro
Neil Lazarus
Atlantic Studies, volume 16, issue 1 (March 2019), pp. 7–20

Chapter 2
Three early modern genres: A microhistorical approach to "world literature"
William Boelhower
Atlantic Studies, volume 16, issue 1 (March 2019), pp. 21–37

Chapter 3
Contesting slavery in the global market: John Brown's Slave Life in Georgia
Michael J. Drexler and Stephanie Scherer
Atlantic Studies, volume 16, issue 1 (March 2019), pp. 38–53

Chapter 4
On transnational analogy: Thinking race and caste with W. E. B. Du Bois and Rabindranath Tagore
Yogita Goyal
Atlantic Studies, volume 16, issue 1 (March 2019), pp. 54–71

Chapter 5

"Time's carcase": Waste, labour, and finance capital in the Atlantic world-ecology
Michael Niblett
Atlantic Studies, volume 16, issue 1 (March 2019), pp. 72–89

Chapter 6

From the Novela de la Caña *to Junot Díaz's "cake-eater": World-literature, the world-food-system and the Dominican Republic*
Kerstin Oloff
Atlantic Studies, volume 16, issue 1 (March 2019), pp. 90–107

Chapter 7

Water shocks: Neoliberal hydrofiction and the crisis of "cheap water"
Sharae Deckard
Atlantic Studies, volume 16, issue 1 (March 2019), pp. 108–125

Chapter 8

From fishery limits to limits to capital: Gendered appropriation and spectres of North Atlantic fishery collapse in The Silver Darlings *and* Sylvanus Now
Michael Paye
Atlantic Studies, volume 15, issue 4 (2018), pp. 523–538

Chapter 9

Feminist politics and semiperipheral poetics: Eavan Boland and Aislinn Hunter
Sorcha Gunne
Atlantic Studies, volume 16, issue 1 (March 2019), pp. 126–141

For any permission-related enquiries please visit:
www.tandfonline.com/page/help/permissions

Notes on Contributors

William Boelhower, Department of Comparative Literature, Louisiana State University, Baton Rouge, LA, USA.

Sharae Deckard, School of English, Drama and Film, University College Dublin, Ireland.

Michael J. Drexler, Department of English, Bucknell University, Lewisberg, PA, USA.

Yogita Goyal, Department of African American Studies and Department of English, University of California, Los Angeles, CA, USA.

Sorcha Gunne, Centre for Gender Research, University of Oslo, Norway.

Neil Lazarus, Department of English and Comparative Literary Studies, University of Warwick, Coventry, UK.

Michael Niblett, Department of English and Comparative Literary Studies, University of Warwick, Coventry, UK.

Kerstin Oloff, Department of Hispanic Studies, Durham University, UK.

Michael Paye, Department of English, College of Education for the Future, Beijing Normal University, Zhuhai, China.

Stephanie Scherer, Department of English, University of Pennsylvania, Philadelphia, PA, USA.

INTRODUCTION

The world-literary system and the Atlantic

Neil Lazarus and Sorcha Gunne

The wording of the "Call for Papers" for this collection of essays was taken directly from *Combined and Uneven Development*, a book which scholars at the Warwick Research Collective (WReC) published in 2015, and which proposed a new theory of "world-literature" as the literature of the (modern, capitalist) world-system. We called for a dialogue between some of the new considerations of literary comparativism, international literary space and world-literary systems that have emerged since the turn of the century and the older theory of combined an uneven development – a theory that has a long pedigree in sociology and political economy, and that continues to stimulate debate across the social sciences, but whose implications for culture have received less attention, even as what it highlights draws attention to a central arc or trajectory of modern or modernist production in literature and the other arts worldwide.

What we were then hoping to promote with this project was an explicit extension or application of some of the comparative modes and methods evident in the "new" world-literary studies (of which the WReC volume was one example) to the Americas. We called for submissions that would grapple with the sorts of issues to which we had gestured in our statement, "with a particular focus on the Atlantic region and Atlanticism." The specific agenda of our Call for Papers was to call attention to the latent contradiction between the ideas of "world-system" (or "world-literary studies") and "America" (or "American literary studies"). Conceptually, this contradiction between the nation-centredness of "American" studies and the global logic of "*world*-system" seems clear enough – it being understood that, among other things, "American" here is typically not (even) the continental or hemispheric concept that it ostensibly denotes, but rather an abstracting alternative for the "United States." But to put things in this way is insufficient, since it might seem to direct us to the ideological problem of *exceptionalism* rather than to the methodological question of *systematicity*. That exceptionalism is a deeply rooted problem in American Studies is true, of course. In *Culture in the Age of Three Worlds*, Michael Denning goes so far as to describe it as the field's constitutive gesture,

> in many ways the foundation of the discipline of American Studies; whether the answers are cast in terms of the American mind, the national character, American myths and symbols, or American culture, the founding question of the discipline [has been] "What is American?"[1]

But while a "de-exceptionalizing" of "America" – somewhat akin to the "unthinking" of Eurocentrism or the "provincializing" of Europe that many postcolonial theorists have called for – would undoubtedly represent a welcome theoretical development, it would not necessarily trigger the "epistemological break" between nation-centred and world-systemic thinking that we are proposing and attempting to promote.[2] After all, scholars passionately committed to anti- or counter-exceptionalist perspectives continue to work perfectly comfortably with the idea that what is identified by "world-system" might just be the global aggregate of all the nation-states – they continue to work, that is to say, with the idea that the "world" in "world-system" is merely the product of all of the nation-states that make it up. So that, for them, the way to pursue comparative studies is simply to put (more and more) comparators onto the table (or into the frame) in relation to "America." Consider the following, for instance (an example chosen almost randomly from literally thousands that might have been cited): it is the online "Department Overview" of the Comparative American Studies program at Oberlin College:

> Comparative American studies (CAS) examines the range and diversity of American experiences, identities and communities. From interdisciplinary perspectives, students study social, political, economic, and cultural processes within the United States as well as explore the role of the nation in a global context. By placing the United States in a transnational and comparative framework, the program invites students to consider the relationship of different communities to the nation-state, ranging from issues of colonialism and empire building to social justice movements.[3]

Impeccably progressive though it is, this overview quite clearly leaves the substantialist idea of the nation as the fundamental unit of sociological analysis intact, whereas world-system theory insists that "system" precedes and indeed altogether displaces "nation" as the conceptual ground of analysis. The point has been made repeatedly by Immanuel Wallerstein in his numerous espousals and defences of "world-system" *as an analytical perspective*:

> World-systems analysis mean[s] ... first of all the substitution of a unit of analysis called the "world-system" for the standard unit of analysis, which [is] ... the national state. On the whole, historians [have] ... been analysing national histories, economists national economies, political scientists national political structures, and sociologists national societies. World-systems analysis raise[s] ... a sceptical eyebrow, questioning whether any of these objects of study really exist ... , and in any case whether they [are] ... the most useful loci of analysis. Instead of national states as the object of study, they substitute ... "historical systems" which, it [is] ... argued, [have] ... existed up to now in only three variants: minisystems; and "world-systems" of two kinds – world economies and world-empires.[4]

To propose the concept of "world-system" is to call into question the methodological protocols of nation-centred scholarship. "Nation" and "world-system" are not on all fours with one another, to adapt the striking phrase that Fredric Jameson has used in describing the disconnect between the literary critical terms of "modernism" and "realism": "the two terms, whether considered to be concepts or categories, are drawn from two unrelated systems, and like those two well-known lines which, prolonged into infinity, never meet, they are incommensurable with each other," Jameson has written about realism and modernism.[5] So too with "nation" and "world-system": drawn from unrelated conceptual systems, incommensurable, opposed and mutually contradictory. One cannot get from "nation" to "world-system" additively or quantitatively. *Pace* Harsha Ram, what is at issue here is not a "question of scale."[6] It is a question, rather, of conceptuality, of problematics or ways of seeing. The world-system is not the nation writ large.

Ram writes:

> To posit the modern world as a singular system has the undoubted merit of acknowledging the structural connectedness of its operative inequalities, arising from the territorial partition of the globe by the imperial powers during the final decades of the nineteenth century and from its simultaneous unification in the wake of accelerating trade and new infrastructures of transport and communication.[7]

But he evidently misunderstands both the genealogy and the epistemological thrust of the category of "world-system." It is not that the world becomes progressively more "unified" or "connected," binding nations and countries and regions into ever larger units and associations and polities. The reality is the reverse of this: (world-) system comes first; the institutions through which its force is expressed – new institutions as well as older ones that predate its emergence: markets, states and the interstate system, households, classes and so on – are integrated, shaped and determined by it. And it is not that this supposed "unifying" happens in the nineteenth century. As Wallerstein makes clear,

> [t]he proponents of world-systems analysis ... have been talking about globalization since long before the word was invented – not, however, as something new but as something that has been basic to the modern world-system ever since it began in the sixteenth century.[8]

It is interesting that both the Oberlin overview and Ram use the term "transnational" in a mediatory way, as a means of moving from individual nation(s) to an idea of the global. It seems to us, however, that both usages represent attempts to go beyond "nation" while at the same time extending its logic rather than superseding or breaking with it. Certainly, they never touch on the idea of systematicity. Whether this is always the case with what has been called "the transnational turn" in (American) literary studies is open to debate. Such recent works as *Transnationalism and American Literature* (Boggs), *Global Matters: The Transnational Turn in Literary Studies* (Jay), *Race, American Literature and Transnational Modernisms* (Patterson) and *A Transnational Poetics* (Ramazami) are sensitive, imaginative and perceptive, but all four studies seem to lack the centrifugal energy that would have derived from a systemic rather than a merely "trans-national" perspective. In the Introduction to her *Cambridge Companion to Transnational American Literature*, Yogita Goyal – one of the contributors to this collection – fair-mindedly reprises both the various arguments that have been levelled against the idea of the "transnational" and the various defences that have been mounted of the concept over the course of the past couple of decades. "If the key motivation behind transnational study is to decenter the nation, does not the very notion of transnational American emerge as an oxymoron?" she asks, before providing her own pragmatic justification: "Why then a volume on transnational American literature ... ? For me, the urgency comes from the fact that critics of the transnational turn have not succeeded in outlining a satisfactory alternative."[9] This pragmatic formulation helps to bring the strategic intent of this collection of essays into relief: might it be the case that the comparative modes, methods and concepts being developed in the "new" world-literary studies (the ideas, mobilized in many of the essays here, of world-literary system or world republic of letters, for instance, of combined and uneven development, singular modernity, critical "irrealism," commodity frontiers, semi-peripherality, world-ecology, etc.) do finally provide the resources for that "satisfactory alternative" to nation-centric (or even transnational) literary enquiry that Goyal is looking for – the "better transnationalism" that she thinks might be possible?[10] Our hope is that the essays collected here will give some food for thought concerning these broad conceptual and methodological matters. The interview with Stephen Shapiro that begins this collection acts to frame key questions about how American Studies – and the Atlantic region in general – engages with these emergent debates in world-literary systems. In a wide-ranging discussion, Shapiro takes off from Denning's comments about "exceptionalism" in American Studies (cited above), but goes on to frame American Studies, post-1945, in world-system. William Boelhower's "Three Early Modern Genres: A Microhistorical Approach to 'World Literature'" demonstrates the openness of the periodization of world literature as it adopts a microhistorical approach to the formation of three inter-related genres of the first half of the sixteenth century – the travel collection, the naufra-gium and the utopia – to provide a perspective on an instance of world literature as it becomes entangled in a variety of geocultural scales representing the complexities of the modern world-system. Michael Niblett's contribution to the collection, "'Time's carcase': Waste, labour, and finance capital in the Atlantic World-ecology," compares two very different literary texts – Thomas Hardy's short-story "On the Western Circuit" (1891) and José Américo de Almeida's novel Trash (A Bagaceira, 1928) – in an exploration of the connections between the degradation of labour and the environment-making dynamics of commodity frontiers. The essays in the volume by Niblett, Kerstin Oloff, Sharae Deckard and Michael Paye all exemplify the turn to "world-ecology" in contemporary world-literary studies. Concerned with the ways in which capitalist modernization advances through the production, consolidation and exploitation of "commodity frontiers," a process involving very particular forms of territorialization and deterritorialization, these essays trace and theorize the aesthetic registration and encoding of differential times/spaces of world-systemic "development" (and "under-development"). Oloff's "From the Novela de la Caña to Junot Díaz's 'Cake-eater': World-literature, the world-food-system and the Dominican Republic" focuses on Dominican and Dominican-American literary aesthetics, reading these in the light of their registration and conceptualization of the rapid integration of the Dominican Republic into the world market through the sugar industry. Deckard's "Water shocks: Neoliberal hydrofiction and the crisis of 'cheap water'" examines world-literary representations of neoliberal hydroculture. Investigating how water functions as a thematic element in literary works from Latin America and China, it explores the critical thrusts and diagnostic capacities of contemporary "hydro-irrealism" and "hydrocli-fi" fiction. Paye's "From fishery limits to limits to capital: Gendered appropriation and spectres of North Atlantic fishery collapse in The Silver Darlings and Sylvanus Now" considers the North Atlantic "commodity frontier" by analyzing literary depictions of fisheries as an extractivist practice commensurate to silver mining and oil in two diverse novels from Scotland and Canada. In "Contesting Slavery in the Global Market: John Brown's Slave Life in Georgia," Michael J. Drexler and Stephanie Scherer explore how John Brown, author of Slave Life in Georgia, proffered a radical approach to ending slavery in the United States in step with Marxian economics. Despite his failure to execute his design, they argue, Brown remains an important voice committed to economic intervention rather than moral suasion. Yogita Goyal's essay "On Transnational Analogy: Thinking Race and Caste with W.E.B. Du Bois and Rabindranath Tagore" similarly attempts to reconfigure "American" debates in global terms, as a transnational conceptual enterprise. Goyal's juxtapositioning of Du Bois and Tagore recovers a submerged history of sustained dialogue between India and the United States over whether race and caste can be thought of as analogies. Finally, in "Feminist Politics and Semiperipheral Poetics: Eavan Boland and Aislinn Hunter," Sorcha Gunne puts world-systems and materialist feminist schools in conversation with work about the "Celtic Tiger" in an article that engages with critical conversations about capitalist modernity in Ireland, contending that it cannot be delinked from gender and sexual politics. The collection of essays overall is intended to contribute to the collective task of reimaging American Studies in transnational, hemispheric and global terms – a project that requires us, we believe, to grasp the actuality of the United States as a constituent (and core) formation in a wider, over-determining, world-system.

Notes

1. Denning, *Culture*, 175.
2. It is worthy of note that when we asked Stephen Shapiro, in the interview published here, to comment on "contemporary initiatives to 'unthink' exceptionalism in American Studies," he answered that he was not

   > entirely persuaded that the task is merely a matter of "unthinking" American exceptionalism, so much as the need to change material and institutional arrangements. It's easier, perhaps, to desire decolonial studies [...] than to have them concretely enacted. Today, for instance, there are very strong countervailing forces to the project of decementing American exceptionalism.

3. Oberlin College, online.
4. Wallerstein, *World-Systems Analysis*, 16.
5. Jameson, *Singular Modernity*, 124.
6. Ram, "Global Modernisms," 1372.
7. Ibid.
8. Wallerstein, *World-Systems Analysis*, x.
9. Goyal, *Transnational American Literature*, 1–2.
10. Ibid.

Disclosure statement

No potential conflict of interest was reported by the authors.

Bibliography

Boggs, Colleen Glenney. *Transnationalism and American Literature: Literary Translation 1773–1892*. New York: Routledge, 2009.

Denning, Michael. *Culture in the Age of Three Worlds*. London: Verso, 2004.

Goyal, Yogita, ed. *The Cambridge Companion to Transnational American Literature*. Cambridge: Cambridge University Press, 2017.

Jameson, Fredric. *A Singular Modernity: Essay on the Ontology of the Present*. London: Verso, 2002.

Jay, Paul. *Global Matters: The Transnational Turn in Literary Studies*. Ithaca, NY: Cornell University Press, 2010.

Oberlin College, Comparative American Studies. Accessed August 8, 2017. http://newoberlin.edu/arts-and-sciences/ departments/comparative_american/.

Patterson, Anita. *Race, American Literature and Transnational Modernisms*. Cambridge: Cambridge University Press, 2008.

Ram, Harsha. "The Scale of Global Modernisms: Imperial, National, Regional, Local." *PMLA* 131, no. 5 (2016): 1372–1385.

Ramazani, Jahan. *A Transnational Poetics*. Chicago, IL: University of Chicago Press, 2009.

Wallerstein, Immanuel. *World-Systems Analysis: An Introduction*. Durham, NC: Duke University Press, 2004.

The world-literary system and the Atlantic: Combined and uneven development – an interview with Stephen Shapiro

Neil Lazarus

Stephen Shapiro is Professor of English and Comparative Literature at The University of Warwick, UK. Before joining Warwick, he taught at Harvard University, the New School, and John Jay College for Criminal Justice (CUNY). He has also been a Fulbright scholar at the University of Saarland, Germany, a Royal Shakespeare Company/Capital Fellow in Creativity and Performance, and a visiting Professor and University of California Humanities Research Institute fellow at the University of California, Irvine. He has published widely, including The Wire: Race, Class, and Genre *(with Liam Kennedy, 2012)*, The Culture and Commerce of the Early American Novel: Reading the Atlantic World-System *(2007)*, How to Read Marx's Capital *(2008)*, How to Read Foucault's Discipline and Punish *(with Anne Schwan, 2000). He has also published a number of books with Philip Barnard including* Pentecostal Modernism: Lovecraft, Los Angeles, and World-systems Culture *(2017). Together with Neil Lazarus and the Warwick Research Collective, he co-wrote* Combined and Uneven Development: Towards a New Theory of World-Literature *(2015).*

Neil Lazarus (NL): In Culture in the Age of Three Worlds (2004), Michael Denning wrote that "The notion of American exceptionalism is in many ways the foundation of the discipline of American studies; whether the answers are cast in terms of the American mind, the national character, American myths and symbols, or American culture, the founding question of the discipline was "What is American?"" In Combined and Uneven Development, we in the Warwick Research Collective cited this statement in discussing what we called "the belated "worlding" of American literature." "Where US writing is concerned," we wrote, "the liabilities of nationalist exceptionalism are widely recognized today. But if the contemporary desire, as Lawrence Buell reminds us in his essay, "Ecoglobalist Affects," is to think ""against" or "beyond" nationness," critical practice has tended to lag behind this desire; for many of the "[d]iscourses that aspire self-consciously to transnational or global reach [...] end up recontained by nation-centered mentalities." The converse is also true: the search for larger frameworks often leads to a decisive underestimation of the roles played by nation-states in the trajectory of the world-system."[1] Could you comment on the success or failure of contemporary initiatives to "unthink" exceptionalism in American Studies?

Stephen Shapiro (SS): It's useful to begin with Denning's discussion of exceptionalism as the "problematic" around which the discipline of American Studies has been organized. But to respond to your question, it would be even more useful to look at his precursor work, especially *The Cultural Front* (1997). In this magisterial study of American left culture, largely in the 1930s, Denning argues that a set of cultural productions, narratives, and "styles" coalesced due to larger changes within the global political economy that brought three groups together: second generation ethnic immigrants along with North-ward bound African-Americans; Europeans fleeing the rise of Nazi, Fascist, and Falangist power; and a smaller set of somewhat privileged WASP (white, Anglo-Saxon Protestant) agents chafing at the American legacy of Puritanical cultural asphyxiation. This coalition brought together particular domestic concerns, such as those regarding Jim Crow racism, with international ones, like the defence of the Soviet Union. These different cam-paigns found expression within a national-popular form that celebrated American "popular democracy" as its *raison d'être*. In addition to this basic claim, Denning also attempts to reconsider the periodization of the Cultural Front and the ways in which its energies circulated and later became cemented within other formations.

The consolidation of American Studies in the US academy in the 1950s and 1960s (often in what were named "American Civilization" programmes – some of the earliest estab-lished programmes, centres and departments still go by this name!) can be seen as one of the legacies of the Cultural Front, bringing together many of its strengths and weak-nesses. In the field's self-historicization, it has become commonplace to argue that Amer-ican Studies is not defined by a particular methodology but by a shared commitment to an evidentiary body of texts and events that are known by an unexamined confirmation bias as "American" (meaning always the USA and, like the proverbial definition of pornography, recognized when seen without needing definition). This tactical incoherence came about as American Studies strove to be neither English Literary Studies (which was in fact already radically more selective than the word "English" might suggest, since it focused overwhel-mingly on writing from London, the Midlands and the south of England), nor Comparative Literature.

"Eng. Lit" was in the US a field dominated by right-wing perspectives that insisted on a constricted realm of themes and topics, thereby (and often quite deliberately) obstructing the enfranchisement of non-elite groups. A neat illustration here would be the duel between T. S. Eliot and Leo Marx over how best to interpret *Huckleberry Finn*. In 1950, Eliot insisted that Twain's novel was fundamentally about a transcendental encounter with the Mississippi River God: "it is the subjection of Man [to the River God] that gives to Man his dignity."[2] In his 1953 reply, Marx insisted that Twain's core theme was not fetishized Nature, but the impact of slavery as a phenomenon that denied dignity not only to Black but also ultimately to White Americans. Marx's riposte was meant to raise the flag for an American Studies dedicated to egalitarian concerns, even if it pitched towards a centrist liberalism.

Comparative Literature in the post-war US, on the other hand, might best be perceived in analogy with post-war Italian politics. Italian governments used to be mocked, in the half-century between 1945 and 1989, for how frequently they collapsed. This fragility was a direct effect of the intricacy of the machinations required to prevent the Italian Com-munist Party from entering into State power. Crazy and irrational governmental coalitions were repeatedly created with the sole purpose of excluding the Communists. So too, ana-logously, Comparative Literature arose in the US as a Cold War initiative to contain and isolate the work of scholars whose fluency in European and Slavic languages was regarded suspiciously as a means through which communist perspectives might be introduced to American undergraduates. It is not that Marxists did not exist in the post-war US academy; the point is that the architecture of Comparative Studies was constructed to keep them at bay.

So, in a sense, American exceptionalism emerged as a rhetoric deployed to create a space different from both Eng. Lit and Comp. Lit, a slogan that might best be understood as a resultant of complex accommodations with higher education institutions and with the energies of the Old and then New Left, where the price paid was often a jettisoning of alternative slogans of communist-spirited internationalism. Exceptionalist language was settled on by those seeking to differentiate the US from the European left and the European right alike; as Michael Paul Rogin has explained, it was often taken up as the price of admission into the American academy for non-WASP scholars.[3] If the 1950s and 1960s were still shaped by the legacy of the 1930s, in many ways, we today remain formed by the patterns of the Cold War.

This seemingly round-about way of beginning my answer is meant to suggest that any attempt to respond to American exceptionalism needs to begin with a many-sided review of how categories that today seem self-evidently insufficient and damaging have also been resilient because they arose as perceived progressive locations within the context of their historical constitution. Today we must insist on disassembling American exceptionalism, but we need also to recognize that we are in a position to do so not because we are any cleverer or more insightful than prior scholars. By no means! Foundations for the so-called "Atlantic Turn" were already laid by R. R. Palmer's *The Age of the Democratic Revolution* (1959–1964) and Jacques Leon Godechot's *France and the Atlantic Revolution of the Eighteenth Century* (1963, translated 1965), but these were never built upon because the institutional conditions for these works to receive their proper recognition were not present, given the still large commitment to the form of American Studies that arose under the Cold War. It is not entirely coincidental that Paul Gilroy's *The Black Atlantic* (1993) was able to appear from a leading American university press and to receive the acclaim that it did only *after* 1989, in the brief space of decongestion occasioned by the fall of the Berlin Wall and the collapse of the Soviet system.

One of the most fruitful approaches to American exceptionalism, I think, is a world-systems perspective, associated with Immanuel Wallerstein among others. This approach allows one to balance regional particularity within a larger framework of historical capitalism. The nation-state, in this view, is a necessary unit of analysis – not least due to its manifold of political, legal, and military outlines; but this unit makes sense only within a larger systemic ecology. Much as Marx began his study of capital with the unit of the commodity, the nation-state remains a material form of appearance and substantive effects that cannot be ignored or washed away with slogans. As Gramsci said, "[l]t is one thing *to be* particular, another thing to *preach* particularism. Herein lies the ambiguity of nationalism [...]. In other words, national is different from nationalist."[4]

The challenge for us is to be able to clarify how the nation-state is constructed, or granted a space of operation, by the constantly changing configurations of the capitalist world-system. In this, I am not entirely persuaded that the task is merely a matter of "unthinking" American exceptionalism, so much as the need to change material and institutional arrangements. It is easier, perhaps, to *desire* decolonial studies, for example, than to have them concretely enacted. Today, for instance, there are very strong countervailing forces to the project of decementing American exceptionalism. Three, in particular, strike me as noteworthy. Let me discuss these separately:

(1) First, we see the contemporary restructuring of the university system according to neoliberal predicates of privatization, financialization, and profit-generation. Heavy pressure is being brought to bear on academics today – especially those working within public universities – to undertake research that can be monetized and ploughed back as capital into the local and regional economies. The progressive, historically entrenched commitment to public higher education finds itself being weakened and compromised by the countervailing imperative to redirect research towards competitive regional and national uniqueness in the marketplace. The demand placed upon academics to ensure that their research has economic impact can envelop and limit otherwise emancipatory scholarship.

We also see this with the revaluation of the term "professionalism." In *Keywords* (1976), Raymond Williams illustrated how capitalism intervened at the level of a single word. He listed numerous examples of a keyword being recoded against its prior meaning so as to create a new common-sense rife with capitalist prerogatives. So the roots of "culture" in agricultural manual labour became lost as it was turned into a descriptor for the values of "high" culture, something usually, and effortlessly, possessed by class elites. The same can be said for "professionalism." It once stood, for instance with Weber, as a standard of market-resistant objectivity and requiring such an adherence to autonomous protocols that it could be seen as a secular calling, a "vocation." But this bureaucratic ideal of civil service is now turned against itself as doctoral programmes are pressured to "professionalize" their students, meaning now to instil the fear of a fetishized job market. To direct one's research in this way is fundamentally the reverse of professionalism as it was conceived in Humboldt's notion of a research university based on academic freedom.

Additionally, considerable pressure has been placed on university presses to become profit generating, as though the subsidization of research was somehow incompatible with the idea of a research university. I once read that 95 per cent of all Anglophone scholars work within US institutions. This factoid is possible only if we exclude situations, like in India, where media communication and the exchange of ideas are in English even while the language is not the first one for most of its locutors. Yet whatever the exact number, it has become clear that US university presses, as institutions of knowledge-production, have tended to become increasingly embedded within a kind of intellectual national protectionism. Because of the tightly self-referential nature of promotion and peer review within the academy, it has become difficult for US-based scholars to operate outside the large echo chamber that is the American conference and university-publishing complex and its self-reinforcing *doxa* of what is considered significant new research. By this I mean one can find the power of American exceptionalism even within the study of other national traditions, since in the US the former's logistic shapes what is published and disseminated within the latter. So the need is not simply to *translate more*, but to alter the structures of evaluation and dissemination that are today increasingly territorialized by neoliberal ideology. Many of our younger colleagues face a grim employment horizon that reflects the larger imbalances of social inequality in our time. If they often seem to adopt a self-promotional persona, this is not an individualized moral weakness, but the continued social force of the marketized university.

(2) Second, the deployment of new technology as a form of communication has reinforced national exceptionalism in the guise of pseudo-universalism. It is an axiom that every new means of communication technology allows for all the errors and prejudices of the past that were thought to have been safely superseded to return as if innocent

and fresh all over again. Let me give an example: One of the great achievements of early anti-imperialist, anti-capitalist Culture Studies was Dorfman and Mattelart's *How to Read Donald Duck* (1971), which exemplified a long-gestating critique of the "soft power" of American popular culture, in terms of which the international children of Coca-Cola had their realms of leisure and fantasy contoured to uphold a sense of self-evident American authority. All that prior work now seems to require reconstruction in a contemporary moment in which US graphic novels and their intercalation within its "prestige" television – to use one example – are taken as defining the standards of excellence. We are experiencing something of a golden age, to use the cliché, of both televisual production *and* critical commentary on television, but very little of it seems aware of the predeterminations of the American parameters within the chosen televisual narratives and responses to these works. It would be vastly simplifying to consider digitalized culture as leading in one direction only, but conversely it would also be an error not to perceive how the *new* excavates power differentials that were thought to be *residual* or *obsolete*, but were always only stored to be ready for use again. Sometimes, even the international can be turned against itself. Apple has usefully packaged itself through a fiercely Americo-centric public image, yet the roots of this image lie in the importation and fusion of minimalist Japanese design aesthetics (from Sony, primarily) and in the Maoist insistence on a homogenizing cultural revolution. It is not only in Beijing but also in Cupertino that official secrecy and the control of consumption by limiting choice and personalization ("hacking" or "detailing") have proved successful.

(3) Finally, "unthinking" American exceptionalism faces the challenge of a new cosmopolitanism with the advent of a certain form of world literature. We already know the difference between cosmopolitanism and internationalism. Cosmopolitanism is the notion that the consumption of cultural objects beyond one's national location is inherently emancipatory and egalitarian. In a simplified version, this is the idea that if we eat the world on expanded à la carte menus, then we are removing social inequality. Internationalism, in the Marxist idiom, means a different kind of social solidarity based on class alliances and the intersection of race, sex-gender, physical ability, and generational domination with a system of labour-exploitation. To paraphrase the *Theses on Feuerbach*, cosmopolitanism looks to the creation of a *civil society*, but internationalism seeks out a *social humanity*. A fair amount of the new world literature has not submitted itself to a self-critique wherein reading novels in translation can remain tied to aestheticist principles, which were often, *in the first instance*, built on nation-states' efforts to establish tariff-protective singularities within the free trade realms developed by the capitalism of the long nineteenth century. Furthermore, historians of photography now recognize the Cold War interests deployed in the Museum of Modern Art's *The Family of Man* (1955, curated by Edward Steichen) travelling exhibition. We must guard against a similar sort of anthology humanism, which buttresses the prestige of the core through a media capture of the periphery, from being renewed through the rubric of world literature.

NL: In our call for papers for this special issue, we advertised our special interest in the following topics: Modernisation/modernity/modernism; Combined and uneven development; Atlantic networks and systems; Atlanticism; Locating the Atlantic in the modern world-system; New modes and models of comparative literary studies; Connections between the Atlantic, Pacific and other oceans. Could you speak about some of the contemporary work that you think is most exciting in its contribution to American Studies in the light of these and related interests?

SS: The above are obstacles facing the moves to evade American exceptionalism. These challenges are many and they are powerful. Yet there are also some tremendously exciting developments relating to the themes of this issue. Four in particular strike me as especially pertinent. Although these strands are not isolated from one another, for the purposes of clarification, let me momentarily separate them out.

(1) We are seeing new inquiries into the reach of Atlantic slavery and the significance of the Haitian Revolution. The Haitian revolution has long been an instance of historical amnesia within American Studies. Thanks to recent work, the influence of Haiti's struggle for independence is being recognized and interwoven with accounts of the eighteenth and nineteenth century. To increasing perceptions of the fabric holding together all aspects of the Atlantic, we see the Haitian revolution as neither simply sequential nor supplemental to the French Revolution, but as a constitutive feature of developments within France from the start. For example, the Vendée revolt and the siege of Nantes cannot be easily disarticulated from that port's role as a chief slaving harbour for French interests, much like Bristol or Liverpool in England. In the wake of Susan Buck-Morss's *Hegel, Haiti, and Universal History* (2009), recent writing that captures the relocation of Haiti includes work by the contributors in collections like David Geggus and Norman Fiering's *The World of the Haitian Revolution* (2009) and Elizabeth Maddock Dillon and Michael Drexler's *The Haitian Revolution and the Early United States* (2016), as well as Manisha Sinha's *The Slave's Cause: A History of Abolition* (2016). A more Atlantic comprehensive viewpoint appears with Philip Kaisary's *The Haitian Revolution in the Literary Imagination* (2014).

(2) As American Studies begins to revise our understanding of the early American republic and national periods with reference to Haiti, it likewise begins to establish the sort of Atlantic perspective that Palmer and Godechot telegraphed long ago. Tied to this has been a tremendously improved horizon on the particular scope of Atlantic slavery. Two important aspects involve work on Northern slavery and Critical Prison Studies/Prison Abolitionism.

The first chips away long-standard exculpatory and self-aggrandizing narratives of Northern moral superiority as it explores the fundamental role of profits from the slave trade as they flow into the endowments and material architecture of older Northern universities. The elements of slavery have always been a known secret for Southern universities, but in works such as Craig Steven Wilder's *Ebony and Ivy* (2013), the same is being shown for the North. Here it is not simply a matter of indicating how dirty money was handed over to universities by men in clean business suits to finance American scholarship and so on, but to cast light on how the flesh trade also shaped the conditions of what was allowed to be presented in seminar rooms and lecture halls. To celebrate a more Haitian-aware Atlantic Studies means not simply giving testimony to Caribbean suffering and audacity, but to unravel the constituent role of Atlantic slavery in establishing the lifeworld of the Atlantic capitalist world-system, including its conditions of thought, social interaction and education.

The significance of binding the plantation complex to the intellectual foundations of the modern university so that we see the architecture of American intellectual life as *entirely* imbricated within the Atlantic slave trade also has a theoretical insight for historical materialism that helps explain the necessity of a world-systems perspective. One understanding of the nineteenth century has it as a period of relatively uniform transfer from capital's *formal* subsumption of older modes of production (mainly through the prolongation of the work-day) to a *real* subsumption involving the reorganization of work (mainly by increasing its intensity and productivity). But Marx does not actually limit or simply sequentialize his terms, for he mentions other kinds of capitalist subsumption, including *hybrid* subsumption, involving activity like merchant trade or usury that interlace core capitalist regions or activity with more peripheral ones. Today we might have reached peak patience with hybridity as a term, so it might be better to call it *mixed* subsumption. In any case, the expansion of our understanding of terminology that was incompletely fleshed out in *Capital* means that we can now better recognize the simultaneous co-existence of different valences or aspects of subsumption as a fundamental feature of capitalist accumulation. Instead of seeing these modes of inequality as sequential (i.e., as progressing from mixed to formal to real), we can understand them as necessarily meshed together so that activities in the core and the periphery are mutually constitutive. In other words, *combined and uneven development*. A world-systems approach prepares the way for a better theoretical basis for what has perhaps been conveyed in more descriptive or persuasive efforts: the foundational role of Atlantic slavery to the phase of large-scale industry. This is a point that Marx actually makes narratively in *Capital*, but does not sufficiently buttress in his conceptual framework.

If readers wonder what a world-systems approach *concretely* brings or enables, one answer may be that it helps unpack Marx's planned for but unwritten treatment of capital as it circulates within a global horizon. Marx is explicit on this need for a more expanded conceptual apparatus. When moving to consider the large circuit of capital as it flows around the world in the second volume of *Capital*, he says that a more complete analysis *"requires a different mode of investigation*. Up till now [that is in *Capital* Volume I], mere phrases have been taken as sufficient in this respect, although, when these are analysed more closely, *they contain nothing more than indefinite notions*, simply borrowed from the intertwining of metamorphoses that is common to all commodity circulation."[5] Here Marx's German is more suggestive than the standard English translation. While *Verschlingungen* is given to us as [the] "entwining," the word would be better parsed as the "tangle," "kink," or "convolution" of commodities. Since a synonym for convolution is "spiral," Marx seems to be using a descriptively rich term as a placeholder to follow his point that the reproduction of capital "is conditioned [or enabled] by modes of production lying outside its own stage of development."[6] Hence the tangle of combined and uneven development, the messy yoking together of different conditions of exploitation and domination, is not simply a static scene of capital, but is, in fact, what creates the contradictions of generating its overall historical process, the spiral of capitalist development.

Thus, tracking the flow of profits from the flesh trade through the endowments of older Northeastern universities, and the ways in which the Haitian Revolution's anti-systemic disruption had to be contained therein, will not only be determinative in reshaping the history of American ideas with regards to the institutional silences on reaping the rewards of slavery, but also contrapuntally to help make our notions *more definite* when considering the material social geography intertwining different lands and peoples under capital's aegis.

Linked to the work on slavery is that of critical prison abolition studies. While a great deal of prison abolitionism within American Studies is geared towards the particularities of the legacies of US slavery, there are useful links to extra-territorial matter, such as exploring how the War on Drugs that has so amplified the prison-industrial complex also involves a new Monroe Doctrine of American intervention into Central and South America population flows. To use a more traditional Marxist lexicon, the regiments of the army of surplus labour (floating, latent, and exceptional) today intertwine Border Studies and the production of domestic carcerality. For all the acclaim given to Ruth Gilmore's 2007 *Golden Gulag: Prisons, Surplus, Crisis, and Opposition in Globalizing California*, less attention has been given to "globalizing" in the subtitle and her use of David Harvey's spatial fix and Neil Smith's work on uneven development. Lisa Marie Cacho's *Social Death: Racialized Rightlessness and the Criminalization of the Unprotected* (2012) is also attentive to the interlacing of US domestic conditions with international ones. While it has only just been published, Andrés Reséndez's *The Other Slavery: The Uncovered Story of Indian Enslavement in America* (2016) may have great impact in overturning an older framework that depended on accidents of disease, rather than structured brutality, in order to interlink Native American Studies and African-American Studies.

(3) Work on environmental matters and energy-regimes has grounded American events and phases within larger transnational contexts and the global markets of Nature extraction. The phases of American transportation and movement as depending on particular energy resources are being explored not only in terms of petroculture, but with reference to earlier modes as well. *Moby Dick* is an Atlantic Studies text as much for its description of structural crises involving an energy regime of living animals in the moments before the onset of fossil fuel and consequent reshaping of sea transportation lanes as for its portrayal of the psychopathologies within nautical capitalism. Matthew Huber's *Lifeblood: Oil, Freedom, and the Forces of Capital* (2013) is excellent for petroculture as a structure of feeling, as is Ross Barrett and Daniel Worden's edited collection, *Oil Culture* (2015) and Stephanie Le Menager's *Living Oil* (2014). And Jason Moore's work, especially the recently published *Capitalism in the Web of Life* (2015), has become a major point of reference, at least for many Atlantic-oriented scholars in the UK and Ireland, such as Sharae Deckard, Mike Niblett, and Kerstin Oloff. We look forward to Moore's forthcoming monograph of historical studies, including work on Atlantic commodity frontiers.

(4) A third initiative, tied to the new environmentalism, involves studies of the circulation of particular commodities across borders. Sven Beckert's *Empire of Cotton* (2015) is one excellent example of the new commodity chain history, as is Gregory Cushman's *Guano and the Opening of the Pacific World* (2013). It might be worthwhile adding that the nascent field of Pacific Studies should be welcomed in Atlantic Studies, especially as the matter of the import and then policing of (Chinese) coolie labour is interlaced with the pulses of Atlantic slavery. Although its capaciousness means that it cannot be simply pigeonholed in one category Jürgen Osterhammel's *The Transformation of the World* (2014) is required reading, especially given its sustained conversation with world-systems assumptions.

(5) Lastly, let me mention the rise of criticism on the alternative life worlds depicted in speculative and para-natural (aka science fiction and fantasy) fiction and televisual narrative. Noteworthy here is work like the Gerry Canavan and Kim Stanley Robinson collection *Green Planets: Ecology and Science Fiction* (2014), Mark Bould and China Miéville's collection *Red Mars: Marxism and Science Fiction* (2009), and, of course Fredric Jameson's magisterial *Archaeologies of the Future* (2005), a work whose subtitle links to more recent collection, *An American Utopia* (2016). These concerns now often converge with some of the above with

studies on Afro-futurism, seen in more generally-directed surveys, such as Ytasha Womack's *Afro-futurism: The World of Black Sci-fi and Fantasy Culture* (2013). Simply said, these works and the critical commentary on them has become a vibrant field for a geopolitical criticism beyond the exceptionalist nation-state.

NL: Your own new book, Pentecostal Modernism: Lovecraft, Los Angeles, and World-Systems Culture, *co-written with Philip Barnard, has just been published (2017). Could you say something about the contribution that this book makes to the emergent theory of "world-systems culture"?*

SS: A frequent criticism of world-systems approaches has been its weak treatment of culture. That criticism is not entirely without foundation. In a 1990 discussion, Wallerstein insisted that "culture" was, like "politics" and "economics," a "non-subject, invented for us by nineteenth-century social science. The sooner we unthink this unholy trinity, the sooner we shall begin to construct a new historical social science that gets us out of the many cul-de-sacs in which we find ourselves. Emphasizing "culture" in order to counterbalance the emphases others have put on the "economy" or the "polity" does not at all solve the problem; it in fact just makes it worse. We must surmount the terminology altogether."[7] At roughly that same period, a 1989 conference brought Stuart Hall and Wallerstein together in Binghamton, an encounter edited for publication by Anthony King in 1991 as *Culture, Globalization and the World-System.* Wallerstein's contribution asked, "Can there be such a thing as World Culture?" His answer was that there could not be, insofar as one took the question as proposing the existence of a universalized, homogeneous, conflict-free realm – "world culture" without a hyphen. The encounter reads retrospectively as a missed opportunity, since neither Hall, Wallerstein, nor any of the other participants, seems to have taken up the possibility of a "world-culture" as the manifold and many-sided culture of the capitalist world-system. Indeed, Janet Wolff's summative statement at the end of the volume accurately bemoans the presentations as lacking in awareness about the matter of cultural representation;[8] she faults the facile usage by some participants of such "concepts as "West" and "Third World," "center" and "periphery," "metropolitan" and "local" cultures, as if the objects they described were coherent, identifiable entities," rather than dynamic social relations, each with their own internal tensions.[9]

In a certain sense, *Pentecostal Modernism,* as well as my earlier *The Culture and Commerce of the Early American Novel* (2008) responds to that failed conjunction between Raymond Williams's cultural materialism as it flowed through Birmingham School Cultural Studies and Wallerstein's World-Systems theory. *Pentecostal Modernism* seeks to forge a new toolkit of conceptual frameworks and terms to discuss world-culture (with a hyphen) to indicate the relationality of cultural production within a world-system that is both unifying and making unequal due to capitalist forces. We discuss the emergence of American Pentecostalism within urban settings in the first decade of the twentieth century, the weird fiction of Lovecraft, and the Protestant theology of Social Gospel through the perspective of Trotsky's concept of combined and uneven development. The study seeks to make four contributions to what we hope is a further collective work on world-culture.

(1) While we focus only on US evidentiary material, this is to insist on it as comprehensible *only* as a particularized aspect of a capitalist world-system, and neither *outside* nor

autonomous from it. American or English cultural productions *are part* of *world-culture* as much as those from Africa or Latin America. To paraphrase Wallerstein, we need to junk the older terminology that separates Anglophone work from that previously listed as "comparative" or "postcolonial." Instead we need to develop a set of studies of analogous registrations. There truly is no such thing as "world culture," in the sense of a transcendental aesthetic, but there is a "world-culture" of the modern world-system, which is, in Franco Moretti's words, one and unequal.[10] If Jameson reminds us to always historicize,[11] we want to add, always hyphenate!

(2) We want to make an argument about modernism as the cultural registration of the thresholds marking new class geographies resulting from the boom period between the Long Depression of 1873–1896 and the Great Depression of 1929–1940s. In so doing, we begin with Williams's comments in *Politics of Modernism* (1996) on the role of urban immigration and the fixed capital of telecommunications and transport to modernism in order to suggest that his arguments are best understood when integrated with a world-systems approach. In this, we seek silently to respond to Wolff's critique and move beyond the categories of core and periphery to chart modernism through a cartography of the semiperiphery, exemplified in our study by the cities of Topeka, Kansas, Houston, pre-Hollywood Los Angeles, and Rochester, New York. As I had argued already in *The Culture and Commerce of the Early American Novel*, the notion of the semiperiphery seems to me a more supple way of thinking through blockages caused by reified notions of the core and periphery, the West and the Rest. Though this claim did not make the final version, it might be useful here to telegraph the "death of the paradigm."

Thomas Kuhn influentially argued that when data that cannot be explained through existing frameworks accumulates, a creative destruction comes as a new explanatory framework is produced. We believe this notion of a homogeneous "paradigm" as a category of analysis remains beholden to bourgeois stagist historiography and its notion of clean slate. Within the *long spiral*, our preferred replacement for the *long wave*, of the world-system's expanded reproduction, analogous conditions reappear to reprocess what had seemed to be residual. For instance, perhaps the most efficacious way to approach the California ideology of Silicon Valley is through a similar moment at the end of the nineteenth century of cartels and monopolies. Google and Amazon as the revivified Standard Oil. Similarly, the so-called "gig" economy restages the piecework of sweatshops. To propose something of an awkward neologism, we rely on neither a paradigmatic nor a syntagmatic approach, but a *spiragmatic* one. An example of this for American Studies might be to reconsider the so-called "myth and symbol" school of literary criticism that sought to establish transhistorical and quasi-essential themes of American expression, usually through reference to US writing of the 1840s. This approach has been thoroughly discredited now but what if these critics' errors were ones of linear continuity? Rather than extrapolate the representations of the 1840s in order to insist on an untroubled lineage, perhaps they ought to recognize this constellation as interpolated at certain phases of the long spiral and that become recalled at later similar ones, like our own. If we were to replace "symbol" studies with that of "genre" then an analysis of the 1840s cultural production might cast better light on this period. The "myth and symbol" school was heavily criticized during the 1980s for making transhistorical and essentialist claims, but the fault might have been less with the school's reading of 1840s culture than with the difficulty experienced by critics at that point, at a time greatly out-of-sync with the conditions of the 1840s, in appreciating the analogous features of similar moments, such as obtain between the 1840s and the present day.

In like fashion, we reject paradigmatic manoeuvres by insisting on the need to re-read work by Trotsky or Williams, which seem obsolete to current fashions but remain necessary resources. Their utility might not have been as evident, though, in the recent past, but as the capitalist world-system seems to becoming more aligned with the conditions of their composition, this older work does not seem to us as belonging to a superseded (critical) paradigm.

(3) We combine literary fiction, social movements, and discursive monographs to suggest that world-literature is not a textualized end-game, but a pathway to the study of world-culture. The "worlding" approach has initially occurred unevenly within different disciplines, such as literature, music, theology, and sociology. Within literary studies, prose, and particularly the novel, has been the first port of call. This has led some erroneously to assume that a world-systems perspective is limited in its application or reach. By no means! To show the possible expansion of world-systems applications, we sought to intermingle social movements with commentary on fiction by a named author. We use the term "world-culture" to suggest that world-literature and world-music, and so on, are subsets within the overarching study of social labour-power in its lived, inscribed, and performed modes in relation to the capitalist long spiral and governmental arrays.

(4) Finally, we exhume Thomas Szasz's addition to conventional (Saussarian) semiotics in his discussion of protolanguage. Szasz argued that when exposed to conditions of social exclusion and marginalization, subjects tended to use a weakly symbolic form of speech, one that was more dependent on iconic and indexical features. He felt that this modality, called protolanguage, conveyed informative, affective, and promotive claims. We feel this captures the particular expressions in regions that are in-between the core and periphery, and hence call it *semiperipheral speech*. Highlighting the emergence of a particular form of social expression helps us constitute a particular *experience-system* (our preferred replacement for Williams's *structure of feeling*) that conveys the frustration of the petit bourgeoisie in times of ostensible wealth. In this, we contend that Affect Studies has left itself unable to respond to historical locations or political possibilities because it has left out two other features, the informative and the promotive. Our claim rests on an approach involving the study of capital's cultural manifolds that is dependent on neither the deep reading of hermeneutics, nor surface (Stephen Best and Sharon Marcus) or "postcritical" ones (Rita Felski). We believe this allows for a technique that can be applicable to macro forms, like genre, as well as micro ones, like word choice.

NL: How do you see the relation between world-systems and other approaches towards system, such as actor-network theory? What is the role of world-literature within the so-called Digital Humanities?

SS: I do not see network theory as easily compatible with world-system approaches. Network theory seems to be the child of Quesnay's *Tableau économique* and its dream of a self-contained circulation free from (class) contradiction or crisis. World-systems approaches are not haunted by the vision of a perfect system; instead they seek, like Marx, to comprehend the systematicity of a regime dedicated to expanding accumulation for accumulation's sake. World-systems approaches have explanations for why and how the circuits of capital alter shape due to crises in the falling rate of profit. Network theory finds it difficult to imagine historical transformation or have a functioning theory of the structuring of inequality.

The role of the computational turn is, on the other hand, more complex. There is no doubt that the forces of algorithmic governmentality and neoliberalism find the informatics of the everyday a useful instrument of domination and exploitation. On the other hand, let us consider what Marx's *Capital* would look like were it not for the information collected in the Blue Books. Or how the inputting of formerly dispersed information about the Atlantic slave trade has allowed for a new granularity and revitalization of the field.

Conversely, it is true that a kind of glottal shift is happening in talks one hears. Few use the word "canon," while many speak of their "archive." One hears less about the "text" and more about the "data." This turn may be due to current pressure even, or especially, among scholars to have a "curated self," a self that is not based on the depth-subjectivity of the nineteenth-century bourgeois, but on surrogate markers of what one chooses to "like" (in the social network sense) or cluster in study. We might call this a cultural form of bourgeois Foucauldianism, the devaluation of interiority as a means of marking consumer privilege. The deployment of mathematics might be read as a self-protective retreat from the risk of having a political orientation. The computational turn sometimes seems as if it functions to exculpate the speaker from declarations of (emancipatory) intent. Williams argued that we would always have selective traditions involving what was chosen to read and talk about, but that the statement of selection always helped constitute our values and social aspirations.

World-culture approaches are in their early days, though, as is the place of cultural computation. The exploration into the possibilities and shortcomings of both remain open to further collective work and discussion.

Notes

1. WReC, *Combined and Uneven*, 42.
2. Eliot, "Introduction," 23.
3. Rogin, "American Political Demonology," 272–300.
4. Gramsci, *Prison Notebooks*, Vol. II, 6.
5. Marx, *Capital: Volume 2*, 194 (emphasis added).
6. Ibid., 190.
7. Wallerstein, "Culture Is the World-System," 65.
8. Wolff, "The Global and the Specific," 166.
9. Ibid.
10. Moretti, "Conjectures on World Literature," 56.
11. Jameson, *The Political Unconscious*, 9.

Disclosure statement

No potential conflict of interest was reported by the author.

Bibliography

Barrett, Ross, and Daniel Worden. *Oil Culture*. Minneapolis: University of Minnesota Press, 2014.

Beckert, Sven. *Empire of Cotton: A Global History*. New York: Vintage, 2015.

Best, Stephen, and Sharon Marcus. "Surface Reading: An Introduction." *Representations* 108, no. 1 (Fall 2009): 1–21.

Bould, Mark, and China Miéville, eds. *Red Planets: Marxism and Science Fiction*. London: Pluto Press, 2009.

Buck-Morss, Susan. *Hegel, Haiti, and Universal History*. Pittsburgh, PA: Pittsburgh University Press, 2009.

Cacho, Lisa Marie. *Social Death: Racialized Rightlessness and the Criminalization of the Unprotected*. New York: New York University Press, 2012.

Canavan, Gerry, and Kim Stanley Robinson. *Green Planets: Ecology and Science Fiction*. Middletown, CT: Wesleyan University Press, 2014.

Cushman, Gregory. *Guano and the Opening of the Pacific World: A Global Ecological History*. Cambridge: Cambridge University Press, 2013.

Denning, Michael. *The Cultural Front: The Laboring of American Culture in the Twentieth Century*. New York: Verso, 1998.

Denning, Michael. *Culture in the Age of Three Worlds*. New York: Verso, 2004.

Dillon, Elizabeth Maddock, and Michael Drexler, eds. *The Haitian Revolution and the Early American United States*. Philadelphia: University of Pennsylvania Press, 2016.

Dorfman, Ariel, and Armand Mattelart. *How to Read Donald Duck: Imperialist Ideology in the Disney Comic [1971]*. Translated by David Kunzle. New York: International General, 1984.

Eliot, T. S. "An Introduction to *Huckleberry Finn*." In *Bloom's Major Literary Characters: Huck Finn*, edited by Harold Bloom, 17–24. Philadelphia: Chelsea House, 2004. Originally published as "An Introduction to Huckleberry Finn." *The Adventures of Huckleberry Finn* (Mark Twain), vii–xvi. London: Cresset Press, 1950.

Felski, Rita. *The Limits of Critique*. Chicago: University of Chicago Press, 2015.

Geggus, David Patrick, and Norman Fiering, eds. *The World of the Haitian Revolution*. Bloomington: Indiana University Press, 2009.

Gilmore, Ruth Wilson. *Golden Gulag: Prisons, Surplus, and Opposition in Globalizing California*. Berkeley: University of California Press, 2007.

Gilroy, Paul. *The Black Atlantic: Modernity and Double Consciousness*. Cambridge, MA: Harvard University Press, 1993.

Godechot, Jacques. *France and the Atlantic Revolution of the Eighteenth Century, 1770–1799 (1963)*. Translated by Herbert H. Rowen. New York: Free Press, 1971.

Gramsci, Antonio. *Prison Notebooks*, Vol. 2. Edited and translated by Joseph A. Buttigieg. New York: Columbia University Press, 1996.

Huber, Matthew T. *Lifeblood: Oil, Freedom, and the Forces of Capital*. Minneapolis: University of Minnesota Press, 2013.

Jameson, Fredric. *An American Utopia: Dual Power and the Universal Army*. Edited by Slavoj Žižek. London: Verso, 2016.

Jameson, Fredric. *Archaeologies of the Future: The Desire Called Utopia and Other Science Fictions*. London: Verso, 2005.

Jameson, Fredric. *The Political Unconscious: Narrative as a Socially Symbolic Act*. Ithaca, NY: Cornell University Press, 1981.

Kaisary, Philip. *The Haitian Revolution in the Literary Imagination: Radical Horizons, Conservative Constraints*. Charlottesville: University of Virginia Press, 2014.

Kuhn, Thomas. *The Structure of Scientific Revolutions*. Chicago: University of Chicago Press, 1962.

LeMenager, Stephanie. *Living Oil: Petroleum Culture in the American Century*. Oxford: Oxford University Press, 2014.

Marx, Karl. *Capital: Volume 2*. Translated by David Fernbach. Harmondsworth: Penguin, 1978.

Marx, Leo. "Mr. Eliot, Mr. Trilling, and "Huckleberry Finn." *The American Scholar* 22, no. 4 (Autumn 1953): 423–440.

Moore, Jason W. *Capitalism in the Web of Life: Ecology and the Accumulation of Capital*. London: Verso, 2015.

Moretti, Franco. "Conjectures on World Literature." *New Left Review* 1 (January-February 2000): 54–68.

Osterhammel, Jürgen. *The Transformation of the World: A Global History of the Nineteenth Century*. Translated by Patrick Camiller. Princeton, NJ: Princeton University Press, 2014.

Palmer, R[obert]. R[oswell]. *The Age of the Democratic Revolution: A Political History of Europe and America 1760–1800*. Princeton, NJ: Princeton University Press, 2014. Originally published in two volumes: *The Age of the Democratic Revolution: The Challenge* (1959) and *The Age of the Democratic Revolution: The Struggle* (1964).

Reséndez, Andrés. *The Other Slavery: The Uncovered Story of Indian Enslavement in America*. Boston: Houghton Mifflin Harcourt, 2016.

Rogin, Michael Paul. *Ronald Reagan, the Movie: And Other Episodes in Political Demonology*. Berkeley: University of California Press, 1987.

Shapiro, Stephen. *The Culture and Commerce of the Early American Novel: Reading the Atlantic World-System*. University Park: Pennsylvania State University Press, 2008.

Shapiro, Stephen, and Philip Barnard. *Pentecostal Modernism: Lovecraft, Los Angeles and World-Systems Culture*. London: Bloomsbury, 2017.

Sinha, Manisha. *The Slave's Cause: A History of Abolition*. New Haven, CT: Yale University Press, 2016.

Steichen, Edward. *The Family of Man*. New York: Simon & Schuster, 1955.

Wallerstein, Immanuel. "Culture Is the World-System: A Reply to Boyne." In *Global Culture: Nationalism, Globalization and Modernity*, edited by Mike Featherstone, 63–66. London: Sage, 1990.

Wallerstein, Immanuel. "The National and the Universal: Can There Be Such a Thing as World Culture?" In *Culture, Globalization and the World-System: Contemporary Conditions for the Representation of Identity*, edited by Anthony D. King, 91–106. [rev. ed.]. Minneapolis: University of Minnesota Press, 1997.

Weber, Max. *From Max Weber: Essays in Sociology*. Edited and translated by H. H. Geerth and C. Wright Mills. Oxford: Oxford University Press, 1953.

Wilder, Craig Steven. *Ebony and Ivy: Race, Slavery and the Troubled History of America's Universities*. New York: Bloomsbury, 2013.

Williams, Raymond. *Keywords: A Vocabulary of Culture and Society*. New York: Oxford University Press, 1976.

Williams, Raymond. *The Politics of Modernism: Against the New Conformists*. Edited by Tony Pinkney. London: Verso, 1996.

Wolff, Janet. "The Global and the Specific: Reconciling Conflicting Theories of Culture." In *Culture, Globalization and the World-System: Contemporary Conditions for the Representation of Identity*, edited by Anthony D. King, rev. edn., 161–174. Minneapolis: University of Minnesota Press, 1997.

Womack, Ytasha L. *Afrofuturism: The World of Black Sci-fi and Fantasy Culture*. Chicago: Chicago Review Press, 2013.

WReC (Warwick Research Collective). *Combined and Uneven Development: Toward a New Theory of World-Literature*. Liverpool: Liverpool University Press, 2015.

Three early modern genres: A microhistorical approach to "world literature"

William Boelhower

ABSTRACT
This essay adopts a microhistorical approach to the formation of three interrelated genres of the first half of the sixteenth century in continental Europe (the travel collection, the naufragium, and the utopia) – roughly speaking, the period of first globalization when the city-state of Venice was not only a dominant power in the spice trade and the continent's major printing centre, but also an immediately involved witness to the shift from a Mediterranean-centred to an oceanic-centred economy. By focusing on a single site, I hope thereby to provide a privileged perspective on an instance of "world literature" as it becomes entangled in a variety of geocultural scales representing the complexities of the modern world-system.

Recent discussions about Comparative Literature's foray into "World Literature" have refined our sense of the challenges of cultural globalization by introducing such concepts as world-systems analysis, planetary consciousness, "world texts," geographical scale, translation and untranslatability, and the world republic of letters.[1] Rather than engage directly with this extremely rich field of conceptual distinctions, I prefer here to address the totality of the issues they raise in terms of a site-specific and historically delimited approach to the emergence of three interrelated, world-embracing genres during what the historian Geoffrey Gunn has called *First Globalization* (2003).[2] As Thomas Bender recently remarked, "local history can only be understood in the light of the history of the world."[3] Indeed, the text-types I will analyse – the travel collection, the naufragium, and the utopia – are all involved in a problematic relation of interdefining scales of European imperial expansion, so-called colonial peripheries, and local metropoles. The three literary formations emerged in historical concert, as direct responses to an explosive technoscientific, economic, and geopolitical period of Portuguese and Spanish exploration into *Mare Occidentalis*. As a result of these imperial probings into the Atlantic and Indian oceans, a major world-historical shift began to materialize in western European metropoles. While this essay adopts a small-scale focus by choosing Venice as its standpoint, the city's cultural range and interests were decidedly cosmopolitan. Indeed, no metropole was more sensitive to the Portuguese advances in Southeast Asia. As imperial histories would soon recount, a new oceanic order was dawning.

In order to avoid what Edward Said in 1993 called "the idealist historicism which fuelled the comparatist 'world literature' scheme" and at the same time recognize "the concretely imperial map of the same moment,"[4] I will focus on the privileged site of the island Republic of Venice during the relatively brief period of 1490–1560, when its own hegemony as the major trade emporium between northwestern Europe and the Orient came under challenge. Due to the Italian peninsular wars, the occupation of parts of Italy by the Spanish and the French, the gradual loss of its colonial bases to the Ottoman Turks along the eastern coast of the Adriatic and the Eastern Mediterranean, the Venetian Republic was forced to acknowledge its shrinking access to the land routes of the spice trade and the diminished status of its famed *Stato da Mar*. The critical moment arose when its ambassadors in Portugal and Spain sent urgent reports home about these two countries' recent maritime exploits leading to new routes to the Indian Ocean and the southeast Asian archipelago. As Donald Weinstein succinctly put it, all of a sudden "the Venetians were outflanked and undercut."[5]

When the Venetian Senate received the startling report sent by Pietro Pasqualigo, its ambassador at the court of Manuel I of Portugal, the significance of Cabral's voyage to Calicut hit hard. Girolamo Priuli, a powerful Venetian merchant and patrician, wrote of the occasion in his *Diarii*:

> Therefore, now that this new route has been found by Portugal this King [...] will bring all the spices to Lisbon and there is no doubt that the Hungarians, the Germans, the Flemish and the French, and all the people from across the mountains who once came to Venice to buy spices with their money will now turn to Lisbon. [...] [I]n this I clearly see the ruin of the city of Venice. (29–30)

Although Venice now had a major competitor in a volatile trade network which it had successfully managed for centuries, it continued to thrive economically for another 150 years. At the beginning of the sixteenth century, Venice was still hailed as "a world city" with a fluid and multi-ethnic population.[6] Having over 150,000 inhabitants, only Paris and Naples rivalled it in numbers on the continent.[7] The wondrous array of commodities available in the city's shops and warehouses between Rialto and Saint Mark's Square was also due to the presence of its immigrant populations. In the words of Joanne Ferraro, "They [the products] resulted from Venice's hosting and absorbing an array of peoples, including Germans, Slavs, Mamluks, Arabs, Greeks, Albanians, Jews, and a great variety of immigrants from mainland Italy."[8] Even today the city itself is visibly oriental in many of its architectural and urban features, beginning with its labyrinthine *calli* and walled gardens. As John Ruskin observed, "[T]he Venetians merit a special note as the only European people that sympathized fully with the great instinct of the oriental races."[9] Over centuries, the city's merchants developed an essentially pragmatic relation with the Muslims of Aleppo in Syria, Alexandria (Egypt), and the Ottoman capital of Istanbul. There were also Venetian merchant colonies at Corfu, on the islands of Crete and Cyprus, and along the Dalmatian coast. Their presence extended to trading colonies as far as the Black Sea. According to Stefano Carboni, the city itself functioned as a "liquid frontier" between two apparently antithetical worlds.[10] In truth, there was an ongoing collaboration and spirit of mutual respect among the competing commercial powers of these multiple worlds.

Venice's extensive trade network was matched by its cultural reach and renown. In particular, it proved to be an ideal location for Europe's nascent printing industry. As skilled

German, French, and Italian printers moved to the city in the second half of the fifteenth century to take advantage of its liberal policies, they found ideal material conditions: a ready supply of paper, translators, excellent Levantine scholars, linguists, and authors, as well as easy longterm credit.[11] The University of Padua – with its constant demand for scholarly editions in the fields of law, medicine, and philosophy – looked to Venice to satisfy its needs, just as the Serenissima relied on the University to prepare not only its ruling oligarchy but also its large ambassadorial and secretarial classes. The city's governing elites, many of them active in Humanist circles, were enthusiastic patrons of publishing initiatives that included both the Italian classics and contemporary authors in the vernacular and the Greek and Latin classics. In 1448, the Byzantine scholar-in-exile Cardinal Bessarion (1403–1472) donated his priceless collection of Greek manuscripts to the city, which was immediately housed in the Ducal palace. This considerable library became a treasure trove for the critical editions published by Aldus Manutius, the renowned Hellenist, scholar, and printer who came to Venice around 1480.[12]

In his study of the Venetian press, Alessandro Marzo Magno draws a flourishing picture of its activities that confirms the felicitous conjuncture between the city's trading networks and the widespread circulation of its Humanist texts. Venice's fame as a centre for the production of authoritative editions of classical works was due largely to the efforts of Aldus Manutius, whose Aldine Academy and scholarly printshop were famous throughout Europe and beyond. Over a 20-year period, Manutius published 132 books, 73 of which were classics (34 in Latin and 39 in Greek). He also wrote and published 12 scholastic manuals, all in Greek.[13] Manutius is also famous for having introduced italic script and the ottavo format (the popular paperback size) in book production as well as the title page and the end-of-text index. In the first years of the sixteenth century, Erasmus of Rotterdam came to Venice to meet Manutius and stayed and worked with him for a year. During that time, Aldus published Erasmus' translation of Euripides and his second collection of *Adagia*. Many other reputable scholars from abroad also collaborated with the printer. For example, Thomas Linacre, from England, worked with Aldus on a number of scholarly editions; and William Grocyn, the dean of English Humanists, also passed through Venice, after studying at the University of Padua.[14]

Translation (*translatio studii*) was a central collaborative activity among Venice's printers. The effort to create authoritative editions required scholars skilled in philology and the comparison of multiple manuscripts. Due to the presence of the Greek diaspora from what was once "Venetian" Crete, printers did not lack proofreaders and men of learning to assist them. According to Martin Davies, during the sixteenth century Venetian printers produced over 60 editions of the Greek classics, which were shipped to northern Europe by sea and to the markets of southern Germany by land.[15] From 1480 to 1560, Venice functioned as the major European point of diffusion for works in Greek, Latin, Hebrew, and Italian. *Translatio studii* was also a major activity for cartographers, geographers, and compilers of travel collections. To cite just one example, exotic place-names from the Venetian Marco Polo's popular account of his travels to China, *Milione* (1298), appeared on Martin Behaim's important globe of 1492 and on maps used by Columbus in his voyage to the Caribbean islands that same year.[16] Travel accounts from this period were structured by dense strings of place-names.[17] In Antonio Pigafetta's account of Magellan's circumnavigation of the globe, these amount to fascinating phonetic transcriptions based on the authority of local speakers. But more than just these linguistic primitives are at stake in intercivilizational encounters, where interpreters became key players of cultural transmission.

Paradoxically, in the early 1500s, at the outset of the economic and political shift from the Mediterranean Sea to the Atlantic Ocean, Venice stood as the major European centre for the production of news and information – in the form of printed maps, letters, treatises, and travel collections – dealing with the new sea routes, commercial bases, geographical discoveries, and colonization projects in the Indian Ocean, the southeast Asian archipelago, and the Americas. The city assumed this role with incomparable acumen and métier, but it did so essentially as an onlooker, by gathering data through its ambassadorial network, merchant colonies, and ubiquitous mariners. To its advantage, and unlike Portugal and Spain, it had no maritime secrets to maintain and no need to hide the flow of cartographic corrections coming from oceanic travel in the Atlantic, Indian, and Pacific oceans. Indeed, Venice's effusive publishing interests in the fields of cartography and geography served as a beacon light for the rest of Europe. As Thomas Bender remarks of this historical moment, "[W]e have not sufficiently recognized how profoundly important was the shift of the centre of the world from the Mediterranean Sea to the oceans."[18] There was, of course, no *one centre of the world*, and as for the Serenissima's merchants, governing elites, and scholars involved in monitoring the shift that pushed the city from the economic and political core of Eurasian globalization to what Immanuel Wallerstein would call the semi-periphery of the modern world-system, they could not help but recognize the opening of new worlds.[19]

Roughly, for a 50-year period Venice reigned as the European capital of Humanist printing, at the very moment that Portugal and Spain made their startling state-sponsored voyages into the Atlantic and Indian oceans. Thus, in 1498, the very year Vasco da Gama reached Calicut by rounding the Cape of Good Hope, Aldus Manutius dedicated his edition of the works of Politian to his friend Marin Sanudo with these words: "Most excellent Marin Sanudo, it often comes naturally to me to find myself full of admiration for our Venice, perhaps due to the almost infinite variety of its aspects, by which it seems to me not so much a city as an entire world."[20] Not the least part of this "entire world" was the city's efforts to duplicate European expansion on paper, thanks to printers' interest in charting the new maritime routes, place-names, encounters, and transactions. As a waning "core city" in the Eurasian world-system, Venice joined other Italian cities in publishing major editions of Ptolemy's *Cosmographia* (*Geography*) and *Almagestum* (*Almagest*).[21] Early modern geography and cartography can be dated to the recovery of these two influential classics. In the first, the Greek geographer set forth his method for transposing a representation of the Earth's ecumene on a flat surface, based on mathematical and astronomical principles. The result was a lucid abstract grid of longitude and latitude lines cast over a spherical surface.[22] This method led to "the crucial non-descriptive tradition for representing the world in the Renaissance," a way of seeing that is already evident in the travel accounts of Amerigo Vespucci, José de Acosta, Antonio Pigafetta, and countless others.[23]

Globus versus mundus

In his essay "The Age of the Modern World Picture," Martin Heidegger discussed the Ptolemaic effect on Renaissance geography and characterized the early modern period as one in which the world was reduced to an image and, thus, to a measurable object.[24] Following immediately upon European exploratory expeditions, cartographers took the lead in depicting the world as a fully conceived anthropocentric *figura*. Their highly prized globes and mathematically-structured world maps reflected the epoch's new Humanistic confidence. In his *Geography*, Ptolemy had defined his subject in a highly disenchanted way:

> Geography is a representation in picture of the whole known world together with the phenomena contained therein [...] The task of Geography is to survey the whole world in its just proportions [...] It is the great and exquisite accomplishment of mathematics to show all these things to the human intelligence.[25]

This anthropocentric turn is immediately evident in the paradoxical homage early modern geographers paid to Ptolemy as more and more travel accounts and sea voyages proved the Ptolemaic view of the world obsolete. In his important edition of Ptolemy published in Venice in 1548, Giacomo Gastaldi – who collaborated with Ramusio on his multivolume *Delle Navigationi et Viaggi* project – added a goodly number of *tabulae modernae* at the end of it, thus promoting a post-Ptolemaic and modern geography.[26] This supplementary practice, common to geographers across Europe, converted the closed text of Ptolemy's *Geography* into an openly expansive corpus. This same practice also characterized the travel collection genre, as it inevitably broke away from the restrictions of medieval geographical encyclopaedias.

Whether in terms of possible or real consciousness, the world in the three Humanist genres under examination – the travel collection, the naufragium, and the utopia – corresponds to the world of the *tabulae novissimae* of post-Ptolemaic geography, a world of mathematical points, lines and zones converted, respectively, into a heterogeneous surface of places, itineraries, and areas of colonial contact and conquest. In short, the globe as cartographic ideal and reflection of imperial possibilities was inherently contested by a surprising spectacle of non-European worlds, each with its own environment, people, customs, and beliefs. The economic and political tensions running through the burgeoning modern world-system can be identified as a tension between the dominant metaphors of *globus* and *mundus* – technoscientific globe and phenomenological world, if you will. All three genres are thoroughly embedded in Renaissance geography and are largely structured by the rhetorical figure of description (in Latin, *evidentia*), which, through generic exertion, they transform from a local *ductus* into an all-embracing textual practice. Deployed in semantically different ways and to different effect, the figure of description in all three genres functions as a worlding and concretionary figure, although this *mundus* application is continuously challenged by the imperial and globalizing aims that usually define (in the case of utopia, counter-define) their textual mission.

Early modern travel collections reach outward, cartographically and icnographically,[27] and would even seem dispersive but for the fact that they explicitly cling to a sustaining imperial centre. This, however, is not the case of the prototypical collections of Venice's Fracanzio da Montalboddo or Giovanni Giambattista Ramusio. As for the shipwreck formation, it registers an interruption, or a rent, in the otherwise continuous surface of the epic-minded itineraries of the travel collection; while the utopia, in its radical quest for a polity of right order and social justice, places itself outside the modern world-system. But it does so from the very heart of a realm of economic disparity, legal unfairness, and monarchical territorial ambitions. In its sixteenth-century beginnings, the travel collection tends to frame the naufragium and the utopia as the opposite extremes of a single semantic continuum that, respectively, checkmates and motivates modern intercivilizational travel. It is worth repeating that as a genre the travel compendium tended to be vocationally involved in upholding the prince's world map. If Europe's monarchs nurtured ambitions on a global scale, it was because their pilots and cartographers quite literally competed with each other to complete the Ptolemaic globus.

The stunning feat of circumnavigation was accomplished in 1522 by a meagre 18 survivors aboard the Spanish ship *Victoria*, after a fleet of five ships set out from Cadiz in 1519. As Venice's Ramusio declared in "Discorso Sopra Il Viaggio Fatto Dagli Spagnuoli Intorno al Mondo," his introductory note to the second volume of *Navigazioni e Viaggi*, "The voyage made by the Spanish around the world is one of the greatest and most wondrous things that our times have witnessed: and although we surpass the ancients in many things, this goes well beyond all the others so far discovered."[28] He then mentions the journey's diligent scribe, Antonio Pigafetta from nearby Vicenza, "who, having encircled the ball of the world, then described it in great detail."[29] This literary theme of circling "the ball of the world" deserves to be given its proper range of significance. Those who, like Pigafetta, Oviedo, Jacques Cartier, and Sebastian Cabot, appeared in early modern travel collections did for their time what nineteenth century realist writers did for theirs: they provided their publics with a new descriptive map of the contemporary world. Nineteenth-century historians learned to write social history from the novelists. Of course, travel collections like Montalboddo's and Ramusio's had a larger frame that was steeled by a new thought-projection, that of the globe as the new "world ground." As we have seen in Ramusio's admiration for the Spanish feat of circumnavigation, Pigafetta was considered a "globe-thinker."[30]

In his book *Globes*, Peter Sloterdijk offers a number of insights that are relevant to my discussion of the three literary genres, the latter all deeply involved in the imperial processes of the early sixteenth century and sharing the internal conditions of a persistent "globus – mundus" tension. As news of the circumnavigation of 1522 spread across Europe, a radically new thought-image began to appear on western world maps and globes reflecting the heady potential of new trade and maritime opportunities. Corresponding to Heidegger's notion of a new world picture, this thought-image featured the Earth as globus, which now occupied the very centre of Humanist knowledge formation. Suddenly, the world-as-globe seemed both politically and intellectually at-hand, and this new construct inevitably became "a power-image" in the hands of the powerful. Sloterdijk discusses this new spirit running through all strata of society as a form of "spheropoiesis" – according to which cartographers and kings began to view the world as a completed image. In effect, not only monarchs and mapmakers, but also merchants, priests, scholars, and pilots began to think in terms of "the world-whole," as if suddenly the new oceanic order made the most distant Edenic island fully accessible.[31] But Sloterdijk's rather benign-sounding "spheropoiesis" must also acknowledge the regularly violent scenarios of early modern European globalization. In short, Magellan's circumnavigation stands as a fitting emblem of the nascent capitalist world-system. While Sloterdijk handles the globe as if it were an absolute metaphor of the early modern period, Joyce Chaplin deals with it exclusively in terms of stories of circumnavigation. These stories remind us that such global thinking was accompanied by an undiluted dose of fear and terrestriality.[32]

THE WORLD-LITERARY SYSTEM AND THE ATLANTIC

While the post-Ptolemaic world view confidently took hold at the techno-scientific and political levels, the three literary genres involved in recording European colonial expansion revealed a different picture of what global inclusivity meant when faced with a corresponding intercivilizational mundus. The travel-collection, which tracked and promoted European expansion more than any other genre, undoubtedly shared the new "circumspective intelligence"[33] that presumed immediate disclosure of the spaces captured by the totalizing geometries of the world map, but it also simultaneously introduced a dense, often untranslatable, and inferential world based on description. The tendency to think "oneworldness" on the part of European colonial agents meant that their accompanying scribes were encouraged "to practice circumspection in all directions."[34] As is evident from Ramusio's prototypical, three-volume collection *Delle Navigationi et Viaggi* (1550–1559), circumspection meant not only a political programme of exploration and colonization, but also a more mundane practice of recording the infinite variety of peoples, customs, languages, cities, flora, fauna, climates, winds and ocean currents, not to mention the cornucopia of spices and commodities and their accompanying artisan and agricultural skills. Tucked away in the interstices of several of Montalboddo's and Ramusio's travel accounts are intense glimpses of distant utopias (most famously, parts of Vespucci's *Mundus Novus*) as well as the periphrastic difficulties of recounting shipwreck, mutiny, and other unforeseen rents in the imperial programme. What the travel collection genre does incomparably well is provide a sense of what it meant for various Portuguese, Spanish, Dutch, French, Italian, and English travellers to be-in-the-world in other core areas (Asia and India) of "their" modern world-system. By reading with and against the grain in these collections, differently situated readers – such as Thomas More, Erasmus, Francesco Sansovino, Ortensio Lando, Anton Francesco Doni, Tommaso Campanella, Francis Bacon, Vasco de Quiroga, Bartolomé de Las Casas – could find a counter-figure of the global programme and an explicit appreciation of "the value of contingency."[35]

Venice: publishing the literature of travel, naufragium, and utopia

Venice's most famous merchant-traveller, Marco Polo, lived and travelled in China for almost 20 years and wrote his highly detailed account while in prison in Genoa in 1298.[36] Edited and published by Ramusio from manuscripts that have since been lost, this popular narrative belongs to a tradition of Venetian travel unequalled by any other European country in the medieval and early modern period. Just 30 years after Marco Polo, Odorico da Pordenone visited China and on his deathbed dictated *De Rebus Incognitis* to a fellow friar. Full of appreciative anthropological observations and reflecting the encyclopaedic culture of his time, his travelog also appeared in the second volume of Ramusio's collection, thus providing, along with *Milione*, an important historical perspective on modern travel. The Polo and the Odorico narratives were well-known throughout the continent and continued to be read by merchants, mapmakers, and scholars well into the modern period. During the course of the sixteenth century, many newsworthy travel narratives in manuscript from Portugal, Spain, and France were printed for the first time in Venice and subsequently used by Ramusio and then other European compilers.[37] Another important account that made its way into *Delle Navigationi et Viaggi* was that of the Venetian Alvise Cadamosto, whose eye-witness narrative of the Portuguese exploration of the

Cape Verde islands in 1455–1456 was fundamental in launching that nation along the west coast of Africa. Mixed in with Portuguese, Spanish, French, and other travel accounts, these Italian and Venetian texts gave Ramusio's *Delle Navigationi et Viaggi* an aura of impartiality which subsequent, more ethnocentric collections in other languages lacked, driven as they were by pronounced national and imperial interests.[38]

Before focusing on Ramusio and his scholarly standpoint, I should briefly mention Fracanzio da Montalboddo's influential print compendium *I Paesi Novamente Ritrovati et Novo Mondo da Americo Vespucio Florentino Intitolato* (Vicenza, 1507; Venice, 1513), which included travel accounts by Cadamosto, Columbus, Cabral, and Vespucci and was quickly translated and reprinted in other European languages. Ramusio, too, borrowed from Montalboddo but went well beyond him in providing a veritable *summa* of maritime and geographical travels illuminating the European paradigm shift from the thalassic to the oceanic order.[39] Prestigious secretary to Venice's ruling Council of Ten, Ramusio was undoubtedly an organic intellectual in the Republic's bureaucratic elite, but he was also deeply involved in the city's Humanist circles, including the Academy of Aldus Manutius. Like other compilers of travel collections, Ramusio relied upon a considerable network of friends who shared his consuming interest in geography as a science. Altogether, as edition followed edition, the three volumes of his collection grew to include over 70 travel accounts, the first and most popular volume dealing with the spice worlds in and around the Indian Ocean, the caravan routes of the Middle East, and northern and western Africa. From the introductions and "Discorsi" that he added to the first volume of his collection, his Humanist-scientific focus is patently dominant. This is confirmed in the dedicatory note to his friend Girolamo Fracastoro, famous for his work on syphilis, where he declares that he aims to correct Ptolemy's observations on Africa and India as set forth in *Geography*.

A major contributor to the formation of sixteenth-century geographical culture, Ramusio chose texts that best reflected his Humanist interests and edited them according to the standards of Aldus Manutius.[40] He knew several languages and translated many of the texts in his collection. His detached interest in geography is evident in the fact that he published the first volume anonymously. For the excellent maps that appeared in his collection, particularly that of Africa, he collaborated with Giacomo Gastaldi, a major cartographer in Venice in this period. Given his important role in the Serenissima's political bureaucracy, Ramusio's interest in following other European countries' maritime exploits appropriately reflected the bystander position Venice itself assumed. As the city's premier Humanist geographer, we might describe his standpoint as a form of "situated universalism," shared by other European cosmopolitans. It led him to shun as much as possible the so-called heroic and triumphalist accounts of self-serving travellers, in favour of those reports that helped fill in the blank spaces of the latest European world map.[41]

What made the travel-collection genre so indispensable throughout the sixteenth century is its omnivorous, accumulative ambitions to recount the formation of a new world-system, both as an activist form of "spheropoietic" curiosity and as an entangled catalogue of microcosmic worlds filled with peoples, events, scenes, and commodities. These new worlds, captured in episodic narrative segments, rarely added up to a single storyline. Meant to be enjoyed as a totalizing sequence, individual accounts invariably revealed a capitalist culture of risk, in which investment-loss in ships, men, and goods (but rarely ideology) was a regular occurrence. Thus, at one end of the travel collection's semantic continuum, generic episodes of shipwreck (particularly popular in Portugal, where so many of its small population were connected with maritime activities) mark its progress at regular narrative intervals. There is enough panic on the periphery to make this genre more compelling than medieval romances. This brief overview can be exemplified by Pigafetta's account of the circumnavigation of the globe, which Ramusio considered the highlight of his collection. Undoubtedly, the secretary was present when Pigafetta enthralled the Venetian Senate with his oral account of this watershed event.

If we read Pigafetta's narrative for a sense of Spanish maritime ambitions in the Indian Ocean and southeast Asia, we immediately realize how superficial this country's globalizing claims were. In the end, Magellan's large-scale vision came at an extravagant cost in ships and men, although this was evidently balanced in 1522 by a chorus of hurrahs and a stunning new world map. Pigafetta's fascinating narrative nicely captures the *currendi libido* of Spain's imperial project. While *Viaggo Attorno al Mondo* is at times fervent with globalizing intentions, its dialectic of land and sea frequently gives way to a monody of existential panic and arrest. Above all, Pigafetta's literally globe-spanning narrative, always sensitive to longitude and latitude, line and point, is equally saturated with the kind of descriptive concretion capable of turning words into worlds and "there" into "here." As a metric of his worldliness, his famous word lists and catalogues of village names, chiefs, islands, commodities, and foods represent a Humanist curiosity that reinforces his scribal intentions "to gain some renown [...] [and] to discover the spicery in the islands of Malucca."[42] As for his now priceless word lists in various languages, they were recorded *in loco* and reflect his many contacts with the peoples encountered along the way: Tehuelche of Patagonia, Bislayan, and Malay (Pigafetta's list of over 140 words being "one of the oldest extant specimens" of this language[43]). Some of his lists provide both the names of villages and their chiefs, with colonial lucubrations such as, "All those villages rendered obedience to us and gave us food and tribute."[44] Of course, there are also the rituals of gift exchange and diplomatic attempts at alliances: "Then the captain-general [...] [said to the king] that he desired to be *casicasi* with him, that is to say, brother." *Casicasi* referred to a ceremony of blood brotherhood practiced among the Malays. The words mean "To be one and the same."[45]

The role Pigafetta plays in intercivilizational encounters is one we readily recognize from Columbus's letter of 1492, but there is another, less condescending dimension to his account that reflects an ethnographic and linguistic interest of some value. While we easily infer the play of force and mercantile circumspection in many of the Spaniards' encounters, it is also true at the phenomenological level of "mundus" that a series of apparently untranslatable place-names is worth as much as any imperial overreaching: "Proceeding on our way we passed amid the islands of Caioan, Laigoma, Sico, Giogi, and Caphi [...], Laboan, Tolimau, Titameti, Batjan [...], Latalata, Tabobi, Maga, and Batutiga."[46] Island hopping occasionally led to skirmishes and the unleashing of brutal Spanish violence. Here and elsewhere in Ramusio's *Delle Navigationi etViaggi* the topos of shipwreck is always just around the corner. As Pigafetta and the majority of Ramusio's authors are fully aware, one must be ready to risk all if they intend to travel across "the Ocean Sea, where furious winds and great storms are always reigning."[47]

Creation of the modern naufragium genre complements the dawning of the new oceanic order and is framed by a world view in which planet Earth is reduced to the status of a cartographic picture. This perspective conquest and its cultural-technical implications allowed for the aesthetic appreciation of shipwreck as evidence of a heroic age of European explorers. Its genre formation is due to the explosion of maritime voyages of exploration, discovery, and colonization in the early modern period. At first a local topos salted into the folds of travel collections like Ramusio's, the naufragium gradually gave way to complete narratives (Nuñez Cabeza de Vaca's *Naufragios y Comentarios*, 1555) and then to independent collections (see Book Fifty of Gonzalo Fernández de Oviedo's *General and Natural History of the Indies*, 1548, and Bernardo Gomes de Brito's *The Tragic History of the Sea 1559–1565*).[48]

In "Shipwreck," one of his *Colloquies* from 1518, Erasmus uses the genre to ridicule those who express false piety at sea. In a conversation between Adolph and Antony, we learn of a ship torn apart by an indescribably infernal storm and the distress of those on board, who pray to their favourite saints and pledge to change their lives if saved. As Antony says to Adolph, "O mad Folks that trust themselves to the sea."[49] The basic narrative structure of the shipwreck is quite simple: an opening frame of departure, the event of shipwreck, and the aftermath in which the survivors reach a safe harbour and take stock of their good fortune and losses. One of the challenges of the naufragium is credibility, so in the incipit the narrator usually takes pains to establish his credentials and specify the time and place of departure, the name of the captain and the ship, and his own role as eye-witness and survivor. For what he is about to recount defies truth. The fact that he survives also allows the narrator a certain aura of wisdom and this is often spent to good advantage, in terms of praising virtue and reconfirming a cosmos ruled by Providence. In the Prologue to Book Fifty of his *Historia General*, Oviedo writes, "In this last book I have decided to summarize some cases of misfortune, shipwreck, and things that happened at sea because those that have come to my attention are worthy of hearing and note, and also so men may know the many perils that accompany sea travel." He explicitly limits himself to "events in the seas from Spain to these Indies and parts farther west of here [Santo Domingo] since the year 1492." As for a moral, he provides two, one from Seneca ("We live in the tempest; let us die in port") and the other a common refrain ("If you want to know how to pray,/Learn to sail the ocean seas").[50]

In theory, the shipwreck would seem to be an obvious literary formation of the early modern period, but it is also a paradoxical one. On one hand, it seduces by trying to describe the event of absolute thrown-ness, when a metropolitan world view, full of optimism and economic promise, suddenly implodes. The entire globus of colonial circumspection now takes the form of an intensely narrow "here" and an ejaculatory "Oh!" Needless to say, many of the travel narratives Ramusio collected can be read as survivor accounts, from Columbus and Vespucci to Pigafetta and Cabot. Broken masts, leaking hulls, a baffled and mutinous crew, a scattering of cargo and plans, physical and mental suffering, loss and endless wild weather – these are all written into the very fabric of travel in the oceanic order and the modern world-system. With its anti-descriptive abysses, the naufragium records the countless rents in the fabric of European hegemonic planning; its expressive "Oh!" alludes to a certain emptiness at the heart of empire. Conversely, the naufragium also seeks to console, by celebrating the narrator-survivor's status as a new kind of middling hero for the modern age. Both a minimal and maximal sign, the shipwreck account remains an ominous formation in the literary system of sixteenth-century European culture. Too popular to be ignored, it makes such claims as

THE WORLD-LITERARY SYSTEM AND THE ATLANTIC

this by Cabeza de Vaca, "[S]uffice it to say that I have offered the account [*Castaways*] to Your Majesty as truth. And I entreat Your Majesty to receive it as a mark of service, for it is the only thing that a man who left those lands naked could bring out with him."[51] Having translated Cabeza de Vaca's account around 1555, Ramusio placed it in the third volume of his collection. Later, Samuel Purchas made a condensed version of it for his own travel compendium, *Purchas his Pilgrimes* (1625).[52]

The semantic continuum of Montalboddo's and Ramusio's travel collections can be defined by the two extremes of the naufragium and the utopia. The three genres work in close tandem, with and against each other as the case may be. As the sixteenth century unfolded and Venice survived the concerted attack of the League of Cambrai (1508), a mythic historiography celebrating the city's centuries-old Republican form of government began to take form. During this same period, the modern genre of utopia was launched with the publication in Louvain (1516) of Thomas More's *De Optimo Reipublicae Statu, Deque Nova Insula Utopia*, a virtual manifesto of cosmopolitan Humanism. We should recall that both Erasmus and More served as counsellors to their King and suffered the contradictions between the contemplative and active life. Based on their own experiences, Venice's Humanists and patrician elite had little doubt that good government could be engineered by wise rulers. A translation of More's book was first published in octavo format in Venice in 1548 and was the first vernacular translation of it. There followed a series of six quarto vernacular editions of Book II of *Utopia* (Venice 1561, 1566, 1567, 1578, 1583, 1607) in the closing selection of *Il Governo*, an anthology on real-world states by Francesco Sansovino. In his discussion of *Utopia* in the general preface, Sansovino alludes to his fellow Venetian Gasparo Contarini's political treatise *De Magistratibus et Republica Venetorum* (1543), in which Venice is projected as "the perfect state." Scholars have argued that Contarini met More in Bruges in 1521 and was influenced by him when he wrote his own political treatise.[53]

There were a number of popular utopian works published in Venice during the first half of the sixteenth century in the wake of More's "libellus aureus," but the germ for utopia as a genre resides more generally in modern maritime exploration and the Portuguese and Spanish "discoveries" of distant islands. In the light of European wars and the tyrannical agendas of its rulers, the so-called New World and the southeast Asian archipelago became staging grounds for projections of political renewal. As Peter Giles tells More by way of introducing Raphael Hythlodaeus, a Portuguese sailor who lived in Utopia for several years, "[T]here is no mortal alive today can tell you so much about unknown peoples and unexplored lands."[54] In Tommaso Campanella's utopia *La Città del Sole* (1602), a Genoese mariner, who sailed with Columbus and has travelled around the world, recounts that on the island of Taprobana (Sumatra or Ceylon) he discovered a city with perfect laws and customs. On March 28, 1521, Magellan's fleet met up with a number of islanders who, according to Pigafetta, spoke the Taprobana tongue. As for Francis Bacon's utopian city in *New Atlantis* (1621), Bensalem lies somewhere in the Pacific Ocean, west of Peru.[55]

There is a crucial fact about *Utopia*'s Raphael Hythlodaeus that leads indirectly to what may be the founding script of this early modern genre: "He was Vespucci's constant companion on the last three of his four voyages, accounts of which are now common reading everywhere."[56] In his letter to Lorenzo di Pierfrancesco de Medici of 1502, Vespucci recounts the marvels of his third voyage. In the region of the Antipodes, Vespucci's ship came to a land (today's northeast coast of Brazil) that "must be near the Earthly Paradise." The weather was temperate and the fruits and flowers were indescribably beautiful. As for the inhabitants:

> They have no law or religious faith, they live as nature dictates, they do not know of the immortality of the soul. They have no private property among them, for they share everything. They have no borders of kingdoms or province; neither have they a king or anyone they obey: each is his own master. They do not administer justice, which is not necessary for them, since greed does not prevail among them. (31)

The letters of Vespucci were printed by Montalboddo, Martin Waldseemüller, and Ramusio and quickly became one of the sixteenth century's best-sellers. The outstanding features of More's *Utopia*, which mirror in part the "Brazilian" Tupinamba "commonwealth," are the suppression of private property, life in common, the elimination of money and the market economy, and a radical simplification of the legal system. Utopia's denizens live in a radically egalitarian society, where family and father form the backbone of government. Many sixteenth-century utopias are patriarchal constructions, often with a compromising script of colonial conquest as their incipt. Such is the case with More's *Utopia*.

This literary and philosophical genre was nurtured into life by travel reports like Vespucci's *Mundus Novus* and Columbus's letter of 1493, *De Insulis Meridiani Atque Indici Maris Nuper Inventis*. They shared the same readership and the same concern for exploring other worlds, including the risks. But in the background were the great architectural treatises of Alberti (*De Re Aedificatoria*) and Filarete (*Sforzinda*).[57] In the hands of a Vasco de Quiroga, More's *Utopia* became a practical manual for planning pueblo-hospitals in Michoacán and Santa Fe de México in the early 1530s. One scholar even claims that Las Casas was inspired by More's *Utopia* in writing his "Memorial de Remedios para las Indias" (1516). The similarities are many. Later on, Kouru, in French Guiana, became the site of a cosmopolitan experiment to create a perfect colony, although the results were disastrous.[58]

While Venice's economic hegemony over trade in the eastern Mediterranean was challenged by the new Atlantic sea routes of the Portuguese, the Dutch and the English, the city's printers were busy publishing the very reports that recounted the paradigm shift from Europe's Mediterranean system to that of a new oceanic order. At the end of the same year that the *Victoria* circumnavigated the globe, Gasparo Contarini, Venice's ambassador to Spain, sent a dispatch from Valladolid to the Council of Ten telling of a secret meeting he had with the accomplished mariner Sebastiano Caboto, then in the service of the Spanish king. Evidently, Caboto was willing to switch his allegiance to the city, offering it exclusive information on a new sea route to as yet undiscovered western lands across the ocean. But after some discussion, the Republic's leaders decided to forgo Atlantic ambitions, fearing they would interfere with Portuguese and Spanish interests. Ramusio, "who [in the words of Richard Hakluyt] had taught the best Cosmographers of this age," died in 1559, but editions of the three volumes of *Delle Navigationi et Viaggi* continued to be published throughout the sixteenth and well into the seventeenth century.[59] When Hakluyt published his travel collection *Divers Voyages* in 1582, he relied heavily on Ramusio's authority as well as several of his texts, citing him on Caboto's claims to have discovered a northwestern route to Cathay. The bait was enough to get England to join the other European nations in the heady chase to build a capitalist world-system.

THE WORLD-LITERARY SYSTEM AND THE ATLANTIC

Hopefully, England would avoid "the troubles and warres, which dayly are used in Europe among the miserable Christian people." These last words were originally Ramusio's, but Hakluyt liked them so much that he decided to make them his own.[60] The semantic tug of war between shipwreck and utopia would continue in the pages of the nation's swelling travel collections. But by then the Venetian Republic had been eclipsed by other commercial and cultural centres like London and Amsterdam.

Notes

1. Palumbo-Liu, Tanoukhi, and Robbins, "Introduction," 1–23; Spivak, "World Systems & the Creole," 102–12; Moretti, "World-Systems Analysis, Evolutionary Theory, *Weltliteratur*," 67–77; Tanoukhi, "The Scale of World Literature," 78–98; Apter, *Against World Literature*, 1–114; Casanova, "Literature as a World," 71–90; Prendergast, "The World Republic of Letters," 1–25.
2. On case study methodology, see Passeron and Revel eds, *Penser par cas*; for a history of Eurasian globalization, see Gunn, *First Globalization*, 1–58.
3. Bender, "Foreword" to *The Atlantic in Global History 1500–2000*, xviii.
4. Said, *Culture and Imperialism*, 56.
5. Weinstein, *Ambassador from Venice*, 23.
6. See Ferraro, *Venice*, 29–50.
7. See Marzo Magno, *L'Alba dei Libri*, 9.
8. Ferraro, *Venice*, 11.
9. Ruskin, *The Stones of Venice*, 97, quoted in Deborah Howard, "Venezia città 'orientale,'" 79.
10. Stefano Carboni, "Istanti Visionari," 7.
11. Martin Davies notes that in the decade 1470–1480, there were 50 printers active in the city. This number almost doubled during the time of Aldus Manutius in the early 1500s (Davies 6).
12. See von der Heyden-Rynsch, *Aldo Manuzio*, 69–72; Brown, *The Venetian Printing Press*, 40–50.
13. Marzo Magno, *L'Alba Dei Libri*, 46.
14. Davies, *Aldus Manutius*, 22, 55–7.
15. Ibid., 6–13.
16. See Marina Montesano, *Marco Polo*.
17. With the rediscovery of Ptolemy's *Geographia*, a new, mathematical approach to geographical place was introduced. The *Geographia* was largely composed of a list of some 8000 places located according to longitude and latitude (see McLean, *The* Cosmographia *of Sebastian Münster*, 45–141).
18. Bender, "Foreword," xviii.
19. Wallerstein, *World-Systems Analysis*, 54–9.
20. Aldus Manutius quoted in von der Heyden-Rynsch, *Aldo Manuzio*, 161–2.
21. The first printed edition dates to 1475 in Vicenza; other printed versions appeared in Bologna (1477), Rome (1478), and elsewhere. By the end of the sixteenth century, Ptolemy's *Geography* had been printed 41 times, 18 of them in Italy. In 1548, Pietro Andrea Mattioli published a new translation in Venice and, in the same city, this was followed by Girolamo Ruscelli's many editions (1561, 1564, 1574, 1598). Petrus Lichtenstein published a Latin *Almagestum* in Venice in 1515 (Shalev, "Main Themes in the Study of Ptolemy's *Geography* in the Renaissance," 1–14).
22. See Cattaneo, "Map Projections and Perspective in the Renaissance," 51–80.
23. McLean, *The* Cosmographia *of Sebastian Münster*, 50.
24. Martin Heidegger, "The Age of the Modern World Picture," 115–54.
25. Ptolemy, *Geography*, quoted in McLean, *The* Cosmographia *of Sebastian Münster*, 49.
26. Weiss, "The Geography in Print: 1475–1530," 98; Tessicini, "Definitions of 'Cosmography' and 'Geography'," 46.
27. Icnography is the science of description. Travel turns description into a science of dynamic traces and figures, typical of the travel collection genre. The movement of global exploration via ocean-going ships and imperial missions is in a sense offset by the icnographic work of reportage.

28. Ramusio, "Discorso Sopra Il Viaggio Fatto Dagli Spagnuoli Intorno al Mondo," 826 (my translation).
29. Ibid.
30. See Sloterdijk, *Globes*, 18.
31. Ibid., 51, 46, 48.
32. Chaplin, *Round about the Earth*, 5–138.
33. Sloterdijk, *Globes*, 84.
34. Ibid., 71. In *Voyages in Print*, Mary Fuller discusses the instructions travellers were given in the early modern period, 2–17.
35. Palumbo-Liu, Robbins, and Tanoukhi, "Introduction," 11–12. The descriptive work of travel narratives inevitably records the contingencies of intercivilizational encounters.
36. Montesano, *Marco Polo*, 61–73.
37. See Ambrosini, *Paesi e Mari Ignoti*, 3–34.
38. The Venetian Nicolò de' Conti revived Polo's myth of "Catai" in his narrative about his travels around the Indian Ocean (1419–1444). Polo remained a major source of information on China in the early modern period, thanks to the Venetian cartographer Fra Mauro and Ramusio.
39. See Parks, "The Contents and Sources of Ramusio's Navigationi"; Donattini, "G. B. Ramusio e le sue *Navigazioni*," 55–100; Milanesi, "Giovanni Battista Ramusio," 75–101.
40. See Milanesi, "Giovanni Battista Ramusio," 75–83; on Ramusio's editing practices, see Romanini, *"Se fussero più ordinate,"* 19–58.
41. See Milanesi, "Giovanni Battista Ramusio," 81–2.
42. Pigafetta, *The First Voyage Around the World*, 4.
43. Ibid., 174 n.344.
44. Ibid., 56.
45. Ibid., 36, 154 n.155, 162 n. 233.
46. Ibid., 110. The strings of place-names evoke a multitude of worlds in which different peoples, with their unique customs and religious beliefs, live and trade in a world-economy of their own. Such onomastic strings capture the tension between a smooth-sailing imperial project and endless local worlds that beg to be understood anthropologically and geographically. This globus/mundus tension can be found in the histories of an António Galvão (Portuguese Captain in the Moluccas, 1536–1539) and a João de Barros (author of an official chronicle of Portuguese activities in Asia, 1563). For Ramusio's interest in de Barros, see Marcocci, *Indios, Cinesi, Falsari*, 69–72, 83–7.
47. Ibid., 5. On the naufragium, see Boelhower, "Christopher Columbus," 13–32 and Blumenberg, *Shipwreck with Spectator*; for primary collections: Oviedo y Valdés, *Misfortunes and Shipwrecks*; Nuñez Cabeza de Vaca, *Castaways* [original title *Naufragios y Comentarios*, 1555]; Gomes de Brito, *The Tragic History of the Sea 1559–1565*.
48. See Blackmore, *Manifest Perdition*.
49. Erasmus, "The Shipwreck," n.p.
50. Oviedo, *Misfortunes and Shipwrecks*, 1, 4.
51. Nuñez Cabeza de Vaca, *Castaways*, 4.
52. See Milanesi in Ramusio, *Navigazioni e Viaggi*, vol. VI, 373.
53. See Kristin Gjerpe, "The Italian *Utopia* of Lando, Doni and Sansovino," in *Thomas More's* Utopia *in Early Modern Europe*, 47–66.
54. More, *Utopia*, 43.
55. See Campanella, *Città del Sole*, 3; Bacon, *Nuova Atlantide/Nova Atlantis/New Atlantis*, 195–6.
56. More, *Utopia*, 45.
57. See Davis, *Utopia & the Ideal Society*, 63–83.
58. See Warren, O.F.M., *Vasco de Quiroga*; Baptiste, *Bartolome de Las Casas and Thomas More's* Utopia; Kupperman, *The Atlantic in World History*, 104–5.
59. See Mancall, *Hakluyt's Promise*, 89, 333, n.48.
60. Ibid., 98–9.

Disclosure statement

No potential conflict of interest was reported by the author.

Bibliography

Ambrosini, Federica. *Paesi e Mari Ignoti: America e Colonialismo Europeo Nella Cultura Veneta*. Venice: DeputazioneEditrice, 1982.

Apter, Emily. *Against World Literature: On the Politics of Untranslatability*. London: Verso, 2013.

Baptiste, Victor N. *Bartolomé de Las Casas and Thomas More's Utopia*. Culver City, CA: Labyrinthos, 1990.

Bender, Thomas. "Foreword." In *The Atlantic in Global History 1500–2000*, edited by Jorge Cañizares-Esguerra and Erik R. Seeman, xvii–xxi. Upper Saddle River, NJ: Pearson Prentice Hall, 2007.

Blackmore, Josiah. *Manifest Perdition: Shipwreck Narrative and the Disruption of Empire*. Minneapolis: University of Minnesota Press, 2002.

Blumenberg, Hans. *Shipwreck with Spectator: Paradigm of a Metaphor for Existence*. Translated by Stephen Rendall. Cambridge, MA: MIT Press, 1997.

Boelhower, William. "Christopher Columbus, Limina Americana, and Global Literary Culture." In *The American Columbiad: Discovering America, Inventing the United States*, edited by Mario Materassi and Maria Irene Ramalho de Sousa Santos, 13–32. Amsterdam: VU University Press, 1996.

Brown, Horatio Forbes. *The Venetian Printing Press: An Historical Study*. New York: G. P. Putnam's Sons and John C. Nimmo, 1891.

Carboni, Stefano. "'Istantivisionari': Venezia e l'Islam (828–1797)." In *Venezia e L'Islam 828–1797*, edited by Stefano Carboni, 3–27. Venice: Marsilio, 2007.

Casanova, Pascale. "Literature as a World." *New Left Review* 31 (January 2005): 71–90.

Cattaneo, Angelo. "Map Projections and Perspective in the Renaissance." In *Ptolemy's Geography in the Renaissance*, 51–80. London: Warburg Institute, 2011.

Chaplin, Joyce E. *Round about the Earth*. New York: Simon and Shuster, 2012.

Davies, Martin. *Aldus Manutius: Printer and Publisher of Renaissance Venice*. Tempe: Arizona Centre for Medieval and Renaissance Studies, 1999.

Davis, J. C. *Utopia & the Ideal Society: A Study of English Utopian Writing*. Cambridge: Cambridge University Press, 1983.

Donattini, Massimo. "G. B. Ramusio e le sue Navigazioni. Appunti per una Biografia." *Critica Storica* XVII, no. 1 (1980): 55–100.

Erasmus, Desiderius. "The Shipwreck." In *The Colloquies of Erasmus, Vol. I*. Translated by Nathan Bailey, edited by Rev. E. Johnson. London: Reeves and Turner, 1878. Accessed June 6, 2015. http://oll.libertyfund.org/title/549.

Ferraro, Joanne. *Venice: History of the Floating City*. New York: Cambridge University Press, 2012.

Fuller, Mary C. *Voyages in Print: English Travel to America 1570–1624*. New York: Cambridge University Press, 1995.

Gjerpe, Kristin. "The Italian Utopia of Lando, Doni and Sansovino: Paradox and Politics." In *Thomas More's Utopia in Early Modern Europe: Paratexts and Contexts*, edited by Terence Cave, 47–66. Manchester: Manchester University Press, 2008.

Gomes de Brito, Bernardo. *The Tragic History of the Sea 1559–1565*. Translated by C. R. Boxer. Cambridge: Cambridge University Press (for the Hakluyt Society), 1968.

Gunn, Geoffrey C. *First Globalization: The Eurasian Exchange, 1500–1800*. Lanham, MD: Rowman and Littlefield, 2003.

Heidegger, Martin. "The Age of the Modern World Picture." In *The Question Concerning Technology and Other Essays*, translated by William Lovitt, 115–154. New York: Harper and Row, 1977.

Howard, Deborah. "Venezia Città 'Orientale.'" In *Venezia e L'Islam 828–1797*, edited by Stefano Carboni, 79–105. Venice: Marsilio, 2007.

Kupperman, Karen Ordahl. *The Atlantic in World History*. New York: Oxford University Press, 2012.

Mancall, Peter C. *Hakluyt's Promise*. New Haven, CT: Yale University Press, 2007.

Marcocci, Giuseppe. *Indios, Cinesi, Falsari: Le Storie del Mondo nel Rinascimento*. Bari: Laterza, 2016.

Marzo Magno, Alesandro. *L'Alba dei libri:Quando Venezia ha Fatto Leggere il Mondo*. Milan: Garzanti, 2012.

McLean, Matthew. *The Cosmographia of Sebastian Münster: Describing the World in the Reformation*. Farnham: Ashgate, 2010.

Milanesi, Marica. "Giovanni Battista Ramusio e le Navigazioni e Viaggi (1550–1559)." In *L'Epopea delle Scoperte*, edited by Renzo Zorzi, 75–101. Venice: Leo Olschki, 1994.

Montesano, Marina. *Marco Polo, Un Esploratore Veneziano Sulla Via Della Seta*. Rome: Salerno Editrice, 2014.

Moretti, Franco. "World-Systems Analysis, Evolutionary Theory, Weltliteratur." In *Immanuel Wallerstein and the Problem of the World*, edited by David Palumbo-Liu, Nirvana Tanoukhi, and Bruce Robbins, 67–77. Durham, NC: Duke University Press, 2011.

Nuñez Cabeza de Vaca, Alvar. *Castaways*. Translated by Frances M. López-Morillas. Berkeley: University of California Press, 1993.

Oviedo y Valdés, Gonzalo Fernández de. *Misfortunes and Shipwrecks in the Seas of the Indies, Islands, and Mainland of the Ocean Sea (1513–1548)*. Edited and translated by Glen F. Dils. Gainesville: University of Florida Press, 2011.

Palumbo-Liu, David, Nirvana Tanoukhi, and Bruce Robbins. "Introduction." In *Immanuel Wallerstein and the Problem of the World*, edited by David Palumbo-Liu, Nirvana Tanoukhi, and Bruce Robbins, 1–23. Durham, NC: Duke University Press, 2011.

Parks, G. B. "The Contents and Sources of Ramusio's Navigationi." *Bulletin of the New York Public Library* 59 (June 1955): 279–313.

Passeron, Jean-Claude, and Jacques Revel, eds. *Penser par Cas*. Paris: École des Hautes Études en Sciences Sociales, 2005.

Pigafetta, Antonio. *The First Voyage around the World*. Edited by Theodore J. Cachey, Jr. New York: Marsilio, 1995.

Prendergast, Christopher. "The World Republic of Letters." In *Debating World Literature*, edited by Christopher Prendergast, 1–25. London: Verso, 2004.

Ramusio, Giovanni Giambattista. "Discorso Sopra il Viaggio Fatto Dagli Spagnuoli Intorno al Mondo." In *Viaggi e Navigazioni. 6 volumes*, edited by Marica Milanesi, Vol. 2, 826. Turin: Einaudi, 1978–1988.

Romanini, Fabio. "Se fussero più ordinate, e meglio scritte … " Giovanni Battista Ramusio Correttore ed Editore delle Navigationi et Viaggi. Rome: Viella, 2007.

Said, Edward. *Culture and Imperialism*. London: Vintage, 1994.

Shalev, Zev. "Main Themes in the Study of Ptolemy's Geography in the Renaissance." In *Ptolemy's Geography in the Renaissance*, edited by Zur Shalev and Charles Burnett, 1–14. London: Warburg Institute, 2011.

Sloterdijk, Peter. *Globes. Volume II of Spheres*. Translated by Wieland Hoban. South Pasadena, CA: Semiotexte(e), 2014.

Spivak, Gayatri Chakravorty. "World Systems & the Creole." *Narrative* 14, no. 1 (January 2006): 102–112.

Tanoukhi, Nirvana. "The Scale of World Literature." In *Immanuel Wallerstein and the Problem of the World*, edited by David Palumbo-Liu, Nirvana Tanoukhi, and Bruce Robbins, 78–98. Durham, NC: Duke University Press, 2011.

Tessicini, Dario. "Definitions of 'Cosmography' and 'Geography' in the Wake of Fifteenth- and Sixteenth-Century Translations and Editions of Ptolemy's Geography." In *Ptolemy's Geography in the Renaissance*, edited by Zur Shalev and Charles Burnett, 31–50. London: Warburg Institute, 2011.

Vespucci, Amerigo. *Letters from a New World*. Edited by Luciano Formisano, translated by David J. Jacobson. New York: Marsilio, 1992.

Von der Heyden-Rynsch, Verena. *Aldo Manuzio, le Michel-Ange du livre. L'art de L'imprimerie à Venise*. Translated by Sébastien Diran. Paris: Gallimard, 2014.

Wallerstein, Immanuel. *World-Systems Analysis: An Introduction*. Durham, NC: Duke University Press, 2004.

Warren, Fintan B., O.F.M. *Vasco de Quiroga and his Pueblo-Hospitals of Santa Fe*. Washington, DC: Academy of American Franciscan History, 1963.

Weinstein, Donald. *Ambassador from Venice: Pietro Pasqualigo in Lisbon, 1501*. Minneapolis: University of Minnesota Press, 1960.

Weiss, Benjamin. "The Geography in Print: 1475–1530." In *Ptolemy's Geography in the Renaissance*, edited by Zur Shalev and Charles Burnett, 91–120. London: Warburg Institute, 2011.

Contesting slavery in the global market: John Brown's *Slave Life in Georgia*

Michael J. Drexler ⓘ and Stephanie Scherer

ABSTRACT

John Brown, author of *Slave Life in Georgia*, published in London in 1854, proffered a radical approach to ending slavery in the USA in step with Marxian economics. In this paper, we will explain how Brown's representation of subjectivity may have caused critics to neglect it. Brown treats freedom as something foreign and external. He has to learn what freedom means, first through exposure to a model of liberal citizenship and then through the experience of several modulations of fugitive liberty. Brown's social world is wholly determined by external forces. Whether slave or freeman, he faces ambiguous situations. Is one master better than another? Will he join a community of fugitive slaves in Indiana? Will he seek refuge from slavery as a labourer in a copper mine? Will he accompany a patron to England? Brown's hesitancy at each of these modalities of freedom takes him to Canada West, where he serves as a carpenter among other fugitives. These Canadian model communities, designed under the purview of white benefactors, also ultimately displease Brown. He finally leaves for England, where he takes up a new charge: a systematic attack on the economic conditions that support the slaveocracy. He aims to undersell southern cotton and dismantle the Southern economy through competition. Despite failing to execute his design, Brown remains an important voice committed to economic intervention rather than moral suasion.

By the middle of the nineteenth century, white abolitionists fully embraced fugitive slave narratives as devices of moral suasion. The narratives' accounts of cruelty, the separation of families and methods of torture would, they believed, evoke sympathy and generate support from recalcitrant white northerners. However, the genre had also long been a broad canvas for demonstrating black agency, recording cultural practices, describing farming techniques and showcasing accomplishments. Authors did not abandon such motivations, even after the unprecedented success of Harriet Beecher Stowe's sentimentalized anti-slavery fiction. Nor did slave narrators embrace any one approach to combatting institutional slavery. In this paper, we attend to one narrator's materialist critique of cotton production to render slave-produced cotton profitless; but before turning to John Brown's *Slave Life in Georgia* (1854), we offer an astonishing coincidence where

Brown's story intersects with the more famous writer at the very centre of the sentimental turn, Josiah Henson.

In the twenty-first chapter of Henson's second autobiographical narrative, *Truth Stranger than Fiction: Father Henson's Story of His Own Life* (1858), the author describes his encounter with the Queen of England in 1851. Henson was the only black exhibitor at the London exhibition of that year. Inside the Crystal Palace, an empire celebrated itself as the world's cultural, industrial, and, most importantly, moral centre. By 1851, England had not only abolished the slave trade, but had endeavoured to "modernize" India and emancipated slaves in its Caribbean colonies.[1] The Exhibition would showcase the self-professed benevolent Empire.[2]

Though Henson concedes that his "complexion" may have attracted attention to his "humble contribution," his polished lumber was undoubtedly striking. Passersby inevitably "paused to look at me, and at themselves, as reflected in my large black walnut mirrors."[3] What then did these gazers see? A showcase to elicit sympathy for a fugitive slave? A stage for moral self-aggrandizing? A product of free labour? The black walnut, both mirror and representative for the exoticized, black body, drew in white consumers' gaze and their stereo-optic demand for evidence of good works and exhibits of world-wide exotica. The Queen herself visited and exchanged pleasantries.

A cultural studies approach to Henson's anecdote would have us dwell on the local, mirror-like finish of the boards. Their reflective surface would be a virtual space juxtaposing subjects from wildly different backgrounds. What animates this study, however, cannot be readily seen. Its coordinates lie not on the shiny veneer, but abroad where a sawmill sits in a Canadian landscape and formerly enslaved black hands rip trees into lumber. Some boards will be used to build houses, churches and schools at this settlement, Dawn Institute, intended to model free black civic life and labour. Others will be shipped elsewhere to publicize this successful communal experiment. The settlements of Elgin, Chatham and Dawn, however, do not stand in isolation on the Canadian plain, but in relation to other dreams and agendas.[4] Abolitionists had proposed various plans: immigration to Haiti or to Africa, armed rebellion and political bargaining. So, too, stands John Brown's personal narrative, *Slave Life in Georgia*, for John Brown was also at Dawn, working as one of the labourers who ripped the very boards that Henson would display overseas. Can we reveal the labourer who disappears once his boards become objects of consumer desire? Brown's narrative rebuts the efficacy of moral suasion. He envisions a direct attack on the bottom line, to make slave-produced cotton unprofitable. We propose a double act of recovery: to reveal the labourer who is displaced when his boards become commodities, and to distinguish his story from popularly marketed abolitionist literature.[5]

Abolitionist propaganda had adapted to consumer taste by mid-century, making Brown's proposals in *Slave Life in Georgia* virtually illegible. Henson, by contrast, leveraged his celebrity after Harriet Beecher Stowe named him as a source for the sentimental hero of *Uncle Tom's Cabin, or Life among the Lowly* (1852). By 1858, Henson addressed a brand-new world. He was no longer marketing a few pieces of fugitive lumber to commoners and queens, but also marketing *himself* as original to Stowe's bestselling masterpiece of moral suasion.[6] We note the titles Henson chose for post-Stowe editions of his *Life*. In its raw form, Henson had christened his narrative, straightforwardly, *The Life of Josiah Henson, Formerly a Slave Now an Inhabitant of Canada* (1849). After *Uncle Tom's Cabin*, he baked the title to suit readers' tastes with the more dramatic *Truth Stranger than Fiction* (1858). The narrative appeared after the Civil War, fully boiled, as *Uncle Tom's Story of his Life* (1876). The anecdotes about the exhibition of the walnut boards at the Crystal Palace first appeared in *Truth Stranger than Fiction*, so it is to that edition we can trace the elision of John Brown.

In his 1858 narrative, Henson presents the mirror-like lumber as a product of his own labour even though his actual work was limited to hiring someone to plane and polish them "in the French style." The anecdote that follows further secures Henson's legitimate claims to the work. When an official representing the American exhibition threatens to commandeer the boards as products of the USA, Henson resists by marring their surface, painting in bold white letters: "THE PRODUCT OF THE INDUSTRY OF A FUGITIVE SLAVE FROM THE UNITED STATES, WHOSE RESIDENCE IS DAWN, CANADA."[7] To underscore for whom this story is told, a group of English gentlemen, "chuckling with half-suppressed delight," bear witness to the scuffle. This audience illuminates Henson's resistance, for the indelible white marks assert both Henson's blackness and his Canadian identity in opposition to white supremacy in the USA. In *Truth Stranger than Fiction*, Henson transforms himself from raw slave, whose body is treated as property, into a producer *alongside* what he has produced. An aide to the Queen amplifies this when he assures her that "Indeed he is [a fugitive] and that is his work" (191).

But of course, even the rough boards were not products of Henson's labour. The credit is due to the black labourers at Dawn Institute, such as John Brown, a fugitive who had gone by the names Fed and Benford while a slave. Brown's narrative, *Slave Life in Georgia*, reclaims those boards and eschews the romantic mode of self-actualization found, perhaps most recognizably, in Frederick Douglass' 1845 autobiography. In *Slave Life*, Brown retells his desperate attempts to reach England after his escape.[8] This story of hapless travel finally rewarded leads Brown to a novel solution to the problem of American slavery. His bid to raise cotton in Liberia and undersell the American South's market is, moreover, no mere "colonizing trick."[9] Instead of emigration and resettlement, a proposition first conceived by the white-led American Colonization Society, Brown's plan does not depend on relocation, but capitalizes on the structural inefficiencies in the slave economy.[10] Brown's proposal is neither ameliorative nor compensatory, but formal and aggressive. His narrative exposes the layers of deception that make slavery corruptly profitable, but also wasteful. His plan is a stunning, Marxist analysis of slavery that puts him in opposition to mainstream abolitionists or those advocating immigration to Canada.[11]

Virtually forgotten beyond offering anecdotal data for historians, John Brown's *Slave Life in Georgia, A Narrative of the Life, Sufferings, and Escape of John Brown, a Fugitive Slave, Now in England* is a complex and unfortunately obscure literary work. For one, it is among the few narratives to recount life in the Deep South. If this has yet to gain Brown readers, we point as well to Brown's intervention in the burgeoning genre of slave narratives. His title emphasizes evidentiary realism, bearing likeness to *The Life or Narrative of Frederick Douglass* (1845) and the titles of Charles Ball's (1837) and Henson's (1849) narratives. But it also engages the impact of the novel-form on the genre. He addresses this directly when he writes, "Mrs. Stowe has told something about Slavery. I think she must know a great deal more than she has told. I know more than I dare to tell."[12] For Brown, the novel-form pretends to reveal a picture of the whole, but a personal narrative *chooses* what to reveal and withhold and thus remains explicitly and purposefully partial. As evidenced with Henson, after *Uncle Tom's Cabin*, several fugitive slave authors changed their titles to reflect shifting marketing strategies – for example second edition titles: Northup's *Twelve Years a Slave* (1853), Douglass's *My Bondage, My Freedom* (1855), Henson's *Truth Stranger than Fiction* (1858), and Ball's *Fifty Years in Chains* (1859). Brown's *Slave Life in Georgia*, by comparison, softens the personal, memoirist's style, but also strikes a more documentary or quotidian pose. The title points to collective experience, not an individual trajectory, whether heroic or sacrificial. This quality of diminishing the primacy of the authorial subject carries over into the narrative content where Brown self-deprecates, aiming less at celebrity than typicality. For Brown, slavery is a totalizing condition of being. Unlike Douglass, who is "free" until he learns what it means to be a slave, or Northup, who knows freedom and loses it, Brown denies any space within which the slave could imagine an autonomous subjectivity, or, as in a novel, a space from which an author could claim omniscience. Freedom for him is neither natural nor inherent. For Douglass, nature is a reservoir of freedom, an antithetical system to slavery, while for Brown it is part of, not apart from, the closed loop of social existence under slavery. "When in Slavery, I was called Fed," he explains, telling us he has no idea how he got the name and that it was "common for slaves to answer to any name, as it may suit the humour of the master" (5). Servitude is a precondition in Brown's lifeworld and nature is within it. This is made clear when he tells of children subject to the assaults of the natural world. Ants and mosquitoes plague his infant brother who had to be in the fields with his mother as she worked. Scenes of torture are metonymically linked to a nature contained within the slave system. Fed's mistress whips slaves with a cow-hide that the slaves call the "blue lizard" and a bull-whip is described as "limber and lithesome as a snake" (7, 110).

In the beginning chapters of the narrative, Fed is punished whenever he tries to insert a gap between himself and the tools for manipulating the natural world. When the milldam overflows or a plough digs too deep, or a mare dies from overheating, Fed is beaten. If he justifies himself when asked why he did not run as fast as he could, or could not plough efficiently, or lost time because of a broken knife, his master Thomas Stevens's punishments reiterate the brutal lesson that the enslaved black body is just another machine of the trade.[13] When Fed tries to explain why a "buzzard plough" ran foul, Stevens kicks him "right between the eyes," breaking his nose, "and cutting the leaders of the right eye, so that it turned quite round in its socket" (28).[14] The use of "leaders," or reins, emphasizes that the eye is either completely useless or, paradoxically, that it can no longer be governed, that it looks backward to interrogate the master. From the master's perspective, however, the injury suits the crime: broken plough, broken eye. The biblical doctrine of an eye for an eye is based on the justice of equation. That is, in the bible, two human beings can retain equality before the law when the suffering of the victim is imposed *ex post facto* on the aggressor. The logic of equation, however, does not hold under chattel slavery. Slave Codes dating back at least to the Barbados Code of 1661 most clearly distinguished chattel from humanity in sections detailing punishment for a master who killed or maimed his own or another's slave. While a slave would suffer execution for physical aggression against whites, whites who maimed or killed slaves were subject to fines. Black bodies, like any commodity, could be exchanged for coin, the universal equivalent for a certain quantity of property. The logic of capital underwrote the relations between master and slave. Slave Codes were an early form of cynical market regulation; while giving the appearance of outlawing the worst excesses of individual slave masters, these codes obscured and thus permitted more quotidian and insidious violence.

Where a morally driven abolitionist might react with horror at the devaluation of an individual slave's humanity in summary punishments like the one Brown describes, Brown chooses instead to highlight how commonplace were violations against slave bodies. In Brown's recollection, when he attempted to rationalize or explain the inefficient functioning of a tool, his defence was met with a violence that effectively rejected the separation of slave and implements.[15] The slave was not a subject who could comment on structurally independent inefficiencies, but an extension of the tool. If the tool broke, then the slave body must be as well. In place of the equation, the slave body was disciplined as a part of a whole. In literary terms, equation works like a metaphor, where two distinct things are yoked to a shared denominator, in this case the quality of both being human. But in the case of chattel, the analogy of "this is equal to that" is not available. Instead, the relationship is metonymic, for the slave body, subjected to the slave master's perverse logic, is *not* dissimilar enough from implements of agricultural production. This metonymic quality is present in the two most disturbing scenes of torture: the picketing of John Glasgow and Fed's subjection to Thomas Hamilton's medical experiments.

John Glasgow was a British seaman, who signed on for merchant service to North America and left his wife and family in Scotland. Upon arriving in Charleston, Glasgow was segregated from the white crew and quarantined in the local jail while the ship remained in port. South Carolina had responded to slave unrest and especially to Denmark Vesey's and Nat Turner's revolts by instituting even tighter restrictions on the importation of slaves and the lives of free people of colour. When Glasgow's captain refused to pay the costs associated with his detention, the managers of the prison foreclosed on Glasgow as collateral, and he was sold into slavery where he eventually met John Brown. Brown recounted Glasgow's story to the British and Foreign Antislavery and Abolition Society Secretary, Louis Chamerovzow, who published this account in the BFAAS's newspaper in 1853. The story was then incorporated into Brown's own narrative, also edited by Chamerovzow, in 1854. Edlie Wong argues that *Slave Life* may be best understood as a vehicle to disseminate Glasgow's story. Embracing Glasgow as a British subject, despite racial difference, British readers could follow a Dantean narrative that invites them on a journey through hell.[16]

Glasgow's beatings are among the most graphic depictions of slave torture from an eyewitness. Using racialized language to underpin the particularity of the violence, the flogging was used to exact "the nigger pride out of him" and "having the look and carriage of a free man," these precisely adumbrated methods objectify the slave body (33). As with the metonymy of slave and tool, the body is reduced to a material part of the machinery of its own punishment, annihilating any signs of individual subjectivity and even separating the victim from the collective identity shared by his fellow slaves. We note that Glasgow's offence was to insist on having been falsely imprisoned and illegally sold into slavery, to insist that he already had a wife and did not need a new one, to insist that he "was free and a British subject" (34). Brown depicts two separate incidents of brutality enacted against Glasgow, comprising two distinct methods of torture: bucking and picketing. That the techniques have colloquial names not only Americanizes the text and authenticates

THE WORLD-LITERARY SYSTEM AND THE ATLANTIC

Brown's credibility, but has the eerie effect of transferring the reader's attention from the victim, reduced to being "the poor fellow," to the method, which is described meticulously. Adding to this effect is the shift in narrative perspective from the first person to the third. The master, seeing Glasgow steal away to visit his second wife Nancy on another plantation, "maliciously allows him to get a good distance off, when beckoning to him three other slaves, *myself*, March, and Jack ... *they* started in pursuit" (35, emphasis added).[17] The focus shifts twice, away from the suffering victim and away from the complicity of the narrating subject. The new perspective brings the torturers into focus, who cruelly play with the body as if it and the machine of torture were part of the same toy. In bucking, the body is restrained so that the torturers can roll it around like a ball; in picketing, the body is impaled on a stake and spun like a top.

A distinctive feature of Brown's language is what one historian calls his understated style.[18] Looking back on his 10-year-old self, Brown can recall feeling terrorized and then stupefied with grief upon seeing his mother for the last time, but he does not pause for a general comment on the system, in which such scenes are embedded, nor amplify the pathos by responding to it as his adult, knowing self. Understatement, however, may indicate something other than the distancing effect of scientific description. We propose that Brown's style recreates the naïve wonder of the child. Where Douglass shows us the transition from man to slave and then slave to man and emphasizes his resilience, craftiness and masculine power, Brown rarely presents himself so favourably. Douglass's rhetorical skill, especially his use of chiasmus, fails to capture the experiential perspective of his much younger enslaved self. Rather than demonstrate his personal triumph over adversity or development of an enlightened, post-slavery self, Brown enacts comedic astonishment. The result is a narrative persona willing to depict his former self as overwhelmed, incapable of critical distance or reflection. How else to capture the world-unmaking trauma of being reduced to property, of proscribed kinship?[19] Fed expresses astonishment: "How I watched them whilst they were driving this bargain!" He then exactingly describes the method through which his owner and the slave-speculator, Finney, arrived at his value: by weighing him on the spot and pricing him by the pound (16). Fed describes the contraption as follows:

> [A] rope was brought, both ends of which were tied together, so that it formed a large noose or loop. This was hitched over the hook of the stilyard [*sic*], and I was seated in the loop. After I had been weighed, there was a deduction made for the rope. I do not recollect what I weighed, but the price I was sold for amounted to three hundred and ten dollars. (16)

Fed expresses a similar sense of wonder when he suffers Dr Thomas Hamilton's Mengele-like medical experiments. Brown presents himself as a passive observer of his own suffering. He reports that he could do nothing to stop it and thus gave himself up for "passive resignation." He marvels at the technical practices that will be used on him:

> Yet, it was not without curiosity I watched the preparations the Doctor caused to be made. He ordered a hole to be dug in the ground, three feet and a half deep by three feet long, and two feet and a half wide. Into this pit a quantity of dried red oak bark was cast, and fire set to it. It was allowed to burn until the pit became heated like an oven, when the embers were taken out. A plank was then put across the bottom of the pit, and on that a stool. (41)

Fed is placed in the hole, which is sealed with blankets, leaving only his head exposed. He is then given various medicines "to ascertain which ... enabled me to withstand the greatest degree of heat" (41). His curiosity at the contraptions designed to violate and degrade his body renders the scenes disjointed, horror balanced by amazement.

The series of escape attempts in the middle chapters of *Slave Life* show Fed gaining a limited understanding of his condition and a marginal ability to react strategically once entitled to fend for himself. But every move forward tends toward a reversal. He escapes and is captured. He escapes from the slave catchers only to decide he would have a more likely chance of success by returning to his master and biding his time. He agrees to have a slave stealer take him away figuring a new master must be better than the present one, but, is eventually returned to his original master when the stealers fear they are about to be arrested themselves.[20] Sold back to Decator Stevens, Brown is subject to one final round of abuse. He is harnessed in the "bells and horns," a wicked inversion of a crown, here constructed of iron bands around the neck and head and four iron rods fixed vertically to each and bent at the end where the bells are attached. The contraption makes escape not only impossible, but also prevents the slave from finding comfort whether working or at rest. Encased in the bells and horns for three months, Fed resolves that once free of this contraption, he will make his final run for freedom.

Reminiscent of Mark Twain's Jim – cruelly ensnared in Tom Sawyer's game before finally gaining his freedom – the scenes that follow uncannily anticipate other plot elements *Huckleberry Finn*, first published in 1884, 30 years after Brown's narrative.[21] Like Huck, Brown's persona is wily and yet still naïve. Fed practises soft deception to prompt a young girl to help him escape; he temporarily dodges slave catchers who send dogs after him through the swamp by tricking the dogs into thinking he is part of the search party; he entertains an internal dialogue about whether to continue in the wilderness or return to "civilization"; and takes a trip on a raft with the object to reach freedom by going *downriver*. Having escaped from Mississippi to Alabama, Fed fears continuing by land. Brown writes:

> I considered what I should do; and concluding at last that the river must run into the sea, and that if I once got to the seaside, I should be sure to find some Englishmen there who would tell me the way to England. (81–82)

A nine-day journey on his raft, running mostly at night and concealing himself by day, has him adapting to the river (fishing, stealing potatoes and disguising himself). Fed also has a frightening, but ultimately comic encounter with a steam-boat. From the perspective of his then-ignorant self, the steam-boat is a devil with "two big, red eyes" belching out a "shower of sparks shooting up in the air, mingling with red fiery smoke" (84). Dupe of his own devices, he arrives in New Orleans, where he expects England to be just beyond the water's edge.

Like Huck and Jim, Fed's journey south only further enmeshes him in the systemic violence and deception of the slaveholding south. On arriving in New Orleans, Fed must face one more horrible decision before making his last and successful break north. Crushed to discover that England was not "only just across the water" and suddenly aware of his precarious liberty, Brown makes a gut-wrenching choice to sell himself back into slavery, rather than be captured as a fugitive. Looking for the slave stealers Buck Hurd or John Murrell, whom he incorrectly assumed he could find just by walking the streets, Brown offers himself as a runaway to a man who looked to be cut from similar cloth. "Young, and indifferently well dressed, his clothes looking dusty and tumbled," the man also appears sleepy with puffy and bloodshot eyes (90). Seeing also that he "walked lazily, with rather an irregular step," Fed puts him down for "a gambler and a drunkard," who might acquiesce to his plan for want of money (90). While still uncertain about freedom and its exigencies, Fed's intuition about the white character proves accurate – this is a skill he has gained from experience, acquitting himself to please when necessary to avoid a master's ire – and he agrees to be sold at auction.

The New Orleans slave market presents yet *another* scene where deceptive practices undermine the efficiency of the slave regime, another occasion where profiteering trumps a regulated institution and its markets.[22] Brown here deceives both as a means of survival and to avoid punishment. His auctioneers command him to perform as saleable property; he is expected to express good cheer and docility, in order to conceal any signs that might reveal the scars of experience and resistance. Brown emphasizes that he chose carefully when to comply and to "take good care to look my brightest and answer my smartest." Convinced if he remained unsellable for much longer he would suffer another round of torture, he decides the time is ripe. With curious pride, Brown writes, "[the] character I gave myself, never a 'nigger' had before" (106). This passage echoes the dominant theme of the end of the narrative, the necessity to combat an institution founded on deception, such as slavery, through like deception. Previously, Brown identified the imperative for assuming such "wicked" practices:

> In fact, we felt we were living under a system of cheating, and lying, and deceit, and being taught no better, we grew up in it, and did not see the wrong of it, so long as we were not acting against one another. I am sure that, as a rule, any one of us who would have thought nothing of stealing a hog, or a sack of corn, from our master, would have allowed himself to be cut to pieces rather than betray the confidence of his fellow-slave; and, perhaps, my mentioning this fact may be taken as a set-off against the systematic deception we practised, in self-defence, on our master. (71–72)

This claim also points to the influence of a corruptive education under slavery. The slave reduced to the brute subject, being "taught no better," can only assimilate what he has experienced and, thus, learned. Yet, this exception for immorality does not extend to relations amongst equals, amongst fellow slaves. Deception must be a practice invested in maintaining or resisting a hierarchy of white versus black in this particular context. Thus, once on the road to freedom, Brown must seek alternative modes of interaction with both blacks and whites.

At last sold to a new master, Brown assumes the name Benford, the name of the plantation where his father had been enslaved. Taken to a prison-like plantation of 150 slaves at Shirt-Tail Bend in Mississippi, Benford endures another cruel master. He spends three months on the plantation as if to bear witness to the especially heinous crimes practised upon slave women. Akin to Dr Hamilton's experiments on the young Fed, Benford testifies to the practice of bull-whipping pregnant women by preparing a hole in the ground "for them to lie in more conveniently, so as not to injure the burden they were carrying" (111–112). Brown's testimony asserts what Spillers reminds us about the "ungendering" of enslaved female flesh.[23] As these related practices echo those experiments inflicted on Fed's body earlier, the narrative depicts the "profitable 'atomizing' of the captive body

... [T]he procedures adopted for the captive flesh demarcate a total objectification, as the entire captive community becomes a living laboratory."[24]

Benford's final escape serves as a foray into freedom through the wilds of the Mississippi River: a journey from the saleable object, through bestial survival, and ultimately to citizenship in Britain. As he makes his way along the banks of the river, Benford describes himself as a "wild man," emphasizing the fear-inducing proximity of "snorting and plashing" alligators. Understandably paranoid about recapture, Brown avoids human contact. He mistrusts everyone he meets, even those he must depend upon for survival. Along the way, Brown adopts a nocturnal existence. He will only risk venturing near to secluded homesteads to inquire about necessary navigational information, and this only under the cover of darkness. It is the colour-obscuring darkness that makes Benford's departure from deceptive practice possible; he writes that as "they could not see [his] colour," these isolated, white homeowners were never "backward in replying" to his applications for information (126). Guided by the kernels of direction from these encounters, Benford finally arrives at a "settlement of coloured people," where he passes for a freedman and works for two weeks. Here, he assumes the name John Brown. This stopover represents Brown's first experience of a self-governing, free black community. He feels he must, nevertheless, maintain his anonymity. Uneasy about suspicions concerning his history, Brown moves on toward Indianapolis. There he learns of the Underground Railroad and the peculiar generosity of the Quakers.

Crediting a kind of "superstition" or "instinct," Brown successfully navigates his way to a northern Quaker family, who harbour and feed him. The "grandness" of the company bewilders him, and Brown struggles to behave appropriately, feeling so out of his element that he feels he has "no eyes, no ears, no understanding" (134). Brown grapples to maintain civility, afraid to touch the food presented to him for fear that he will reveal his bestial voracity. After over a half hour of encouragement, Brown finally gorges himself. Once again, his narrative persona does not hesitate to present himself comically, ill-equipped to perform nicely in polite society. The family must intervene to prevent Brown from over-indulging and injuring himself.[25] After the meal, Brown can sleep comfortably in the security of a "safe retreat" for the first time since the escape. He wakes, uncertain of his surroundings, and describes, "I could see the walls of my room, and the curtains all of a dazzling *whiteness* around me" (135, emphasis added). The whiteness of the room astonishes him and provides a stark contrast to the wilderness through which he has made his way. Enveloped in the comparatively luxurious comfort and freedom of white space and finally "alive to the truth" that he is free and safe, Brown has a brief moment to reflect on his "saviours," and attempts to pray, reflecting: "I had never learnt to pray; but if what passed in my heart that night was not prayer, I am sure I shall never pray as long as I live" (135).

Brown's brief but powerful first-person admission exposes him as yet unformed and uneducated as a properly Christian, liberal subject. He has been deprived of a spiritual education, and thus does not consider prayer natural or intuitive. Stowe's Uncle Tom, by contrast, is a natural at praying. Where Brown's ineptitude at the Quaker dinner table reveals him as a prototypically naturalist protagonist, Stowe sculpts Tom into the defining figure of the sentimental slave hero. Despite Tom's deficiency in education, both general and theological, his natural capacity "of mind," which accounts for his remarkable piety, outstrips that of his fellow slaves and rivals that of "even better educated persons." Uncle

Tom, the "patriarch" and "martyr," is a portrait of the exceptional slave, set apart from and above any of the other individuals within his various slave communities.[26] Uncle Tom's unimpeachable honesty does not waver even in the face of violence or injustice, even against the arguments of fellow slaves, like the desperate Cassy, who point out the futility of morality when locked within a fundamentally amoral system. John Brown's marked disinterest in religious devotion stands in stark relief against Tom's innate belief. Furthermore, Tom's adherence to Christian principles and faith provide him with clear parameters for determining who can be trusted. Brown, however, cannot shake the scepticism inculcated by slave education, that is, the systematic deception practised by both slave and master. When told that he must move on to the next stop on the Railroad, Brown immediately doubts the intentions of his Christian rescuers; he believes they are deceiving him, and he will be sold back into slavery. Finding this to be untrue, Brown repents harbouring such suspicions against his "friends." Yet, the moment of doubt brings Brown's evolving conception of "friendship" into focus. For Brown, unlike Tom, friends are acquired through highly localized interactions, usually involving material exchange. Whereas the slave must rely upon solidarity with his peers and self-defensive deception, the newly free man can develop new parameters for commonality based upon empirical evidence of honest reciprocity. The friendly exchanges of protection and goods Brown experiences along his journey north shape his developing notions not only of equitable market relations, but also of communal citizenship.

The chapter on the Underground Railroad at the very end of *Slave Life* – re-published from *The Anti-Slavery Reporter* by editor Chamerovzow – includes a notable anecdote of inverted deception, one that offers a decidedly divergent portrait of "white saviours" in the North than that found in Brown's own account. Instead of slaveholders or slave stealers practising deception against slaves, the white conductors of the Underground Railroad manage to spoil the pursuit of slave-hunters in northern Ohio by deceiving them in turn. Hearing news that the slave-hunters are nearing a house harbouring fugitives, the white abolitionists quickly smear their skin with soot from the chimney and exchange clothing with the slaves. They successfully trick the hunters into believing that they are indeed black slaves fleeing from pursuit and lure the slave-hunters away from the house with a carriage chase. It is not until the "black faced" subjects are presented before a judge that they are revealed to be free, white American citizens. The abolitionists' antics provide enough diversion for the slaves to escape further north along the Railroad, thereby saving them from certain capture. This sketch concludes the chapter on the Underground Railroad and highlights, more than anything, the ingenuity, not of the escaped slaves, but of their benevolent, white protectors. Chamerovzow's addition of this final section deflects Brown's narrative voice with yet another opportunity for white self-aggrandizement. Polishing off Brown's rough conclusion, Chamerovzow ensures that a British audience will leave the reading experience with the gratifying reflection of themselves in the white heroes working toward the abolition of slavery, a goal already accomplished in England. However, the "switching" of places – inverting the traditional power dynamic – is only attainable for the white subject, who very easily washes off "blackness" in the face of a justice system that privileges whiteness, even in the North.

John Brown, then, develops a much different sense of unified action – that which is grounded not in like deception, but rather in just and open resistance. As he nears the Canadian border, Brown gains confidence in his freedom. He meets a group of fugitive slaves, with whom he takes up work. When the master of one of these fugitives finds them out, he threatens to transport his former slave back South. The master, outnumbered by the group of fugitive slaves and friends, is met by the very real threat of violent resistance. This moment solidifies for Brown both his allegiance to his equals and the strength they have as a united front to thwart the intentions of the white slaveholder.

Having thus experienced how empowering communal resistance in the local sense can be, Brown begins seeking opportunities, which would provide like empowerment and community. The answer it seems lies in combined labour. Brown lands in Detroit, Michigan where he begins employment in the mines, under the direction of the British Captain Teague, "native of Redruth, of Cornwall." In Teague, Brown finds his most promising conduit to the country he has most desperately been trying to reach: England. And yet, when Teague departs for England, Brown does not follow immediately. He decides, instead, to take a visit to a communal living experiment he has heard of: the Dawn Institute of Canada West. In this pivotal decision swerving from what could be envisioned as the powerful climax of the narrative, Brown's brevity, while characteristic of his style through-out, proves especially puzzling. Even if Brown does not ask this of himself, we are left to ponder what could possibly induce him to postpone the fulfilment of his driving wish to reach England. Why Canada? What is he doing, now that his physical liberty seems secure? Recalling that Brown's admiration for the British John Glasgow as a model-free citizen was one of the chief inducements to strike out for freedom in the first place, is the conscious decision to remain in North America a significant redirection of his initial, though misinformed, attraction to England as the pinnacle of escape from servitude? Perhaps, John Brown looks to Canada as the last opportunity to secure the success of his escape without abandoning solidarity with his American fugitive and free black peers. Canada could be Brown's opportunity to continue developing his vernacular and localized theory of what freedom means.

The model communities, like the Dawn Institute of Canada West, were designed to showcase how freed slaves could overcome physical and political disenfranchisement to enact a productive civic life. With this in mind, then, Brown's curiosity appears much less enigmatic or banal. In stark contrast to Douglass's romantic hero, Brown's protagonist resists both the standard tropes of exceptional individualism and innate ability. Instead, Brown's travels are his education about the material experiences of liberty, and it is within the community, not within himself, that he looks to find information about political subjectivity. Free to explore his options, he remains, not merely to "see" the Institute, but to work actively within the Institute's lumber mill for a period of about five to six months. And it is here in Canada West that the historical-biographical trajectories of two fugitive narrators collide: Brown works with Josiah Henson, who was one of the founding members of the Dawn Institute, to produce the boards to be displayed at the Great Exhibition in Hyde Park. This directs our attention back to the constellation of producers and editors, which we identified in the beginning of this essay: first, Brown, who produces the boards that Henson claims as the product of his own craftsmanship, and second, Henson, whose autobiography is appropriated by Harriet Beecher Stowe. Much as Henson had smoothed away the rough parts of the boards that John Brown had originally hewn from logs, Stowe refashions Henson's life, a polishing that ironically places him in a meagre, roughly cut log cabin, for the sentimental marketplace, where, as Uncle Tom, he thrived. After working for a period of a few months at the Dawn Institute sawmill, Brown ultimately expresses displeasure with Henson's community. In the penultimate chapter of the narrative, Brown offers further insight into his impatience with this particular Canadian settlement, expressing his desire to

> show my coloured brethren who are in Canada, that they might do something great for our people in the South, by turning their attention to growing cotton in the West Indies or in Africa. By so doing, they would strike slavery a hard blow, just where it is most likely to feel it. I have been to Canada, and though the coloured people there may, some of them, be doing tolerably well … [t]hey ought to look into the future. They ought to consider those they have left behind them, and how they can help them. My opinion is, they could do so better in the West Indies or in Africa, than in Canada. (171–172)

Brown travels to England, where, like John Glasgow, he may finally assume British citizenship. However, he rejects this opportunity in favour of a more active proposal to combat the economic underpinnings of the slave industry – working to counter slavery by exploiting its inefficiencies and defeating it in the global cotton market. He identifies the inadequacy of moral revolution on the micro-social level: Glasgow's moral "family man"; Stowe's reconstituted Christian family; as well as the well-intentioned, but ineffectual showcase communities in Canada West, built to placate white male abolitionists' paternalistic impulses and not designed to alleviate the sufferings "of the millions of men, women, and children [Brown] has left behind in slavery" (165). Brown neither postures as an individual hero (Douglass's Romanticism) nor falls as a martyr (Stowe's sentimentalism). Macro-social revolution can only be achieved, he argues, through macro-economic intervention.

> But, as I have already said, slaveholders are not sensible to moral arguments, because they believe their interests are bound up in maintaining the system of slavery. I would not advise the anti-slavery party to leave off arguing out the question on moral grounds; but I would urge them to pay a little more attention to the commercial part of the subject. I do not hesitate to say, that so long as anti-slavery people, or those who profess anti-slavery sentiments, continue to use up slave-grown articles, the slaveholders will keep on, thinking their professions are hollow. I do not see how the system is to be put down except by undermining it. I mean by underselling it in the markets of the world. (169)

Brown criticizes the strategists in the abolitionist community as he elaborates his future plans. That slaveholders are not easily swayed by appeals to their morality comes as no surprise; however, Brown must also debunk the myth that moral suasion can push people opposed to slavery beyond indifference when it comes to putting their money where their mouths are. They will pay to read a sensational narrative of suffering, but will not suffer a "small advance on the price of an article of free-labour cotton" (170). If people with anti-slavery sentiments will still look to their purse when buying slave-produced commodities, the southern slaveholder, he writes, will continue to ignore "hollow" abolitionist rhetoric. Knowing he cannot count on changing behaviour by begging for charity, Brown crafts a "commercial" plan that will instead target the capitalist, not the consumer. How will slavery be ended? he asks, before answering his own question:

> I look upon it that slavery is kept up entirely by those who make it profitable as a system of labour. Bad as slave-holders are, if they did not find their account in working slaves, they would soon leave off doing it. Their badness arises out of the system. (165)

50 THE WORLD-LITERARY SYSTEM AND THE ATLANTIC

The only way to bring the system down is to strike at slaveholders' pockets, to sell free cotton for less and thereby make slavery unprofitable. Free cotton production in the West Indies, India, Australia or Africa must be carried out "systematically" (171). Brown devotes chapters 18–20, respectively titled "The Cultivation of Cotton, Tobacco, and Rice," "A Few Words on the Treatment of Slaves," and "My Reflections," to a demonstration of his expansive knowledge not only of agricultural methods, but also of the fundamental inefficiencies in slaveholders' management of their sites of production. In his "Reflections," Brown admits his belief that he has the experience to improve on these wasteful practices, if only he could acquire the "tools" to enact his knowledge. Selling his narrative is only a means to his end of financing his cotton-growing scheme:

> I have no education, and until I can settle down I am not likely to pick much up. But I have just that sort of experience which I believe I could turn to account were the field open. I am what is called a "handy fellow." I am a good carpenter, and can make just what machinery I want, give me only tools. I understand all about the growth of cotton, from the time of preparing the land to receive the seed, till the wool is jinned and packed … My knowledge has not come naturally to me. I have acquired it in a very hard school, and I want to turn it to account. (170–171)

For Brown, the authorial pen is the kind of tool with which he can craft "just what machinery" he wants to yield a profit. The mighty dollar, he recognizes, rules all both north and south: as long as pockets are full "you may talk, but [they] will [keep] on neverminding you." He concludes that the righteous slaveholder will only be swayed as the dollars slip away (166).

Brown's theory hinges on his certainty that slaveholders know that what they do is wrong. They beat their slaves because that is the only way to get them to work for nothing. "Cruelty," he explains, "is inseparable from slavery, as a system of forced labour" (165). And absolute power leads to depravity. "It is not of any use to talk to the slaveholder about the wrongfulness of holding slaves … [for] the chinking of the dollars in his pockets makes such a noise that he cannot hear you" (166). For Brown, the slaves know that their labour power is being stolen from them and that the slaveholders' law governing chattel "unmakes God's work," which would entitle each man "to the use of his own limbs, his own faculties, of his own thoughts" (167). We see that slaveholding, with all its methods of deception and cunningly cruel profiteering, is, at last, a gross form of self-deception. Brown describes witnessing several deathbed scenes where "it is usual for the slaves to be called up on such occasions to say they forgive [their masters] for what they have done" (168). This convinces the slaves that "[slaveholders'] minds must be dreadfully uneasy about holding slaves, and therefore there cannot be any good in it" (168). Though Brown briefly hints at an innate right to freedom, he is also quite direct that it is only by glimpses through "these little chinks" that slaves "learn that there is something wrong in slave-holding." "When we hear them cry out with pain and fear on their death-bed … we understand that they are only poor human creatures like ourselves" (169).

Brown concludes on this note of conciliatory universalism, but it is justification not to preach truth to falsehood, but to deprive the system of the profit motives that cause human beings to treat other human beings as atrociously as they do. This, then, is Brown's final note: the conditions of the system of capitalism, the all-consuming pursuit of profit, create enslavement and degradation. Far from a pre-capitalist mode of production,

THE WORLD-LITERARY SYSTEM AND THE ATLANTIC 51

slavery must be considered an engine of the modern world economic system. Despite never fulfilling his Liberian alternative, Brown remains an important and missing voice from the abolitionist movement, one committed to systemic change not through moral suasion based on sentimental identification, but through active economic intervention.

Notes

1. See Webster, *Twilight* and Drescher, *The Mighty Experiment*.
2. The Great Exhibition of 1851 was a climactic moment for British self-regard, anticipating the British Raj (1858–1947). By coining this British paternalism "the white man's burden" in 1899, Rudyard Kipling invited the post-bellum US to join the "thankless" responsibility to improve the non-white, Third World; the poem's original title was "The White Man's Burden: The United States and the Philippine Islands" (Murphy, *Shadowing*). In 1851, however, the English did not view the slaveholding US as a partner-in-benevolence. See Stephen Knadler, "At Home in the Crystal Palace."
3. Henson, *Truth*, 191.
4. See also Paul, "Out of Chatham."
5. Brown articulates Ed Baptist's recent claim that slavery was the most advanced form of capital accumulation and not a backward economic system to be eclipsed by industrial modernity (Baptist, *The Half*). Despite the renaissance of scholarship addressing the relationship of slavery and capitalism, black radicals (DuBois, C. L. R. James, Eric Williams) had already persuasively argued this case. Brown's work demonstrates an even earlier recognition of the same.
6. For complete digital texts of the several editions, see *Documenting the American South: North American Slave Narratives* (UNC-Chapel Hill), http://docsouth.unc.edu/neh.
7. Henson, *Truth*, 189.
8. One typical way of talking about slave narratives has been to describe them with the literary terms romantic or tragic. The romantic narrative will end with a triumph of the individual over the situation of enslavement. Because most self-emancipated slave narrators continued to fight for a general abolition, even the most romantic narratives end with political expressions about what to do next or lamentations for those left behind. Often, fugitive slaves left their families behind, hoping to earn enough money to buy their relations' freedom. While there can be comedic moments within slave narratives, Brown's is atypical in that his narrative persona is often the self-deprecating butt of the joke. We contend this is more than a tactic of self-presentation, but underscores a more general theme of the whole; Brown eschews the romantic mode almost entirely whether in terms of individual or collective success. Because he is most often the object of the joke, Brown's story is not romantically uplifting, even as he escapes to the North and Canada. Freedom turns out to be less a state of being than a variegated and unclearly defined set of options.
9. The term is from David Kazanjian's book title.
10. *Slave Life in Georgia* was published four years before Benjamin Coates put his own cotton production plan into print with similar arguments and justifications in *Cotton Cultivation in Africa in Reference to the Abolition of Slavery in the United States*. Coates began to develop his plan in the late 1840s, teaming up with freeborn Joseph Jenkins Roberts, who had already settled in Liberia, becoming its first president in 1847. The earliest written evidence of Coates' plan appears in a 1 January 1851 letter to Douglass soliciting his support who, unimpressed and ideologically averse, refused to offer support. Perhaps Douglass would have reacted similarly to Brown's proposal, but no record exists acknowledging that he ever read *Slave Life in Georgia*. See Greene-Power, *Against Wind and Tide* and Lapsansky-Werner, *Back to Africa*.
11. The connection is less to early Marx than to Marx's *Capital*, Volume 1 (1867).
12. Brown, *Slave Life*, 60. Subsequent references to the narrative will refer to F. N. Boney's scholarly edition and will appear in textual parentheses.
13. Hortense Spillers develops this distinction in her widely cited essay "Mama's Baby, Papa's Maybe" (66–67). She distinguishes the captive "body" from flesh, "that zero degree of social

conceptualization that does not escape concealment under the brush of discourse" (67). The "brush of discourse" in Brown's narrative would be the metaphoric and metonymic binding of the body to the machines of plantation agriculture. When Brown graphically describes the tearing of his flesh he asserts that he is not a trope, but flesh.

14. This passage almost inevitably leads readers to check the image of Brown on the frontispiece where the unhealed eye is still apparent.
15. A similar point is made in Johnson, *River of Dark Dreams*, 169.
16. See Wong, *Neither Fugitive Nor Free*, 228.
17. Though Glasgow had relented and remarried, he drew Stevens' ire for marrying another man's property and thus depriving his master the ownership of any of the couple's children.
18. Harriet H. Washington, by contrast, argues that Brown recounts his medical torture at the hands of Thomas Hamilton as a "matter of fact" in Washington, *Medical Apartheid*, 52.
19. See Spillers, "Mama's Baby," 75.
20. Brown describes the machinations of Buck Hurd and the John Murrell gang's operations within a network of stations and safe houses, a seemingly ironic inversion of the Underground Railroad. Instead of routing fugitives north, the Murrell gang transfers their bounty south. Then, in a perversely incentivized conspiracy with the stolen slaves, they sell their contraband to a new plantation, promising to re-steal the slave and start the process of flight and resale over again. Brown reports hearing of a slave being swapped in and out of servitude three or four times before either making an escape or remaining enslaved. The economy of slave stealing is not an equal partnership, as Fed reports that he has known the slave stealers to kill any fugitive they may suspect of revealing the conspiracy.
21. The similarities in plot prompt the question: was Twain familiar with Brown's story?
22. Hartman comments on the preparations for market, noting the

> enormous effort [...] expended in demystifying the ruses of the trade, attuning the reader to the difference between the apparent and the actual, narrating the repression of the "real" that occurs by way of this costuming of the contented slaves – hair dyed, faces greased, preening, primping, smiling, dancing, tumbling, et cetera

to demonstrate the "spry and smart disposition of slaves," *Scenes of Subjection*, 39–40.
23. See Spillers, "Mama's Baby," 68.
24. Ibid.
25. This representation of the freed slave's insatiability, or like an animal, may come dangerously close to negative racial stereotypes and thus contributed to the hesitation to promote this narrative. However, it also draws both a connection and a contrast to a discussion in Douglass's narrative in which slaves are punished for stealing food by being forced to eat the same past the point of sickness.
26. Stowe, *Uncle Tom's Cabin*, 53.

Acknowledgements

The authors wish to thank Ed White and students in English 302 at Bucknell University for their helpful comments.

Disclosure statement

No potential conflict of interest was reported by the authors.

ORCID

Michael J. Drexler ⓘ http://orcid.org/0000-0001-7870-9237

Bibliography

Ball, Charles. *Fifty Years in Chains, or, the Life of an American Slave*. New York: H. Dayton; Indianapolis, IN: Asher, 1859.

Baptist, Edward E. *The Half Has Never Been Told: Slavery and the Making of American Capitalism*. New York: Basic Books, 2014.

Brown, John. *Slave Life in Georgia: A Narrative of the Life, Sufferings, and Escape, of John Brown, A Fugitive Slave* [1854], edited by F. N. Boney. Savannah, GA: Beehive Press, 1972.

Douglass, Frederick. *Narrative of the Life of Frederick Douglass, an American Slave*. Boston: Anti-Slavery Office, 1845.

Drescher, Seymour. *The Might Experiment: Free Labor Versus Slavery in British Emancipation*. Oxford: Oxford University Press, 2002.

Hartman, Saidiya. *Scenes of Subjection: Terror, Slavery, and Self-making in Nineteenth-Century America*. Oxford: Oxford University Press, 1997.

Henson, Josiah. *Truth Stranger Than Fiction*. Boston: John P. Jewett, 1858.

Johnson, Walter. *River of Dark Dreams: Slavery and Empire in the Cotton Kingdom*. Cambridge, MA: Harvard University Press, 2013.

Kazanjian, David. *The Colonizing Trick: National Culture and Imperial Citizenship in Early America*. Minneapolis: University of Minnesota Press, 2003.

Knadler, Stephen. "At Home in the Crystal Palace: African American Transnationalism and the Aesthetics of Representative Democracy." *ESQ: A Journal of the American Renaissance* 56, no. 4 (2011): 328–362.

Lapsansky-Werner, Emma J., and Margaret Hope Bacon, eds. *Back to Africa: Benjamin Coates and the Colonization Movement in America, 1848–1880*. University Park: Penn State University Press, 2005.

Murphy, Gretchen. *Shadowing the White Man's Burden: U.S. Imperialism and the Problem of the Color Line*. New York: New York University Press, 2010.

Northup, Solomon. *Twelve Years a Slave*. Auburn, NY: Derby and Miller, 1853.

Paul, Heike. "Out of Chatham: Abolitionism on the Canadian Frontier." *Atlantic Studies* 8, no. 2 (2011): 165–188.

Power-Greene, Ousmane K. *Against Wind and Tide: The African American Struggle Against the Colonization Movement*. New York: New York University Press, 2014.

Spillers, Hortense J. "Mama's Baby, Papa's Maybe: An American Grammar Book." *Diacritics*, 17, no. 2 (1987): 65–81.

Stowe, Harriet Beecher. *Uncle Tom's Cabin*. Boston: John P. Jewett, 1852.

Washington, Harriet H. *Medical Apartheid: The Dark History of Medical Experimentation on Black Americans from Colonial Times to the Present*. New York: Anchor Books, 2013.

Webster, Anthony. *The Twilight of the East India Company: The Evolution of Anglo-Asian Commerce and Politics, 1790–1860*. Woodbridge, UK: Boydell & Brewer, 2013.

Wong, Edlie. *Neither Fugitive Nor Free: Atlantic Slavery, Freedom Suits, and the Legal Culture of Travel*. New York: New York University Press, 2009.

On transnational analogy: Thinking race and caste with W. E. B. Du Bois and Rabindranath Tagore

Yogita Goyal ⑩

ABSTRACT
This essay takes up W. E. B. Du Bois's theorization of internationalism, focusing on his representation of India as racial kin and anti-colonial herald, especially his suggestion of an analogy between race and caste, by reading him alongside Nobel Prize-winning poet and philosopher, Rabindranath Tagore. I juxtapose Du Bois and Tagore to recover a submerged history of a sustained dialogue between India and the United States over whether race and caste can be thought of as analogies, and what such efforts reveal about transnational method: the politics of comparison outside a core-periphery model, the tangled relations among modernity, race, and caste, and ultimately, the conditions of possibility of the Global South.

"We are in the age of Du Bois," notes Aldon Morris, chronicling the explosion of scholarship on W. E. B. Du Bois's life and work over the last two decades.[1] Although Morris's ground-breaking book focuses on Du Bois's contribution to – indeed his invention of – the discipline of sociology, the same could easily be said of a number of other fields the prolific scholar encountered. Anticipating the solidaristic frames of Bandung, Third Worldism and the Global South, Du Bois was among the first to insist on the connection between racism in the USA and imperialism abroad, and to argue that labour and race are twin faces of the same problem. Throughout his vast career (1868–1963), in such works as *The Souls of Black Folk* (1903), *The Negro* (1915), *Darkwater* (1920), *Dark Princess* (1928), *Black Reconstruction* (1935), *Dusk of Dawn* (1940), *Color and Democracy* (1945), and *The World and Africa* (1947), and as editor of the NAACP's journal, *The Crisis: A Record of Darker Races*, Du Bois insisted that "the problem of the Twentieth Century is the problem of the color-line."[2] As early as 1900, he called for a global racial justice in which neither "class," "privilege," "caste," nor "birth" would fetter a "striving human soul."[3]

Placing African Americans within a larger international setting, Du Bois subtly calibrated local, regional, national, and global scales and frequencies. His world historical sensibilities, already evident in *The Souls of Black Folk*, amplified over time, as the subjects of Africa, imperialism and war, and the relation between race and class came to be increasingly central to his thinking. Key to all of these was his deep and unusual engagement with Asia, which served as a pivot for his conceptualization of what we now term the Global South and its political possibilities. Du Bois was writing the global before the language existed to do so.[4] Even when his formulations may not stand the test of time – the elitism of the Talented Tenth doctrine or the elision of women from his model of black leadership – they code conflicts about race, class, and empire that continue to resonate.[5]

Excavating a pre-history of transnationalism and its possibilities, I focus in this essay on Du Bois's representation of India, and particularly on his persistent suggestion of an analogy between race and caste, by reading him alongside Nobel Prize-winning poet and philosopher, Rabindranath Tagore (1861–1941), to think comparison outside a core-periphery model. Because the idea of India in Du Bois's imagination is so fertile, his shifting dialogues with Tagore help pinpoint larger quandaries of South–South encounters. While we tend to see African-American and colonial modernity as converging only in the era of Civil Rights and Black Power, Du Bois and Tagore both notably attempt to conceive of a non-imperialist universalism prior to Bandung. Both formulate a prophetic vision of transnational politics, negotiating the varying pulls of race, nation and empire, thereby making it possible for us to see what early transnationalism looked like, why and whether it failed, and how it shaped our world.

It is instructive to compare the literary texts of the two men – Du Bois's *Darkwater* (1920) with Tagore's *The Hungry Stones* (1916), say, or *Dark Princess* (1928) with *Gora* (1910) or *The Home and the World* (1915) – where they postulate a template for transnational politics, weighing the potential of anti-colonialism against the lure of the universal, and conducting a vibrant dialogue about the contingent conditions that attend any comparative endeavour. But restricting our focus to these texts alone obscures larger comparative possibilities, as Fredric Jameson argues, encouraging a new form of literary comparativism instead: the "comparison, not of the individual texts, which are formally and culturally very different from each other, but of the concrete situations from which such texts spring and to which they constitute distinct responses."[6] Juxtaposing Du Bois and Tagore helps recover a submerged history of a dialogue between India and the USA over whether race and caste can be thought of as analogies, and what such efforts reveal about transnational method: the politics of analogy, difference or alterity and its shaping of transnational traffic, and ultimately the relations among modernity, race and caste. That race is not caste is self-evident. But re-tracking the history of efforts to construct race and caste as analogies tells us something about what exactly race and caste are – the ontology of each but also how they are historicized, embedded in other social forms, how they become modalities that not only house alterity but code relations of power. Juxtaposing two histories that are not reducible to each other reframes the linear narrative of racial formation in African-American history that takes us from slavery to Jim Crow to Civil Rights to neoliberalism, as well as the notion of caste as an exception, which is said to give India its unique national identity. Exceptionalist claims about race in the USA and caste in India are both thrown into crisis when read as symbiotic histories, mutually formative, and unexpectedly connected.

The scholar and the sage

Du Bois and Tagore are always coded as profoundly representative of the soul of their people, seen as monumental figures in traditions that do not generally intersect. Tagore was famously said to have "sung Bengal into a nation."[7] Du Bois's "electrifying manifesto," *The Souls of Black Folk,* "was one of those events epochally dividing history into a before and an after."[8] Both first espoused and later rejected nationalism, imagining a poetics of internationalism. For Du Bois, the theorization of African Americans as a nation within a nation was fundamentally anchored by an aesthetic sublime. As he moved from racial nationalism to internationalism, his strong belief in cosmopolitan humanism, in the affective and moral power of literature, and his profound interest in romance as a mode for theorizing history aligned him with Tagore's similar trajectory. Tagore's eclectic and productive career as poet, playwright, novelist, lyricist, editor, educational reformer, painter, and composer of songs, including the national anthems of both India and Bangladesh, is uniquely matched by Du Bois's own transformation of various modes of writing and thinking, including history, sociology, fiction, poetry, and economics.

Although he is most often read as a Bengali poet, the "geographical diminution" of Tagore as a "parochial possession" of Bengal overlooks his travels to Europe, North and South America, China, Japan, Iran, and Indo-China.[9] His university, "Visva-Bharati," translates as "India in the World" or "The World in India," signalling his insistence that India "was and must remain a land without a center," a land of confluences of cultures and religions.[10] Animated rather than frustrated by the disjunctions of East and West, tradition and modernity, Tagore, like Du Bois, consistently rejected nativism in favour of looking outward – to Europe, Asia, and the USA – but found challenges in imagining alliance in all these spaces. He also shared an intellectual kinship with Wordsworth and Coleridge and such modernists as Yeats, Pound, Gide, Owen, and Frost, echoing Du Bois's affiliations with American pragmatism, German romanticism, socialism, and black radicalism. Having been promoted by Yeats, Tagore won the Nobel Prize for literature in 1913, becoming the first Asian to do so. He was frequently criticized in India for being too cosmopolitan and friendly to the imperialist West, and insufficiently nationalist or Bengali, though the postcolonial state has successfully elided the memory of his fierce anti-nationalism and invented him into a nationalist icon, recalling the rise and fall of Du Bois's reputation over the years.

A famous encounter between the two demonstrates the difficulty of instantiating Afro-Asian alliances, and their search for a third way, beyond colonizer and colonized, black and white. Du Bois solicited Tagore for a message for *The Crisis* in 1929. He had earlier introduced him as "a great, new voice representing the colored races and speaking with the peculiar authority of a Nobel prize man": Tagore offered a method for the "healing of the nations" and the worldwide "race problem" by asking for "a social unity within which all the different peoples could be held together, yet fully enjoying the freedom of maintaining their own differences."[11] Here, Tagore is positioned as Du Bois's fellow traveller, formulating a critique of Western civilization based on the extermination of difference, and seeking alternative forms of community. But in 1929, when Tagore advocates leaving the "fenced seclusion of our racial tradition" and showing "each in our own civilization, that which is universal in the heart of the unique," Du Bois supposes that readers will not understand why "a man who is colored ... writes practically nothing of ... 'race consciousness.'"[12] Tagore's universalism will make little sense to "provincial" Americans, whether white or black, Du Bois observes. But rather than simply extol Tagore's embrace of universal culture, Du Bois goes on to describe Tagore's reaction to the racism he personally encountered during his American tour, part of the rising tide of white supremacy targeted at so-called Asiatics. Tagore had cut short his tour, arguing that "it was not a personal grievance, but as a representative of all Asiatic peoples I could not remain under the shadow of such an insult."[13] In framing Tagore's comments against the reality of American racism, Du Bois signals his respect for Tagore's universalism, but also criticizes it as idealistic, insofar as it is incapable of reckoning with American realities.

That Du Bois needed to gloss Tagore's message highlights the misreadings and shifting meanings endemic to internationalist encounters.[14] Du Bois's claim of fellowship with India was never simply about imagining an anti-colonial coalition, but gestured to a more densely layered notion of kinship – variously geopolitical and racial, as India appeared to him as a nation that was also distinctively coloured, with a history of "fierce struggles between these whites [Aryans] and blacks [original inhabitants] for ... mastery."[15] For Du Bois, India's caste-based social divisions are instances of miscegenation and race-mixing. In mapping race onto caste, Du Bois is not making a conceptual mistake, nor is he projecting from the American case, but instead is inviting us to unravel the deep historical entanglement between race and caste, long submerged in the name of exceptionalism.

For Tagore, a subtle, flexible, and curious thinker, anti-colonial nationalism became insufficiently supple for an Indian identity that was based neither on imitating nor on rejecting the West. After the First World War, Tagore grew ever more critical of nationalism, and his 1916 lectures in Japan and the USA equated it with a loss of soul, responsible for turning people into machines and leading inevitably to conflict. For internationalism, he looked to what he saw as India's history of the adjustment of races and to China and Japan, searching for a Pan-Asian coalition to counter European hegemony. Remarkably similar to Du Bois's Pan-Africanism, Tagore's vision relied on its romantic articulation of a cultural difference separating the East from the West: the East's special, spiritual wisdom could be opposed to (Western) mechanization and militarism.

While Tagore relentlessly critiqued the imperialist West, he also foresaw that Indian nationalism would not be able to contain in its utopian frame very real Hindu–Muslim, rural–urban, and caste-based divisions. Such contemporary markers of crisis and instability as communal violence, Western imitation, urban–rural tension, and the failure to deliver social justice are presaged in *Gora* and *The Home and the World*. For some, Tagore's criticism of the West sounded like an ethereal Eastern mysticism, jettisoning the world in quest for the soul. Certainly, part of Tagore's appeal to Europeans was that he fulfilled the physical and spiritual function of the Oriental seer.[16] *Nationalism* warns against emulation of Western models of the nation. Its central binary is exactly similar to that found in Du Bois's *The Souls of Black Folk*, which argued that the division between East and West was the division between spirit and machine. But can Tagore's emphasis on Eastern spirituality be anything other than a romantic residualism, a response to what Partha Chatterjee, after Hegel, termed the cunning of Reason?[17] In rejecting colonialist and nationalist frames, Tagore was groping for a third way – beyond the polarities of East and West, traditional and modern – insisting on the value of what Du Bois termed soul force in a "dusty desert of dollars."[18]

The distaste for nationalism and the turn to the universal are precisely what have made figures like Tagore and Du Bois appealing to scholars in World Literature, who read the two writers as cosmopolitan humanists. Ross Posnock and Martha Nussbaum reach this very conclusion about *Dark Princess* and *The Home and the World*, respectively. But this way of interpreting Tagore and Du Bois often evacuates the political questions concerning race, nation, and empire that are at the core of their thinking. Tagore's ultimate disenchantment with nationalism is well documented, just as Du Bois's steady turn towards Marxism requires little preface today. What needs further investigation is the way in which they use the categories of provincialism and universalism to think about racial and colonial power. Both reach – sometimes in convergence with, at other times in contradiction of, one another – for the idea of an analogy between race and caste in their thinking about India and the USA. But before turning to their deeper comparative analysis of race and caste, it is first necessary to recall Du Bois's changing conception of India.

"A land of dark men far across the sea"

India was important to Du Bois in two significant ways, which were to some degree contradictory – as a nation that was racially kin, harking back to days of antiquity prior to colonialism and slavery, and as an anti-colonial example, a herald of modern politics. From his earliest days as editor of *The Crisis* to his last days in Ghana, Du Bois urged African Americans to educate themselves about India's struggles with Britain and its efforts to shape a modern democracy. India's history of hybridization of different "races" – the ability to assimilate difference within a social polity without slavery or genocide – animated Du Bois. In the first issue of *Horizon* in 1907, he wrote about "a land of dark men far across the sea ... the land of India, the land, perhaps, from whence our forefathers came, or whither certainly in some prehistoric time they wandered. There a white race has conquered brown men."[19] The idea of another dark people, an ancient race, that could serve as a counter to Western claims about civilizational achievement supported Du Bois in his vindicationist mode. He frequently aligned Asia with Africa as a bulwark against white supremacy. In 1919, he called on black Americans to sympathize with "colored India and colored Egypt" since

> their forefathers were ancient friends, cousins, blood-brothers, in the hoary ages of antiquity. The blood of yellow and white hordes has diluted the ancient black blood of India, but her eldest Buddha still sits black, with kinky hair [...] we are all one – we the Despised and Oppressed, the "niggers" of England and America.[20]

The second dominant manner in which India occupied Du Bois was as a beacon for anti-colonialism everywhere. He claimed in 1947 that India's independence from Britain was "the greatest historical date of the nineteenth and twentieth centuries," an "epochal" event, more significant than emancipation, the Russian revolution, democracy in England, or revolution in France, that would serve as a "prelude to self-determination for all the darker races":[21]

> American Negroes, particularly, have every reason to hail the new and free India. It ... ends the day in a whole continent, when the white man by reason of the color of his skin, can lord it over colored people; when he can bring his segregation and his cheap habits of superiority, as shown by exclusive clubs, "Jim-Crow" cars and salaams and the other paraphernalia of disgraceful human degradation. The sun of the colored man has arisen in Asia as it will yet rise in Africa and America and the West Indies.[22]

Here, Du Bois understands colonialism as a racial project, indeed a white supremacist one: resistance to it is a victory for the "colored man" across the world.

THE WORLD-LITERARY SYSTEM AND THE ATLANTIC 59

Du Bois returned time and again to the analogy that would come to be called the internal colony thesis: in 1943 he wrote that "we American Negroes are the bound colony of the United States just as India is of England."[23] Part of his broader effort to construct racialized modernity as a counterweight to imperial and racial power, he drew upon analogy to indict the USA as an imperial power in a climate of rising anti-colonial sentiment. Japan's victory over Russia in 1904 had galvanized the imaginations of colonized peoples across the world (including Tagore, who reportedly led his students in a spontaneous dance on hearing the news); India then signalled the possibility of transnational solidarity.[24] Du Bois wrote about Gandhi and the Non-cooperation movement from the 1920s onward, stressing the spiritual aspect of Gandhi's platform, praising him as an "exceptional soul called forth by a great need."[25] India thus became both a land of "saints" and a site of modern politics as "race consciousness" in the USA and "nationalism" in India and other colonies came to name the same thing.[26] Later, Du Bois imagined Gandhi, the apostle of peace, Tagore, the majestic poet, and Ambedkar, the Dalit leader, standing together to oppose Britain, casting independent India as a land where "Prince and Untouchable, Muslim and Hindu, [are] all standing shoulder to shoulder."[27] Here, India becomes a successful nation precisely by removing inequality of caste and religion, finding, as the official government slogan has it, unity in diversity.

At the centre of such shifting imaginaries is Du Bois's conception of race and caste as analogous formations. In equating the two, he echoes what is sometimes termed the two-race theory of Indian civilization, which holds that an "Aryan" people invaded India from the Northwest, conquering the original dark-skinned inhabitants, the Dravidians. Du Bois often described Indian history

> as a story of change and tragedy [where] three or four thousand years before Christ, a black people established civilization in the valley of the Ganges ... Upon them descended invaders ... [Mongolians, Indo-Europeans, Mohammedans] A fine and striking primitive civilization arose in India upon the black Dravidian foundation,

as shown by the "black and crisp-haired Buddha."[28] In *The World and Africa*, Du Bois again claims that the original population of India consisted of "Negrillos," followed by "pre-Dravidians, a taller, larger type of Negro; then the Dravidians, Negroes with some mixture of Mongoloid and later of Caucasoid stocks." On this population "descended through Afghanistan an Asiatic or Eastern European element, usually called Aryan."[29] India thus contains a mixture of at least three races: "Some are Negroes; some are black folk, with straight hair; some are of the Chinese type, and some more nearly the European type."[30] Du Bois frequently speculates that India had a "land connection in prehistoric times" to Africa.[31] Such notions of an ancient Afro-Asian connection signal a latent alternate geography capable of changing the historical record (an idea fictionalized in *Dark Princess*). In *The World and Africa*, Du Bois's claim that "black-Asian exchange was a veiled shaping source of the ancient world" looks forward to modern Afrocentrism; his analysis of imperialism as not just the highest stage of capitalism (Lenin), but along a racial grid in terms of which it is European and American imperialism that devastated great expanses of Africa and Asia, anticipates what Wilson Moses calls Afrocentric Marxism.[32]

It is worth recalling that for Marx and Engels, it was precisely this absorptive capacity that kept India from modernizing – "Arabs, Turks, Tartars, Moguls, who had successively overrun India, soon became Hinduized, the barbarian conquerors, being, by an eternal law of history, conquered themselves by the superior civilization of their subjects."[33] This only ends when Britain arrives, the "unconscious tool of history."[34] In Du Bois's mind, the successive invasions of Arabs or Turks become colonial ones – Portuguese, Dutch, and English, which rhetorically aligns India with an invaded and colonized Africa.[35] This allowed him to construct an Afro-Asian world, in the Afrocentric vein of Blyden and Crummell, who viewed Egypt and North Africa as part of the greater ancient Orient, and argued that ancient black culture was a composite of non-white and non-European sources.[36] An ancient Afro-Asia was a counterweight to such racist tracts as Stoddard's *Rising Tide of Color Against White Supremacy* and Grant's *The Passing of the Great Race*, which merged eugenics, racist ideology, and anthropological "evidence" of African and Asian inferiority.

Assessing Du Bois's vast output from his early defence of distinct racial civilizations to his late embrace of Communism, many scholars have charted a development away from a romantic racialism shaped by nineteenth-century ideas of race, nation, and culture, towards a Marxist radicalism, simultaneously inflected by class and race.[37] The analogizing of race and caste suggests something of a similar arc. Indeed, Mullen and Watson write that Du Bois "turned further East as he turned deeper Red."[38] While much of his writing around the First World War focuses on Indians as another coloured people fighting from freedom, by the 1940s, after his engagement with Gandhi, we see a de-essentialization of race taking place in his writing, and caste becomes an ally in that project. Despite this, it is difficult to discern a clear trajectory: on the one hand, so much of his thinking responds to unfolding political events; on the other, the autodidacticism of his reading on Asia causes him to change his mind and even to contradict himself. Rather than assert a historical arc, therefore, my discussion below traces the variegated itineraries caste allows Du Bois to pursue: some incomplete, others circuitously leading back home, and still others beckoning to new horizons.

Of race and caste, or, one of these things is not like the other

Any attempt to think about India and the USA together comes up against the question of the relation between race and caste, a question that calls variably on biological, cultural, and coalitional politics. The analogy may be used to draw a parallel (as Du Bois typically did) between African Americans and all Indians as fellow coloured peoples or darker races struggling against white oppression, thus linking US racism to British imperialism. For Du Bois, this also increasingly meant viewing racism and imperialism as hydra heads of the same capitalist monster. The analogy may also be drawn to connect two minorities – Dalits in India and African Americans – as the Dalit Panther Party famously did in the 1970s, explicitly modelling its organization on the Black Panthers, and adopting a Marxist analysis of revolutionary transformation. The same analogy may also be used to view the USA and India as common subjects of British imperialism, where India draws inspiration from the US declaration of independence. However, the analogy is called into play, it displays a desire for solidarity and alliance as much as a competition, a ranking or hierarchy of suffering or oppression, to protect the nation from criticism.[39]

While Du Bois frequently used the language of caste to describe African-American experience under Jim Crow, he did so for several different purposes. In 1911, he referred to the US South and especially Booker T. Washington's policy of accommodation in terms of caste, saying that "we have seen grow up in the South a caste system which threatens the foundations of democracy."[40] Even in his 1915 memorial to Washington, he noted that the leader was responsible for "the firmer establishment of color caste in this land."[41] In 1929, he warned that "the logical end of racial segregation is Caste, Hate, and War."[42] Caste becomes a fixed form of discrimination for him, the antithesis of racial uplift, progress, even democracy itself. As he wrote in 1912, when Southerners are "tired of democracy; they want caste: a place for everybody and everybody in their father's place, with themselves on top and 'niggers' at the bottom where they belong."[43] In these instances, caste doubles as a synonym for segregation, a backward form of politics signifying an unequal division of society along lines of birth and descent rather than of merit or human rights.

In 1933, Du Bois writes in "Color Caste in the United States" that marriage, the "restricted chance to earn a living," the retardation of "normal social development" by segregation, the uneven distribution of wealth, transportation, trades, public service, and education are all ways to stigmatize and thwart African Americans. African Americans comprise a *caste* that is denied opportunity, access to public spaces, and entry into the national body politic: "this is a true picture of the caste situation in the United States today."[44] The title of the essay itself combines colour and caste to convey Du Bois's understanding of racism as a system analogous to caste-based discrimination. In the same year, he explains this further:

> We are American Negroes. It is beside the point to ask whether we form a real race. Biologically we are mingled of all conceivable elements, but race is psychology, not biology; and psychologically we are a unified race with one history, one red memory and one revolt. It is not ours to argue whether we will be segregated or whether we ought to be a caste. We are segregated; we are a caste. This is our given and at present unalterable fact.[45]

In this construction, caste signifies something immutable and empirically real, while race is placed in the realm of psychology and shown to be variable and internally differentiated. Something similar occurs a year later when Du Bois explains the history of race and racism in the USA, tracing the arrival of labour from Europe which was contracted into indenture, and separated from uncontracted labour from Africa and the Caribbean. But it was only when "slavery became a matter of racial caste ... [that] white laborers served for definite terms and most black workers served for life" that a society bifurcated along clearly demarcated racial lines was created.[46] The use of the term caste again signals the consolidation of racism, becoming something imprinted on skin, community, and race, and transmitted from one generation to another.

In contrast, Tagore's use of the same analogy of race and caste ascribes permanence and fixity to race in the USA, claiming for caste at times a positive social value, and at others, a dynamic sense of changing relations. In 1916, Tagore notes that "a parallelism exists between America and India – the parallelism of welding together into one body various races."[47] Race and caste function as analogies here. But a disjunction soon occurs. When asked about caste in India, usually with a "superior air," Tagore says that he feels tempted to respond with the question: "What have you done with the Red Indian and the Negro? For you have not got over your attitude of caste towards them. ... You have no right to question India."[48] Transnational comparison, rather than inaugurating the exploration of heterogeneous inequities, can foreclose it, becoming a competition of sorts of each nation's social ills.

Both Du Bois and Tagore converge the language of race and caste to discuss their own societies, even as they insist at other times on separating the two formations as exceptional and local. In a 1912 lecture, *Bharatvarsher Itihaser Dhara* (*A Vision of India's History*), Tagore explains India's history of contact, assimilation of various influences, divisions within Hinduism, and the very birth of Hinduism as a unifying force through the language of race and race consciousness, chiding his "western critics, whose own people" resort to "extermination or expulsion by physical force" in a display of "caste feeling against darker races."[49] In 1910, Tagore wrote to an American lawyer: "It has never been India's lot to accept alien races as factors in her civilization. You know very well how the caste that proceeds from colour takes elsewhere a most virulent form."[50] To drive home the bite of the "elsewhere," he continues, "I need not cite modern instances of the animosity which divides white men from negroes in your country, and excludes Asiatics from European colonies."[51] Tagore reconstructs Indian history as an instance of inclusiveness, enabled by the caste system, a testament to India's greatness:

> When, however, the white-skinned Aryans on encountering the dark aboriginal races of India found themselves face to face with the same problem, the solution of which was either extermination, as has happened in America and Australia, or a modification without the possibility of either friction of fusion, they chose the latter.[52]

Even as he castigates the evils of the caste system, he argues that it enabled "races with widely different culture and even antagonistic social and religious usages and ideals to settle down peaceably side by side."[53]

Such statements rely on a particular logic about the encounter of two cultures or races, either through invasion or settler colonialism, assuming the outcome as either extermination through genocide or subordination through slavery. India offers a third option – a social order that can manage difference because everybody has a place. In Tagore's reiteration of this argument, he implicitly positions African Americans as aboriginal or indigenous to the USA or the New World – aligned with Native Americans rather than with Asian immigrants.

Within India, however, Tagore was a biting critic of caste-based forms of discrimination, after an initial romance with them in his early years. His comic sketch, "Aryans and Non-Aryans," gives a sense of his iconoclastic and subtle critique of upper-caste pretensions. Here, in a conversation between Adwaita and Chintamani (literally, worry-wart), Tagore stages a Socratic dialogue over the question "what is this thing that you call Aryan?"[54] Every affirmative statement about being an Aryan is immediately negated, and the hollowness of the category becomes abundantly clear, as the definition shifts from "Hindu" (715) to "not non-Aryan" to "dynasty" to "glorious ancestors" (716) to "the Aryan blood coursing through my veins" (717). Ultimately, Chintamani proves the glory of Aryans by claiming that such cultural practices of theirs as oil massage, the clicking of fingers while yawning, and the beating of a hand-fan on the floor all stem from "magnetism" (718), which proves Aryan superiority to European science and education. Caste discrimination is then cited as evidence of "the exceptional scientific enquiry pursued by the Aryans" (721). What Tagore achieves, beyond poking fun at upper-caste pretensions, is the hollowing out of the very category of "Aryan" which becomes an empty ontology, a locus of ideological claims alone with no empirical reality. Reminiscent of Du Bois's masterful deconstruction of the category of "Negro" or "black" – with the final answer – "the

THE WORLD-LITERARY SYSTEM AND THE ATLANTIC

black man is a person who must ride 'Jim Crow' in Georgia"[55] – Tagore shows both the persistence of casteism and the absurdity of the rationale behind it. In sharp contrast to his statements on caste in relation to race in the USA, Tagore here presents caste as both mutable and meaningless, except in relation to power. Only in comparison with race, then, does caste appear fixed to him.

Du Bois and Tagore were by no means the only thinkers to pursue the race-caste analogy. In the early twentieth century, as critiques of Western materialism and the assertion of Eastern difference multiplied, anti-colonial thinkers like Aurobindo Ghose (1872–1850) and Swami Vivekananda (1863–1902), frequently contrasted India with the USA and Europe. Vivekananda argued that Western societies were stratified along class lines in a manner similar to the caste system in India: "Your rich people are Brahmans, and your poor people are Sudras."[56] Meanwhile, Ghose likened the relation between the European and the Asiatic to that between "master and slave."[57] Both instances exemplify the malleability of transnational comparison as various categories – class, caste, east, west, master, slave – clash as they move across national contexts.

Even Gandhi, known to be the proponent of "harijan" or god's people, had to join the fray, when asked by an American woman in 1929: "Is the plight of the untouchable as hard as that of the Negro in America?" Gandhi first responded, "There can be no true comparison between the two. They are dissimilar."[58] But he then went on to suggest that the plight of the untouchable was indeed better than that of the Negro, listing four reasons – the lack of legal discrimination in the form of Jim Crow laws, the absence of lynching, the canonization of individual Dalits as saints, and the increasing "wearing out" of caste prejudice while "the tide of colour prejudice" in America flowed unabated.[59]

In contrast, the Dalit leader and scholar, Bhimrao Ramji Ambedkar (1891–1956), argued that "there can therefore be no doubt that untouchables have been worse off than slaves" since "to enslave a person and to train him is certainly better than a state of barbarity accompanied by freedom."[60] Ambedkar initially argued that slavery was beneficial to African Americans, "an exchange of semi-barbarism for civilization."[61] His thinking evolved on the question, and through his later correspondence with Du Bois, the African-American experience appeared to him as an example of historical struggle and potential alliance. Ambedkar, who studied at Columbia University, wrote a series of essays comparing untouchability to slavery.[62] He also focused on Reconstruction as an era and a project that could be mined for insight on how to rebuild after the abolition of slavery. In *What Congress and Gandhi Have Done to the Untouchable* (1945), he drew on Herbert Aptheker's *The Negro in the Civil War* (1938) to extract parallels between Reconstruction-era African-American politics and caste politics after Indian independence. Comparing Lincoln and Gandhi as leaders willing to overlook minority interests to further national unity, he sought a connection with Du Bois. But though sympathetic to the Dalit cause, Du Bois was far more interested in allying with Indian nationalism as a sign of the emerging strength of the coloured world. Just as his desire for an autonomous black nation led him to overlook labour violations in Liberia, and his excitement at the idea of a non-white imperial power led him to celebrate Japan's militarism rather than condemn its treatment of China, Du Bois's interest in India as a parallel anti-colonial force led him to downplay the caste solidarity that Ambedkar desired. His mystic interest in ancient India thus helped gloss over caste inequalities, at times fetishizing the Hindu pure blood lineage, though at others, Du Bois yoked the diversity of India's population to his own conception of a mulatto world, what he imagined in *The Negro* as a world of coloured men as the true bearers of humanism, since "most men in the world are colored. A belief in humanity means a belief in colored men."[63] Shifting across the poles of ancestral purity and mulatto globality, the competing uses of caste in Du Bois's thinking register a historical reality characterized by two distinct visions of alliance – race and caste on the one hand, and racism and colonialism on the other.[64]

Ambedkar himself shifted between various meanings of the race-caste analogy. Because caste was defined as a social, spiritual, and religious system, it was difficult to make it the source of a politics that would not automatically fulfil the prophecy of backwardness. Throughout the early twentieth century, Dalit movements tried to make use of the logic of the two-race theory of Indian history and lay claim to being the original inhabitants or "adi-vasis" of the land. But this often meant that a space for Dalit modernity was difficult to establish on the basis of indigeneity alone.[65] Such difficulties help explain Ambedkar's shifting conceptions of the race-caste analogy. He maintained that Aryans were not a race, and that "to hold that distinctions of caste are really distinctions of race ... is a gross perversion of facts."[66] At other moments, however, he expressed a kinship with African Americans on the basis of a possible shared racial identity. But in his correspondence with Du Bois, he notes that because there is "so much similarity between the position of the Untouchables in India and the position of Blacks in America," he "was very much interested to read that the Blacks of America have filed a petition to the UNO. The Untouchables of India are thinking of following suit."[67] Such a statement is not simply repeating the colonial suggestion of a biological connection, though, as Ambedkar distinguishes between an ontological understanding of caste and race and a recognition of similarities of struggle, what Ralph Ellison had termed "an identity of passions," as analogous histories of exploitation may help generate common strategies for resistance like approaching the United Nations.[68]

Du Bois shifted the meaning of the race-caste analogy further when he wrote in 1935, "American Negroes have in their own internal color lines the plain shadow of a caste system. For American Negroes have a large infiltration of white blood and the tendency to measure worth by the degree of this mulatto strain."[69] Here, the history of miscegenation in the USA is again likened to the caste system, as Du Bois extends his colour line between black and white in two directions at once: internally, among African Americans, and externally between Indians struggling for independence and anti-racist struggle in the USA. Running several understandings of the race-caste analogy together in his writings, especially in a lyrical mode, he often used the phrase "color caste" sometimes splitting it up into "the caste of work" (which meant class) and "the caste of color" (which stood in for race).[70] While at times, the use of "caste" signals permanent subordination, at other times Du Bois makes caste a synonym for physical segregation, situating the evolution of a caste system in the USA in a historical process of the institution of indentured labour, slavery, Reconstruction, and the re-entrenchment of subordinate status.

Unthinking exceptionalism

To recognize that such discussions are not just a forgotten mid-century moment, we need only turn to Michelle Alexander's path-breaking study of the relation between race today and past forms of oppression, *The New Jim Crow* (2010). Alexander uses the phrase "racial caste" on nearly every page of the book, in the blurb, and in chapter titles. She argues that slavery, Jim Crow, and mass incarceration are distinct caste systems in America. She neither takes up the race-caste analogy explicitly, nor does she spend any time discussing convergences with the Indian caste system or justifying the term for an American context. Only at one point does she acknowledge the rhetorical choice, declaring that:

> The aim of this book is not to venture into the long-running, vigorous debate in the scholarly literature regarding what does and does not constitute a caste system. I use the term racial caste in this book the way it is used in common parlance to denote a stigmatized racial group locked into an inferior position by law and custom. Jim Crow and slavery were caste systems. So is our current system of mass incarceration.[71]

In other words, she clarifies that caste for her is a matter of common sense, signifying a systematic form of subordination, based on law and custom, rather than any explicit connection with the Indian caste system in the manner traced above.

But her usage matters more than this apparent dismissal might indicate. That such a careful study would use a seemingly anachronistic reference to caste, or recall the vocabulary current in the 1940s and 1950s to describe race suggests at the very least that the analogy still has useful descriptive value. That is to say, since Alexander draws on such landmark studies as Du Bois's *Black Reconstruction* (1935), Gunnar Myrdal's *An American Dilemma* (1944), and C. Vann Woodward's *The Strange Career of Jim Crow* (1955), all of which refer to race as caste, her use of the term may simply indicate how the analogy has passed into common usage, has become sedimented as historical memory, has become real, in a sense. But I think the opposite is actually true here. Alexander uses the term "caste" precisely because it does not fit, to make her point that racial justice in America is mythical, to highlight the shamefulness of current racial politics, thus drawing on "caste" as a signifier of extreme inequality, subordination based on descent, and a backward, shameful, and shocking form of social and political stratification. Her use of caste is neither unconscious nor disingenuous, but deliberate and pointed. She enters the discussions that have haunted the analogy from the outset – the relations among class, race, and caste. She clarifies that although the "language of caste may well seem foreign or unfamiliar," the American avoidance of caste is exactly the same as the refusal to talk about race or class. She concludes that the "so-called underclass is better understood as an undercaste" – "a tightly networked system of laws, policies, customs, and institutions that operate collectively to ensure the subordinate status of a group defined largely by race."[72] The sociological debates between Myrdal, Oliver Cromwell Cox, and Robert Park thus return in the twenty-first century, as the constellations of caste, class, and race undergo various forms of triangulation and mutation.

Recalling this long history of comparisons between race and caste shows that transnational dialogue requires more than a simple politics of analogy or substitution. One form of discrimination does not translate into another, even as the comparison forces the question of the precise nature of the relation between the different forms. To ask the question – is caste race – is thus to enter into a dizzying set of comparisons, deferred meanings, claims of exceptionalism, declarations of eternal verities of an essential Hindu identity or the biology of race that would otherwise not be raised. In contrast to many of the assumptions of transnational American studies, simply opening up the borders of US literature and looking outside does not always challenge the logic of empire or the defensive essentialisms of race and nation. Rather it is only when the historical specificity of a particular formation (racial or caste-based) is acknowledged, can we start making a comparative study. This does not then mean that we should proceed as if the two have nothing to do with each other. The histories and identities of race and caste are intertwined, but they do not make available any simple paradigm of relation. For Tagore and Du Bois, what do India, Africa, blackness, and caste mean, when juxtaposed? What are the uses of Orientalism for black writers like Du Bois, and of blackness for Asian thinkers like Tagore? Ideologies of race and caste developed in tandem, and reconstructing this history makes possible a genealogy of transnationalism that does not go through the nation, as well as generating new conceptual frames for transnational comparisons, beyond cosmopolitanism. Moreover, Du Bois's anti-racism and Tagore's anti-colonialism reveal differences that are as important as the similarities, and analogy often names a political desire rather than a historical reality. To resolve the difficult question of thinking the postcolonial and American together, we should reckon with the fact that the ideas of these two thinkers are not subsumable within abstractions like Third Worldism, nationalism, or internationalism, but rather move between and across them.

Du Bois's tendency to see Indian history through the two-race theory, to map race onto caste thus untangles a convoluted transnational history – revealing not isolation or substitution, but oblique cross-influence. At first glance both Tagore and Du Bois use transnational comparison as a way to shore up their own orthodoxies, equating race and caste, or dis-aggregating them when politically convenient. But the deeper we go into the dialogue, the more illuminating the schisms and misreadings become, as they shape a textured debate about the very conditions of possibility of something called the Global South. Not only do discourses of race and caste appear estranged in juxtaposition, new conceptions of the valence of nation and globe in Du Bois and Tagore become possible. To internationalize race and caste neither requires exporting First World categories nor relying on colonial or nationalist constructions of Indian exceptionalism, nor resorting to the terrain of biology or phenotype. European ideologies of race drew heavily on caste, and in turn, the colonial reading of race helped codify caste as a racial taxonomy in India. Moreover, the first intellectual histories of Dalit identity explicitly referenced slavery and emancipation in the USA as an exemplar of a successful struggle against discrimination, and the last 100 years have witnessed numerous instances of such appeals between Dalit and African-American circles.[73] Most clearly continuing in Du Bois's footsteps, a basic sense of the commonality between Dalit and black continues to characterize contemporary discussions about affirmation action and caste-based reservations or quotas in the USA and India, the similarity of prohibitions on inter-caste marriage to anti-miscegenation laws, and a common language of pollution or contamination. But at other times, different kinds of coalitions are imagined, as in November 2014, when a protest against racial violence in Ferguson, Missouri was organized in front of the American Embassy in Delhi, with the slogan "Black Lives Matter, Dalit Lives Matter." Such efforts to imagine beyond the national always encounter, indeed rely upon, analogy, pinpointing how race travels, how ideologies of race mutate and transform in translation, across the globe, and whether they might become the site of new alliances.

Notes

1. Morris, *Scholar Denied*, xix.
2. Du Bois, *Souls*, 1.
3. Du Bois, "To the Nations," 639–640.
4. It is thus no surprise that he has proved so central to such efforts to imagine transoceanic paradigms as Gilroy's *The Black Atlantic*. On Afro-Asia, see Prashad, *Kung Fu Fighting*; Lee, *Making a World*; Mullen, *Afro-Orientalism*. For Du Bois as a postcolonial thinker, see Bhabha, "Global." On the Global South as conceptual apparatus, see Levander and Mignolo, "Introduction."
5. See Carby, *Race Men*.
6. Jameson, "Third World," 86.
7. Ezra Pound made this claim in a letter to Harriet Monroe, editor of *Poetry*. Monroe, *A Poet's Life*, 262.
8. Lewis, *Du Bois*, 277.
9. Guha, "Travelling," 152–153. Also, see Chaudhuri, "Foreword," xx.
10. Quoted in Guha, "Travelling," 178.
11. Du Bois, "Tagore," 60.
12. Du Bois, "Message," 333–334.
13. Ibid., 334.
14. See Lahiri, "World Romance"; Ahmad, *Landscapes*.
15. Du Bois, "Asia in Africa," 9.
16. See Guha, "Travelling with Tagore," 163.
17. Chatterjee, *Nationalist Thought*, 167–171.
18. Du Bois, *Souls*, 11.
19. Du Bois, "India," 8.
20. Du Bois, "Egypt and India," 62.
21. Rampersad, *Art and Imagination*, 248, 246.
22. Du Bois, "Freeing," 316.
23. Du Bois, "As the Crow Flies," 10.
24. See Horne, *End of Empires*.
25. Du Bois, "Gandhi and India," 203.
26. Du Bois, "Looking Glass," 229–230.
27. Du Bois, "Magnificent India," 29.
28. Du Bois, "Freeing," 302.
29. Du Bois, *World and Africa*, 176–177.
30. Du Bois, "Wide, Wide World," 8.
31. Du Bois, *World and Africa*, 176.
32. Quoted in Mullen and Watson, *Du Bois on Asia*, 2.
33. Marx and Engels, *On Colonialism*, 82.
34. Ibid., 41.
35. See Basu, "Figurations."
36. See Mullen and Watson, *Du Bois on Asia*.
37. See Robinson, *Black Marxism*.
38. Mullen and Watson, *Du Bois on Asia*, xi.
39. See Pandey, *History of Prejudice*; Slate, *Colored Cosmopolitanism*; Visweswaran, *Un/common Cultures*.
40. Du Bois, "Starvation and Prejudice," 309.
41. Du Bois, "Booker," 82.
42. Du Bois, "Pechstein," 313.
43. Du Bois, "Education," 75.
44. Du Bois, "Color Caste," 59.
45. Du Bois, "Negro College," 177.
46. Du Bois, "History," 86.
47. Tagore, *Nationalism*, 83.

48. Ibid., 78.
49. *Tagore Reader*, 194–195.
50. *Essential Tagore*, 100.
51. Ibid.
52. Ibid.
53. Quoted in Slate, "Translating," 64–65.
54. *Essential Tagore*, 716. Hereafter cited parenthetically.
55. Du Bois, *Dusk of Dawn*, 153.
56. Mishra, *Ruins of Empire*, 222.
57. Ibid., 224.
58. Quoted in Slate, "Translating," 67.
59. Ibid.
60. Quoted in Slate, "Translating," 69.
61. Ibid.
62. Ambedkar, *Writings*, Volume 5: 9–18, 80–88 and Volume 12: 741–759.
63. Du Bois, *The Negro*, 146.
64. As Immerwahr puts it, the debate is over "whether being black is like being colonized or like being untouchable" ("Caste or Colony," 276).
65. See Rao, *Caste Question*.
66. Quoted in Omvedt, *Dalit Visions*, 49.
67. Quoted in Thorat Umakant, *Caste, Race and Discrimination*, xxix.
68. See Anderson, *Eyes Off the Prize*.
69. Du Bois, "Clash of Color," 72.
70. Du Bois, "Evolution," 197.
71. Alexander, *New Jim Crow*, 12.
72. Ibid., 13.
73. See Phule, *Slavery*; Murugkar, *Dalit Panther*; Rajshekar, *Dalit*.

Disclosure statement

No potential conflict of interest was reported by the author.

ORCID

Yogita Goyal ⓘ http://orcid.org/0000-0002-5248-3513

Bibliography

Ahmad, Dohra. *Landscapes of Hope: Anti-colonial Utopianism in America*. Oxford: Oxford University Press, 2009.
Alexander, Michelle. *The New Jim Crow: Mass Incarceration in the Age of Colorblindness*. New York: New Press, 2012.

Ambedkar, B. R. *What Congress and Gandhi Have Done to the Untouchables*. Bombay: Thacker, 1946.

Ambedkar, Dr. Babasaheb. *Writings and Speeches 1891–1956*. Bombay: Education Department, Government of Maharashtra, 1979.

Anderson, Carol. *Eyes Off the Prize: The United Nations and the African American Struggle for Human Rights, 1944–1955*. Cambridge: Cambridge University Press, 2003.

Aptheker, Herbert. *The Negro in the Civil War*. New York: International, 1938.

Basu, Biman. "Figurations of 'India' and the Transnational in W.E.B. Du Bois." *Diaspora* 10, no. 2 (Fall 2001): 221–241.

Bhabha, Homi. "Global Minoritarian Culture." In *Shades of the Planet: American Literature as World Literature*, edited by Wai Chee Dimock and Lawrence Buell, 184–195. Princeton, NJ: Princeton University Press, 2007.

Carby, Hazel. *Race Men*. Cambridge, MA: Harvard University Press, 1998.

Chatterjee, Partha. *Nationalist Thought and the Colonial World: A Derivative Discourse?* Delhi: Oxford University Press, 1986.

Chaudhuri, Amit. "Foreword: Poetry as Polemic." In *The Essential Tagore: Rabindranath Tagore*, edited by Fakrul Alam and Radha Chakravarty, xv–xxxiv. Cambridge, MA: Harvard University Press, 2011.

Du Bois W. E. B. "Asia in Africa." In *W.E.B. Du Bois on Asia: Crossing the World Color Line*, edited by Bill Mullen and Cathryn Watson, 9–32. Jackson: University Press of Mississippi, 2005.

Du Bois, W. E. B. "As the Crow Flies." *New York Amsterdam* News (10 April 1943): 10.

Du Bois, W. E. B. *Black Reconstruction. An Essay Toward a History of the Part which Black Folk Played in the Attempt to Reconstruct Democracy in America, 1860–1880*. New York: Harcourt Brace, 1935.

Du Bois, W. E. B. "Booker T. Washington." *The Crisis* 11, no. 2 (December 1915): 82.

Du Bois, W. E. B. "The Clash of Color." In *W.E.B. Du Bois on Asia: Crossing the World Color Line*, edited by Bill Mullen and Cathryn Watson, 68–73. Jackson: University Press of Mississippi, 2005.

Du Bois, W. E. B. "Color Caste in the United States." *The Crisis* 40, no. 3 (March 1933): 59–60.

Du Bois, W. E. B. *Dark Princess: A Romance*. Jackson: University Press of Mississippi, 1995.

Du Bois, W. E. B. *Darkwater: Voices from Within the Veil*. New York: Dover, 1999.

Du Bois, W. E. B. *Dusk of Dawn: An Essay Toward an Autobiography of a Race Concept*. New Brunswick, NJ: Transaction, 1997.

Du Bois, W. E. B. "Education." *The Crisis* 4, no. 2 (June 1912): 74–76.

Du Bois, W. E. B. "Egypt and India." *The Crisis* 18, no. 2 (June 1919): 62.

Du Bois, W. E. B. "The Evolution of the Race Problem." In *W.E.B. Du Bois Speaks: Speeches and Addresses, 1890–1919, [1909]*, edited by Philip Foner, 209–224. New York: Pathfinder, 1970.

Du Bois, W. E. B. "The Freeing of India." *The Crisis* 54 (October 1947): 301–304; 316–317.

Du Bois, W. E. B. "Gandhi and India." *The Crisis* 23, no. 5 (March 1922): 203.

Du Bois, W. E. B. "History of the Segregation Philosophy." *The Crisis* 41, no. 3 (March 1934): 85–86.

Du Bois, W. E. B. "India." *Horizon* 1, no. 1 (January 1907): 8.

Du Bois, W. E. B. "The Looking Glass: A Word from India." *The Crisis* 30, no. 5 (September 1925): 229–230.

Du Bois, W. E. B. "Magnificent India." *The Crisis* 38 (January 1931): 29.

Du Bois, W. E. B. "A Message to the American Negro from Rabindranath Tagore." *The Crisis* 36, no. 10 (January 1929): 333–334.

Du Bois, W. E. B. *The Negro*. Philadelphia: University of Pennsylvania Press, 2001.

Du Bois, W. E. B. "The Negro College." *The Crisis* 40, no. 8 (August 1933): 175–177.

Du Bois, W. E. B. "Pechstein and Pecksniff." *The Crisis* 36 (September 1929): 313–314.

Du Bois, W. E. B. *The Souls of Black Folk*. New York: Penguin, 1996.

Du Bois, W. E. B. "Starvation and Prejudice." In *The Emerging Thought of W.E.B. Du Bois: Essays and Editorials from the Crisis*, 309–311. New York: Simon & Schuster, 1972.

Du Bois, W. E. B. "Tagore." *The Crisis* 13, no. 2 (December 1916): 60.

Du Bois, W. E. B. "To the Nations of the World." In *W.E.B. Du Bois: A Reader*, edited by David Levering Lewis, 639–641. New York: Henry Holt, 1995.

Du Bois, W. E. B. "The Wide, Wide World." *New York Amsterdam News* (7 October 1931): 8.

Du Bois, W. E. B. *The World and Africa: An Inquiry into the Part which Africa Has Played in World History*. New York: International, 1992.

Gilroy, Paul. *The Black Atlantic: Modernity and Double Consciousness*. Cambridge, MA: Harvard University Press, 2003.

Guha, Ramachandra. "Travelling with Tagore." In *Theorizing the Present: Essays for Partha Chatterjee*, edited by Anjan Ghosh, Tapati Guha-Thakurta, and Janaki Nair, 152–187. New Delhi: Oxford University Press, 2011.

Horne, Gerald. *The End of Empires: African Americans and India*. Philadelphia, PA: Temple University Press, 2008.

Immerwahr, Daniel. "Caste or Colony? Indianizing Race in the United States." *Modern Intellectual History* 4, no. 2 (August 2007): 275–301.

Jameson, Fredric. "Third-World Literature in the Era of Multinational Capitalism." *Social Text* 15 (Autumn 1986): 65–88.

Lahiri, Madhumita. "World Romance: Genre, Internationalism, and W. E. B. Du Bois." *Callaloo* 33, no. 2 (Spring 2010): 537–552.

Lee, Christopher J., ed. *Making a World After Empire: The Bandung Moment and Its Political Afterlives*. Athens: Ohio University Press, 2010.

Levander, Caroline, and Walter Mignolo. "Introduction: The Global South and World Dis/Order." *The Global South* 5, no. 1 (Spring 2011): 1–11.

Lewis, David Levering. *W.E.B. Du Bois: Biography of a Race 1868–1919*. New York: Henry Holt, 1993.

Marx, Karl, and Frederick Engels. *On Colonialism: Articles from the New York Tribune and Other Writings*. New York: International, 1972.

Mishra, Pankaj. *From the Ruins of Empire: The Intellectuals who Remade Asia*. New York: Farrar, Straus, and Giroux, 2012.

Monroe, Harriet. *A Poet's Life*. New York: Macmillan, 1938.

Morris, Aldon D. *The Scholar Denied: W.E.B. Du Bois and the Birth of Modern Sociology*. Oakland: University of California Press, 2015.

Moses, Wilson. *Afrotopia: The Roots of African American Popular History*. Cambridge: Cambridge University Press, 1998.

Mullen, Bill. *Afro-Orientalism*. Minneapolis: University of Minnesota Press, 2004.

Mullen, Bill, and Cathryn Watson. *W.E.B. Du Bois on Asia: Crossing the World Color Line*. Jackson: University Press of Mississippi, 2005.

Murugkar, Lata. *Dalit Panther Movement in Maharashtra: A Sociological Appraisal*. Bombay: Popular Prakashan, 1991.

Nussbaum, Martha. *The Clash Within: Democracy, Religious Violence, and India's Future*. Cambridge, MA: Harvard University Press, 2007.

Omvedt, Gail. *Dalit Visions: The Anti-caste Movement and the Construction of an Indian Identity*. New Delhi: Orient Longman, 1995.

Pandey, Gyanendra. *A History of Prejudice: Race, Caste, and Difference in India and the United States*. Cambridge: Cambridge University Press, 2013.

Phule, Jotirao. *Slavery (in the Civilized British Government under the Cloak of Brahmanism)*, 2nd ed. Translated by Maya Pandit. In *Selected Writings of Jotirao Phule*, edited by G.P. Deshpande, 23–99. Delhi: Left Word Books, 2002.

Posnock, Ross. *Color and Culture: Black Writers and the Making of the Modern Intellectual*. Cambridge, MA: Harvard University Press, 2000.

Prashad, Vijay. *Everybody Was Kung Fu Fighting: Afro-Asian Connections and the Myth of Cultural Purity*. Boston: Beacon Press, 2001.

Rampersad, Arnold. *The Art and Imagination of W.E.B. Du Bois*. Cambridge, MA: Harvard University Press, 1976.

Rao, Anupama. *The Caste Question: Dalits and the Politics of Modern India*. Berkeley: University of California Press, 2009.

Rajshekar, V. T. *Dalit: The Black Untouchables of India*. Atlanta: Clarity Press, 1987.

Robinson, Cedric. *Black Marxism: The Making of the Black Radical Tradition*. Chapel Hill: University of North Carolina Press, 2000.

Sinha, Mrinalini. *Specters of Mother India: The Global Restructuring of an Empire*. Durham, NC: Duke University Press, 2006.

Slate, Nico. *Colored Cosmopolitanism: The Shared Struggle for Freedom in the United States and India.* Cambridge, MA: Harvard University Press, 2012.

Slate, Nico. "Translating Race and Caste." *Journal of Historical Sociology* 24, no. 1 (March 2011): 62–79.

Tagore, Rabindranath. *The Essential Tagore.* Edited by Fakrul Alam and Radha Chakravarty. Cambridge. MA: Harvard University Press, 2011.

Tagore, Rabindranath. *Gora.* Translated by Radha Chakravarty. New Delhi: Penguin, 2009.

Tagore, Rabindranath. *The Home and the World.* Translated by Surendranath Tagore. London: Penguin, 2005.

Tagore, Rabindranath. *The Hungry Stones and Other Stories.* New York: Macmillan, 1916.

Tagore, Rabindranath. *Nationalism.* Delhi: Rupa, 1992.

Tagore, Rabindranath. *A Tagore Reader.* Edited by Amiya Chakravarty. New York: Macmillan, 1961.

Thorat Umakant, Sukhadeo, ed. *Caste, Race and Discrimination: Discourses in International Context.* New Delhi: Rawat, 2004.

Visweswaran, Kamala. *Un/common Cultures: Racism and the Rearticulation of Cultural Difference.* Durham, NC: Duke University Press, 2010.

"Time's carcase": Waste, labour, and finance capital in the Atlantic world-ecology

Michael Niblett

ABSTRACT
This article deploys the category of "waste" as an analytical optic through which to explore the connections between the degradation of labour, the contradictions of the value-form, the environment-making dynamics of commodity frontiers and the whirl of finance capital. This investigation forms the basis of a comparison between two very different literary texts: Thomas Hardy's short-story "On the Western Circuit" (1891), set in England's semi-peripheral West Country; and José Américo de Almeida's novel *Trash* (*A Bagaceira*, 1928), set across northeast Brazil's sugar zone and peripheral *sertão* region.

"Time is everything, man is nothing; he is, at the most, time's carcase." So argued Marx in *The Poverty of Philosophy* as he sought to explain the transformation of labour under capitalism.[1] With the generalization of abstract labour-time as the measure of value, it is quantity, not quality, that is decisive in gauging the worth of an individual's labour. Workers are distinguishable one from another only by "the length of time they take for their work."[2] Marx's description of the labourer as an animated corpse possessed by time (value) emphasizes how superfluous the body of the worker is to capital in a certain sense; for what counts is only abstract social labour – labour abstracted precisely from the concrete labours of specific bodies in the cause of determining a socially average quantity of time. Yet the body in its various concrete activities is fundamental to capital: value, as an immaterial yet objective social relation, needs that carcase. As David McNally observes:

> For all its ghostly objectivity, value flourishes only by [...] temporarily possessing entities whose objectivity is appreciably more palpable. [...] The soul of value strives to capture the bodies of value, to possess them, and to evacuate them of all sensibility and concreteness, indeed to suck the life from them in the case of living labour.[3]

Marx's image thus registers the Gothic monstrosity of capitalism's appropriation of life-energies. But it also encodes the structural ambiguity that characterizes value's relation to what it produces (and treats) as waste. The paradoxical figure of the living dead is required to give expression to the paradox represented by the body in its concrete labours as waste matter that – for all it is integral to production – must be expelled by value insofar as these concrete labours, precisely as matter, cannot enter into value as immaterial relation.

In this article, I deploy the category of waste as an optic through which to analyse the connections between the degradation of labour, the contradictions of the value-form, the environment-making dynamics of commodity frontiers and the whirl of finance capital. This analysis will inform my comparison of two very different literary texts: Thomas Hardy's short-story "On the Western Circuit" (1891), set in England's semi-peripheral West Country; and José Américo de Almeida's novel *Trash* (*A Bagaceira*, 1928), set across northeast Brazil's sugar zone and peripheral *sertão* region. Underlying my comparative approach is an understanding of world literature as the literature of the capitalist world-system. I derive this understanding from the work of the Warwick Research Collective (WReC), for whom capitalism is the "substrate" of world literature (or better, world-literature – the hyphen emphasizing its relationship to the world-system); capitalist modernity is "both what world-literature indexes or is 'about' and what gives world-literature its distinguishing formal characteristics."[4] The effectivity of the world-system, WReC contend, "will *necessarily* be discernible in any modern literary work, since the world-system exists unforgoably as the matrix" within which all such works take shape.[5] To this proposition, however, I would add that the world-system must also be grasped, following environmental historian Jason W. Moore, as a world-ecology – as a specific, systemically patterned way of organizing nature.[6] Capitalism, in this view, develops through successive transformations in human and extra-human natures. Thus, these transformations will also *necessarily* be discernible in any modern literary work, since they too exist as the matrix within which all modern literature takes shape.

My interest, then, is in the way Hardy's and Almeida's texts register the localized articulation of the world-historical forms of life- and environment-making through which the dialectic of waste and value unfolds. This dialectic can be understood more specifically as expressing the contradiction between the reproduction of capital and the reproduction of life. Capital, argues Marx, in its insatiable appetite for surplus labour,

> oversteps not only the moral but even the merely physical limits of the working day. It usurps the time for growth, development and healthy maintenance of the body. [...] Capital asks no questions about the length of life of labour-power. What interests it is purely and simply the maximum of labour-power that can be set in motion in a working day. It attains this objective by shortening the life of labour-power, in the same way as a greedy farmer snatches more produce from the soil by robbing it of its fertility.[7]

The tendency to exhaust not only labour-power, but also the vitality of extra-human nature is not something that overly concerns capital so long as it can secure fresh supplies of both. To the extent that such fresh supplies have been reproduced outside the circuit of capital, they represent a repository of unpaid work that capital can seize upon as a "free gift."[8] This unpaid work is performed both by humans and the rest of nature: it might take the form of, say, the domestic labour required to reproduce the individual, or the biophysical processes through which soil fertility is maintained. By appropriating such unpaid work, capital can ensure a greater throughput of energy within the production process at no extra cost. This is the argument put forward by Moore, who follows Marx in understanding abstract social labour as the substance of the value-form, but contends that whereas "Marxist political economy has taken value to be an *economic* phenomenon with systemic implications, the inverse formulation may be more plausible: value-relations are a *systemic* phenomenon with a pivotal economic moment."[9] The accumulation of abstract social labour is possible only to the degree that unpaid work by humans and the rest of nature can be appropriated. Absent such unpaid work, "the costs of production would rise, and accumulation would slow."[10] The value-form (the commodity) is thus constitutively shadowed by its more expansive conditions of reproduction, which, as unpaid work, are unvalued.

The production of value, therefore, depends on that which is unvalued. Yet from the perspective of capital's logic of endless accumulation, the duration required for the (unpaid) reproduction of human and biophysical natures – precisely because it is not directly subordinate to the metric of abstract labour-time – is a *waste of time* insofar as it runs up against the imperative to turn a profit within the socially necessary turnover time. Seeking, as a result, to more closely control and speed-up the delivery of unpaid work to commodity production, capitalism tends to commodify what it had previously been able to treat as a "free gift," thereby driving up production costs.

Such cost increases may be met with the further reorganization of human and extra-human natures in the sphere of commodity production (paid work). This might involve efforts to improve efficiency and reduce wastes of time by rationalizing work routines or radically simplifying environments. Such productivity increases tend to go hand in hand with new forms of plunder. Crucial in this regard has been the global movement of commodity frontiers – spaces of extraction or production (such as mines or cash-crop plantations) that reorganize human and biophysical natures in such a way as to send vast reservoirs of cheap goods into the global economy. In so doing, they help reduce the system-wide costs of production. Commodity frontiers too, however, tend ultimately to undermine the "cheap natures" they initially mobilize. Propelled by the self-expansionary logic of capital, they exhaust their ecological conditions of possibility, degrading land and labour to the point at which profitability falters and new sites of exploitation must be secured. In this sense, commodity frontiers unfold through the production of waste just as much as the production of value. From over-exploited bodies to toxified soils, every commodity frontier, as Moore observes, "is also a waste frontier."[11]

The movement of commodity frontiers in search of fresh streams of nature's bounty is frequently entwined with another of capital's typical responses to rising production costs: its flight into the realm of fictitious capital. Here, capital seeks to eliminate not merely wastes of time but time itself through financialization. As Joshua Clover has remarked, insofar as the subordination of the circuit of capital (M–C–M') to the logic of financialized accumulation (M–M') involves the removal of the commodity phase (C), it entails the "subtraction of time" since "the commodity par excellence is that of labour power, the value of which is measured in time."[12] The florescence of finance capital might thus be seen as capital attempting to free itself, in the context of declining returns on productive investment, from the whole messy, now wasteful business of the labouring body and its productive activities.

The dates of publication of Hardy's and Almeida's works correspond to a period of transition in the capitalist world-system during which the responses I have outlined above to faltering profit rates were all very much to the fore. Hardy's story takes place against the backdrop of the "Great Depression" of 1873–1896, which marked the "signal crisis" of the British-led systemic cycle of accumulation of the long nineteenth century.[13] The economic downturn encouraged efforts to increase industrial productivity through technical and scientific innovation. This was the era of the "second industrial revolution" as the "age of coal and iron" gave way to that of "steel and electricity, of oil and chemicals."[14] As this periodization suggests, such technical advances were inextricable from the movement of new commodity frontiers, which ransacked the globe in the hunt for cheap inputs. Not coincidentally, of course, this was also the era of the "new" imperialism, itself connected to an efflorescence of finance capital. Both during and after the depression of 1873–1896, declining opportunities for profitable investment in industry led many capitalists (especially in Britain) to pursue "an increasing range of speculative activities."[15] Hardy's "On the Western Circuit," I will argue, can be read in the light of this flight of capital away from production towards that more rarefied economic realm in which money breeds money.

Trash, meanwhile, was published on the eve of the final crumbling of the British-led regime of accumulation, the "terminal crisis" of which was signalled by the crash of 1929 and subsequent depression.[16] Almeida's narrative is bookended by the droughts that hit the *sertão* in 1898 and 1915. It registers the harsh labour conditions in Brazil's Northeast, as well as the modernization of the region's sugar industry – the local expression of the restructuring of the world-ecology following the 1873–1896 crisis. Far less obviously, it also registers the phenomenology of financialization as this was experienced in the peripheries of the world-system. The novel's timeframe corresponds to the period of the Edwardian *belle époque* (1896–1914), one of those "wonderful moments" capitalism periodically experiences as the switch to financialized accumulation eases competitive pressures, allowing for a brief flowering of prosperity.[17] *Trash*, as its title suggests, is an exemplary text for any consideration of how the category of waste might be mobilized to help dissect the relationship between the logic of financialization and the exhaustive plunder of human and extra-human natures.

In recent years, "waste" has become an increasingly significant analytical optic in the humanities and social sciences.[18] Broadly speaking, two main (if substantially overlapping) lines of enquiry can be identified. The first is concerned with waste in the form of refuse, pollutants, excrement and other detritus.[19] The second is concerned with what Zygmunt Bauman calls the "wasted lives" of surplus or "superfluous" populations, including the unemployed, migrants and refugees.[20] Surveying contemporary accounts of unemployment, Michael Denning cautions that for all its rhetorical power, Bauman's "overly glib linking of material waste and human waste [...] repeats one of the oldest tropes regarding the wageless – that they are akin to garbage, rubbish." The logic by which globalization produces redundancy, argues Denning, "would be better understood not through the deceptively concrete image of wasted lives," but through a dialectical account of the relationship between waged and "wageless" life.[21]

Denning's critique of Bauman is salutary. It might usefully be supplemented by Michelle Yates' assertion that Bauman fails "to ground the modernizing process, and waste as outcome of this process, theoretically, in the capitalist system in which it is properly embedded."[22] Crucially, a number of critics (including Yates) have sought to elaborate a dialectical conception of waste that has much to contribute to precisely the kind of analysis Denning advocates. Vinay Gidwani, for example, posits waste as "immanent to capital's becoming-being": on the one hand, it is "capitalist value-in-waiting"; on the other, "it is an omnipresent logic of dissipation that evades or exceeds capital's dialectic, threatening its legitimacy and existence."[23] Waste, thus, is something like the degree zero of value: not "forever outside value's ken, but rather its limit and future possible."[24]

Historically, capitalism could be said to emerge through the elimination of "wastes" in the form of the enclosure of common wastes (recast by advocates of enclosure as "wasted commons"); the seizure and cultivation of the "waste lands" of the colonies; and the disciplining of the "wasteful" bodies of those landless men and women who were branded vagabonds and idlers and forcibly inducted into the new regimens of production.[25] Yet, as Marx observed, for all that it is concerned with eliminating waste, "capitalist production is thoroughly wasteful with human material."[26] We have already touched on capitalism's tendency to degrade and exhaust the labourer. It also tends systematically to generate unemployment. The "greater attraction of workers by capital," wrote Marx, "is accompanied by their greater repulsion"; it is capitalist accumulation itself that "constantly produces, and produces indeed in direct relation with its own energy and extent, a relatively redundant working population, i.e. a population which is superfluous to capital's average requirements for its own valorization, and is therefore a surplus population."[27] The accumulation of surplus-value, then, is the accumulation of wasted labour. Ejected from the circuit of production, the surplus population provides a pool of potential workers for capital to seize upon when necessary (in that sense, they are Gidwani's "capitalist value-in-waiting"). Even in its superfluous state, however, this "wasted" labour remains integral to the continuation of surplus-value production, since "the pressure of the unemployed compels those who are employed to furnish more labour."[28]

Marx's comments on capital's creation of a surplus population were, of course, written in the latter half of the nineteenth century – the very period in which unemployment as an empirical category was "invented" by the "emerging social state [...] in the process of normalizing and regulating the market in labour."[29] As Denning observes, "the word itself emerged just when the phenomenon became the object of state knowledge production in the long economic downturn of the 1880s and 1890s."[30] Significantly, a new discourse on waste also came to prominence at this time. Patrick Brantlinger and Richard Higgins argue that between roughly 1870 and the First World War, an emphasis on the "reversibility of wealth and waste" appeared in the work of thinkers as diverse as Thorstein Veblen, H. G. Wells, John Ruskin and Friedrich Nietzsche.[31] In the case of Veblen and Wells, this interest in waste was tied to a critique of the prodigality of capitalism and the parasitism of a new "leisure class." Veblen's most familiar concept, "conspicuous consumption," also means "conspicuous waste," which serves to "absorb any increase in [...] industrial efficiency or output of goods, after the most elementary physical wants have been provided for."[32] One of Veblen's targets were the exclusive books produced by William Morris's Kelmscott Press. Yet Morris too was concerned with the conspicuous waste generated by capitalism, delivering a series of lectures on the subject in the 1880s.[33] Given the context in which such critiques were articulated – the depression in the world-economy; rising unemployment; the flourishing of finance capital (itself typically connected to an increase in conspicuous consumption[34]) – it is not altogether surprising that they should turn so centrally on the problematic of waste.

This context, broadly speaking, was also the one in which Hardy was writing. His evocations of rural life are marked by the impact had on English agriculture by the growth in unemployment and the fall in prices caused by the depression of 1873–1896.[35] Think, for example, of his description of the difficulties confronting agricultural workers in his essay 'The Dorsetshire Labourer" (1883), or of the initial appearance of Michael Henchard as an unemployed hay-trusser in *The Mayor of Casterbridge* (1886). But his work also

THE WORLD-LITERARY SYSTEM AND THE ATLANTIC

captures the response prompted by the crisis in the countryside, most notably the increasing mechanization of farming as a means to ratchet up the plunder of ecological surpluses from the land and the labourer.[36] Consider the well-known scene in *Tess of the D'Urbervilles* (1891) in which Tess is forced to work on a steam-threshing machine that saps "the endurance of [her] muscles and nerves."[37] Plunged into a "stupefied reverie" by the spinning of the thresher's drum, she is reduced to little more than an animated carcase, her movements determined by the devilish will of the "Plutonic master" she serves.[38] The juxtaposition of Tess's exhausted body with the "immense stack of straw" excreted like "faeces" by the machine suggests the dialectical relationship between waste and value, while also echoing the contemporary discourse of the reversibility of wealth and waste.[39]

Some of these same concerns could be said to haunt Hardy's "On the Western Circuit" (originally published in the same year as *Tess* in the *English Illustrated Magazine*). Here, however, the impact of the Great Depression on labour and production figures only in highly displaced form. The narrative concerns Charles Raye, a junior barrister from London who has come to Wessex to do the rounds of the local assizes. Here he falls in love with Anna, a servant girl he catches sight of at a fair in Melchester. Due to the peripatetic nature of his job, their relationship is conducted largely through the exchange of letters. Yet unbeknownst to Charles it is Anna's mistress, Edith Harnham, who writes the letters for her servant girl since the latter is illiterate. Edith falls in love with Charles in the process of corresponding with him; and, moved by her letters, he in effect falls in love with her. Ultimately Anna's secret is revealed, but not until after Charles has married her. He resolves to stay with her, but with a heavy heart and a sense that he has compromised his life and career.

The story begins with a scene partly reminiscent of the threshing scene in *Tess*. An alien machine, in this instance a steam-powered roundabout, has intruded into Wessex, its presence there coded as hellish and phantasmagorical. The spectacle of the fair at which three such roundabouts are in operation is "that of the eighth chasm of the Inferno":

> A smoky glare, of the complexion of brass-filings, ascended from the fiery tongues of innumerable naphtha lamps [...]. In front of this irradiation scores of human figures, more or less in profile, were darting athwart and across, up, down, and around, like gnats against a sunset.

> Their motions were so rhythmical that they seemed to be moved by machinery. And it presently appeared that they were moved by machinery indeed; the figures being those of the patrons of swings, see-saws, flying leaps, above all of the three steam roundabouts which occupied the centre of the position.[40]

Although not a description of labouring bodies, the scene is nonetheless suggestive of the dislocating, estranging effect of the contemporary modernization of the English countryside. Indeed, the representation of the human figures gestures towards the increasing mechanization of agricultural production. Reduced to, as it were, lifeless bodies animated only by the movement of the machinery, the figures are at the mercy of the steam-engine's "inexorable stoker" (246) who at any moment might bring the contraption to a halt, jettisoning the riders. These riders are mainly country folk of lower status than Charles (himself an intrusive presence into Wessex). For this urban middle-class onlooker, the "revolving figures passed before his eyes with an unexpected and quiet grace in a throng whose natural movements did not suggest gracefulness or quietude as a rule" (245). The movements of the machine are thus perceived to have disciplined the otherwise unruly bodies of the riders, just as the new machineries of production were designed to rationalize the extraction of surplus labour. Anna's place on this carousel is secured by Charles, who repeatedly throws his money into circulation to keep her body governed by the motions of the machine.

For all that the roundabout gestures to the steam-powered machines of modern agriculture, however, it is, of course, a means of leisure. With this in mind, I want to suggest that the whirl of the roundabout alludes not only to the reorganization of production, but also to the reverse face of the economic conjuncture: the whirl of financialization and the rise of a new rentier leisure class. In a compelling analysis of the story, John Plotz argues that the presence of the steam roundabout creates a

> phantasmagoric effect that engenders a thoroughly mistaken love at first sight, a sort of love impossible in *ante*industrial Wessex. The steam circuses do not merely conceal some aspect of reality, but create, in a viewer's eye, an illusion that becomes *preferable* to reality.[41]

This escape into an illusory world wreathed in immaterial steam is suggestive of the contemporary flight of investment away from the sphere of material production towards the more abstract realm of fictitious capital. "On the Western Circuit" registers the phenomenal experience of an increasingly financialized society, one subject to the pressures exerted by volatile money and capital markets. Crucially, the relationship between Charles and Anna hinges not only on the judicial circuit of the title, which brings Charles to Wessex, but also on a form of financial speculation. As Plotz notes, money is present at their initial meeting at the roundabout, if not "producing then at least sustaining the original blur."[42] By throwing his cash into circulation to enable Anna to continue to ride the carousel, Charles "sends their relationship into the realm of possible futurity."[43] He moves from being a spectator to a speculator. His money allows him to go on enjoying Anna's motion, an enjoyment derived from sending her away, not in keeping her near him – much as the finance capitalist profits not from the purchase of labour-power to be set to work, but by sending money out into the world. Moreover, having constructed his initial image of her from the blurred fragments of various girls he sees on the carousel, Charles throws his money not after Anna in any material sense, but after a fiction produced by the whirl of the roundabout.

Speculative financial activity, therefore, is presented by the story as the basis of a deceitful relationship. Indeed, money "precisely *alienates* the two who are using it, deferring the conversation (not held till after the wedding) that would undeceive Charles and Anna as to each other's pre-simulation identity."[44] Tellingly, "On the Western Circuit" appeared in the wake of the financial panic of 1890, otherwise known as the Baring crisis, during which Barings Bank in London was driven to near insolvency following excessive financial risk-taking on poor investments in Argentina.[45] Hardy's portrayal of speculative transactions as the source of personal turmoil might thus be seen as peculiarly inflected by the financial instability of the time. The presentation of Charles is noteworthy in this regard. It should be stressed that he is as much guilty of deceit as Anna, taking advantage of this girl of "limited capabilities" with no intention of allowing what for him is a "summer fancy" to "greatly encumb[er] his life" (253). His pursuit of fleeting romantic pleasures adds to the impression that, despite his status as an aspiring professional, this "end-of-the-age young man" is more akin to a member of Veblen's leisure class (252). He is initially described as having "nothing square or practical about his look, much that was

THE WORLD-LITERARY SYSTEM AND THE ATLANTIC   79

curvilinear and sensuous. Indeed, some would have called him a man not altogether typical of the middle-class male of a century where sordid ambition is the master-passion" (245). Later, he is said to belong "to the classes that live on expectation" (254) and to be "sensuous, and, superficially at least, infested with the self-indulgent vices of artificial society" (261). The text, moreover, persistently describes him or his actions as "idle" – he is an "idle spectator" (246), he has an "idle touch" (250), he is drawn to "idle pleasures" in town (253) and so on. Charles, then, appears to resemble a member of the rentier–financier class more than he does any entrepreneurial, bourgeois captain of industry.

If the relationship established at the roundabout is indicative of the structures of experience of a financialized society, so too is the third circuit on which the story turns, that of the epistolary communication between Charles and Anna. The letters they send one another might be seen as representative of the kinds of speculative cultural forms that, as Ian Baucom contends, flourish at moments of financial expansion.[46] Baucom suggests that the rise of credit "enshrined the imagination as a new force at the heart of economic, political and social life."[47] Fittingly, in the context of a renewed proliferation in forms of credit, Charles and Anna's relationship is one predicated on the imagination – on what Charles imagines Anna to be like on the basis of the imagination displayed in "her" written expressions of sentiment. Indeed, the phenomenology of their relationship is symptomatic of the "phenomenology of transactions, promises, character, credibility" demanded by the credit system to complement its accounting protocols.[48] As part of the transaction between Charles and Anna, he extracts a promise from her that she will write to him, her letters (written by Edith) providing the information on which he ultimately assesses her character and comes to credit her in a way he had not done so before:

> The letter moved Raye considerably when it reached him. The intelligence itself had affected him less than her unexpected manner of treating him in relation to it. The absence of any word of reproach, the devotion to his interests, the self-sacrifice apparent in every line, all made up a nobility of character that he had never dreamt of finding in womankind. (260)

The letter on which Charles bases his decision to continue speculating on his relationship with Anna can be grasped as a form of fictitious capital in a double sense: both insofar as it becomes representative of the symbolic capital Charles believes Anna to possess and wants to invest in (the slip of paper he receives is in effect a share on which he bases his future claim on her); and in the sense that this symbolic capital really is a fiction, since the letter is in fact written by Edith. And in this latter sense, of course, Charles has credited something – invested in something – that is not as well capitalized (in symbolic terms) as he believed. He has over-valued Anna; and when the truth of her illiteracy is revealed – when the speculative bubble bursts, so to speak – his world comes crashing down. Envisioning his future in the aftermath of his marriage, he sees "as it were a galley, in which he, the fastidious urban, was chained to work for the remainder of his life, with her, the unlettered peasant, chained to his side" (268). The speculator who has pursued illusory, immaterial riches (in love) is thus brought down to earth, to the everyday material reality of work and the corporeal.

Charles' appalled vision of himself chained to the body of a peasant – a labourer – can be interpreted with reference to the thematic of waste and value. To return to the opening scene at the roundabout: it could be said that Charles exhibits a kind of double vision here. As he watches the various real bodies of the riders whirling in front of him, his vision constructs an illusory body from the physical motions of three girls in particular, which he then attributes solely to Anna, who he decides on as the "prettiest" (246). Charles' double vision might be likened to the double character of the capitalist value-form. In his essay "Labour, Language, and Finance Capital," Richard Godden follows Moishe Postone in proposing value as a non-identical unity: value, he writes, which "stands in for something else [...], will always be shadowed, in the form of an 'impertinence,' by that which it nominally displaces – or, better, creatively mis-takes."[49] The impertinent shadow to which Godden refers is concrete labour. Such labour is necessary to the creation of value; yet value – as abstract labour-time – must expel the concrete particularity of the labour of the human body, treating this body and its activities as (waste) matter to be displaced in the cause of determining a socially average quantity of time. Here, contends Godden, "in the passage of labour into abstract labour, lies the founding duplicity of capitalist value, whose tension will not go away."[50] Indeed, as Godden emphasizes when turning specifically to the "enchanted world of finance capital," the

> real world of labour under capital inheres as a structural "remainder" and reminder within the formation of capitalist value, existing, therefore, as a "dynamic contradiction" interior to the appearance of enchantment and not simply long gone from a notional "outside", occupied by a receding and redundant essence of labour.[51]

It is precisely the tension generated by concrete labour as the haunting residuum or impertinent shadow of value that Charles, the idle spectator who becomes a speculator, must confront in his betrothal to Anna. Seeking through his illusory image of womanhood, born from abstracting from a series of bodies on the roundabout, to profit from a blissful marriage, he finds he is unable to escape the brute matter of the labourer's body. Anna, once revealed as illiterate, is surplus to his requirements; he wants only Edith, the real author of the letters he credits so much. The servant girl, or the "peasant" as Charles now perceives her, is merely waste. He would gladly dispose of her, but the world of work this "peasant" represents cannot, it seems, be sidestepped. If Charles' situation thereby figures the double character of the value-form, it also speaks to the non-identical unity of this value-form with its necessary value-relations, that is, with the socially necessary *unpaid* work that is the historical condition of socially necessary labour-time. Through his marriage to Anna, Charles had hoped to benefit from the unpaid work she could provide not only in the domestic sphere, but also as an accessory at social gatherings, where she would be expected to perform the role of a "professional man's wife" (262). Part of the crisis he confronts is that due to her status and lack of education, she is incapable of doing so. His effort to accumulate social capital, in other words, is jeopardized by his inability to secure the kind of unpaid work he requires.

The accrual of such social capital is necessary to Charles' career; but his ultimate goal – expressed in his complaint that in being chained to Anna he is "chained to work for the remainder of his life" (268) – would appear to be to break free from the world of work altogether and escape the whole messy business of the labouring body. In the context of the financial panic of 1890, Charles' comeuppance takes on the appearance of a warning to those who would indulge in speculative activities and treat too lightly the realities of (working) life. But if the story might thus be viewed as a kind of moral fable (perhaps significantly, it was first republished in Hardy's collection *Life's Little Ironies*), the same context that encourages such a reading also underscores the narrative's registration, at the level of something like its political unconscious, of the economic logic of the era. For Charles' trajectory recalls the trajectory of finance capital, which similarly wishes to avoid the perils of production, seeking to by-pass the commodity phase (C) of capital's general circuit, M–C–M'. Yet, as Clover emphasizes (echoing Godden), despite finance capital's flight from "the concrete context of its productive geography," the "financialized formula M-M' is in fact always the formula M-M'[C]" since "the labour commodity is not truly routed around" but "must perforce await in the future" as the source of the value upon which those speculative activities ultimately depend.[52]

Clover, then, highlights how the rarefied heights of finance capital remain haunted by the hidden abodes of production. But might it not also be possible to read his statement as indicative of capital's tendency to conjoin financialization with new rounds of plunder? That is, might the C in M–M'[C] equally be the commodity frontier? Commodity frontiers, as noted earlier, function to send vast reservoirs of cheap goods into the global economy, thereby helping to lower production costs. The extension of such frontiers into new territories during periods of faltering profitability tends to go hand in hand with the flourishing of fictitious capital: at the same time as declining returns on productive investment send capital scurrying off into the financial sphere, the pressure to reduce costs and restore profit rates propels the frontier-led search for fresh streams of nature's bounty. The flight to the realm of M–M', therefore, is necessarily shadowed by C, the commodity frontier, as the means by which the underlying stagnation in the productive economy might be overcome.

In "On the Western Circuit" the faint shadow of the commodity frontier can be detected behind the images of steam-driven roundabouts with which the story begins. As I have suggested, these register not only the whirl of financialization, but also (albeit in highly displaced form) the increasing mechanization of the countryside in response to the contemporary depression in agriculture, crucial to which was the relative exhaustion of the English grain frontier and its inability to compete with imports from "the newly opened-up wheat lands of the North American prairies and Argentina."[53] But such frontier movements constitute only a distant background to Hardy's narrative. For a more explicit representation of their unfolding we must leave Wessex and cross the Atlantic to Latin America. Here, in a context overdetermined by imperialist domination, the pressures generated by the metropolitan demand for cheap raw materials precipitated an export boom that lasted roughly from 1870 to 1930. In the final section of this essay, then, I consider Almeida's *Trash*, which captures life on the sugar frontier in Brazil's Northeast in the latter days of the boom.

By the 1920s, Brazil's Northeast had emerged as a specific regional geography with an identity defined by harsh environmental conditions (most notably the periodic droughts that gripped the sertão backlands) and a "problematic if ardent embrace of modernity."[54] The Northeast's experience of modernization in the late nineteenth and early twentieth century has been neatly summarized by Durval Muniz de Albuquerque: "Juxtaposed alongside fields of cotton and sugar plantations," he writes,

> were now telegraph cables, telephone lines, and railroads. Hudson, Ford, and Studebaker automobiles as well as Great Western railway cars sped commerce but catalysed its detrimental impacts on the environment, as mountains were scraped clean of foliage and smoke darkened the sky. Traditional modes and rhythms of life were transformed.[55]

In response to these transformations, as well as to a perceived need to assert the specificity and significance of the Northeast in opposition to the growing dominance of the South (not least its economic powerhouse São Paulo), various regional intellectuals produced work celebrating what were construed as the Northeast's distinctive cultural and social traditions.

Perhaps the most influential of these discourses was that associated with the sociologist Gilberto Freyre, who in books such as *Casa-Grande e Senzala* (1933) and *Nordeste* (1937) located the essential values and identity of the region in its coastal sugarcane plantations. Freyre was concerned by what he viewed as the disruption to social equilibrium caused by modernization and its impact on the sugar industry. In the late nineteenth century, the industry "began a major change in its productive organization with the establishment of large mills (*usinas*), which absorbed many smaller *engenhos* and brought downward mobility for many in the traditional planter class."[56] Exemplifying Brazil's subordination to metropolitan financial hegemony, the owners of the modernized *usinas* were often foreign or foreign-born; indeed, the "northeastern sugar fazendas were the very paradigm of dependence upon British capital."[57] Freyre regarded the *usinas* as a socially and ecologically degrading force. Criticizing the rapacious logic of the sugar frontier, he lamented the devastation of the soil by monoculture and the fouling of rivers by waste from the mills. His response to this state of affairs, however, was primarily a nostalgic, conciliatory one. He "wanted to restore the Northeast as it was before the expansion in scale of the smoke-belching sugar factories with their reeking cauldrons, the 'progress,' the destructive affectations that were changing traditional social relations."[58] Against the image of the filthy *usinas*, Freyre posed the traditional *engenhos* – organized around the patriarchal authority of the master or *senhor* – as the embodiment of a past of power and harmony, one that could steer the development of the Northeast in a direction coincident with its "values." His

> utopia was the return of an idealized society in which technical advancement was not necessarily an enemy of tradition, if it was diligently controlled; in which tradition and modernity strolled together, the latter supported and guided by the firm masculine arm of the former.[59]

Almeida's *Trash* responds to the same historical pressures as Freyre's work, albeit it is animated by a very different political vision. As Albuquerque observes, the novel is "deeply transitional, pivoting between [...] naturalist and modernist aesthetics, just as its subject is the transformation of a patriarchal society to a bourgeois one."[60] But where Freyre lamented the erosion of the quasi-feudal authority of the *senhor de engenhos*, Almeida wished to hasten its decline. For him, the modernization of the Northeast was imperative; and modernization could not be achieved if it were to be guided by the plantation oligarchy, since this oligarchy, along with Brazil's Republican government, were responsible for the region's underdevelopment in the first place.[61] Almeida's vision of modernization instead emphasized the integration and development of the impoverished, drought-stricken lands of the sertão.

In the period following independence, nationalist authors had turned to the sertão in search of landscapes and customs that might be mobilized as images of Brazilian cultural autonomy. However, by the time of the proclamation of the Republic in 1889 (and in the wake of the Great Drought of 1877–1879), the area had shifted from "an idealized repository of national identity toward a danger zone that threaten[ed] the construction of the modern nation."[62] Through its representation in literary texts, newspaper articles and official reports (in which an ideology of racial and environmental determinism was typically present), the sertão emerged as a backward, degraded, constitutively anti-modern space. This discourse helped to enable and justify repressive state policies towards its inhabitants, who came to be associated with mass disorder, banditry and disease.[63] Almeida sought to challenge this presentation of the sertão. Blaming its impoverishment on government neglect and the influence of the local oligarchy, he revived in some measure the earlier representation of the region as a site of authentic Brazilian values. For Almeida, however, if the sertão was to contribute to the development of the nation it required modernization, a task he pursued as minister of transportation and public works in the government of Getúlio Vargas following the revolution of 1930.

Given Almeida's active involvement in the revolution, one might view *Trash* as staging something like a cultural rehearsal of the class politics surrounding Vargas's rise to power. Vargas's movement was supported by the national industrial bourgeoisie and directed "against the agrarian, commercial and metropolitan interests which had shaped and benefited from previous governmental policy."[64] As Mark Anderson notes, Almeida's novel

> constructs a geographic opposition [...] between three conflictive spaces: the *brejo*, or lush mountainous highlands of coastal Paraíba, is placed in opposition to the [...] *sertão* as well as to the metropole [...]. By no means a third meditating space, the *brejo* represents a morally and racially degraded area in which the feudal economy of the [...] sugar plantation prevails and individual initiative is smothered by patriarchal egoism and animal instinct. In a snub to Gilberto Freyre's nascent thesis of an integrated Northeast based on the coastal "sugar civilization," Almeida describes the sugar plantation as a moral and economic wasteland.[65]

Alongside Almeida's corresponding revalorization of the sertão, therefore, the symbolic geography of *Trash* speaks to the political concerns of the industrial bourgeoisie in the lead up to the revolution, imaginatively rehearsing what it would mean to appeal to, and potentially ally with, the popular classes in the struggle against the agrarian oligarchs. This projection of the possibility of a cross-class alliance is manifested in the developing relationship between the characters of Lúcio and Soledade. Lúcio, the enlightened son of a plantation owner, has been educated in the city and advocates the modernization of the rural economy. Soledade, a beautiful young woman from the backlands, arrives on Lúcio's father's plantation with a group of refugees fleeing drought in the sertão. Their union would symbolize the integration of the sertão into the modern nation, with the domestication of Soledade "coincid[ing] with the modernization of the agricultural economy."[66]

Crucially, however, this union fails, with Soledade not only returning to the sertão but doing so with Lúcio's father. Lúcio, meanwhile, marries the daughter of the owner of a *usina*. The text thus abandons its rehearsal of a cross-class alliance, staging instead the possibility of an intra-bourgeois one. (In so doing, it presages the fate of the 1930 revolution, which devolved into compromise between the old agrarian interests and the new industrialists over a share of the spoils of office.)[67] The modernized plantation Lúcio establishes following his marriage becomes an emblem for the new nation. It represents "an oasis of prosperity, a model of agricultural technology whose efficiency contrasted with the old primitive methods" – methods that had earlier been said to impoverish the soil, turn the landscape "into a waste," and rely on exploitative modes of labour regulation that were "unrewarding" and "wasted" the "energy" of the workers.[68] However, just as the symbolic coupling of Lúcio and Soledade misfires, so the symbolism of the modernized plantation is far from unproblematic. Lúcio's idyll of lush cultivated fields and well-adjusted, productive labourers remains haunted by the wasted figures of starving refugees from the backlands, as well as by the continued lack of sympathy displayed by his *brejeiro* workers towards the *sertanejos*.

The haunting quality of the drought-stricken migrants is emphasized by the narrative twist at the end of the novel, when the drought of 1915 brings Soledade, who had been thought dead, back to Lúcio's door:

> The deep shadows under her eyes spread a violet hue over all her face. Her skin was dark and coarsened, showing the lines of the bones, and her cheeks so shrunken she seemed to have three mouths. She looked about her with a sad expression that seemed to make her nose longer. Finally, so as not to fall, she leaned against the wall and remained there looking like a shadow. (159)

Soledade's wasted, disquieting body here stands as a variant on the image of the labouring body as a carcase, a residuum, an "impertinent shadow" (as Godden puts it), which capital exploits, exhausts, and expels as waste, and yet can never jettison fully. For Lúcio, she is a reminder of the suffering, devitalized bodies that had laboured on his father's plantation, a world he had hoped to supersede by his rational reorganization of work routines and his respectful, compassionate attitude to his employees. The suggestion is that he cannot in fact escape the degrading, exploitative dynamics of the sugar frontier: the systemic compulsion to exhaust human (and extra-human) natures will continue to weigh upon his dreams of an enlightened form of labour discipline – a potential return of the repressed foreshadowed perhaps by Soledade's having arrived with a young boy whom Lúcio is forced to recognize as his brother.

Soledade's disfigured body – at once both lacking and excessive, emaciated yet proliferating (her "three mouths," her distended nose) – is but one of many similarly grotesque bodies that stalk the novel. Early on in the narrative, for example, we encounter the "exodus from the drought of 1898":

> A resurrection from ancient cemeteries of resuscitated skeletons of claylike appearance and stinking of the charnel house. Emaciated ghosts, their shaky, unsteady steps seemed like a dance as they dragged themselves along in the manner of one who is carrying his legs instead of being carried by them. [...] They were more dead than alive. [...] They sniffed the sickly smell of the molasses which only exacerbated the pangs of their empty stomachs; but instead of eating, they themselves were eaten by their own hunger, in self-destructive autophagia. (14–15)

Such gritty yet lyrical descriptions of starving bodies – bodies that are "eaten by their own hunger" even as they are surrounded by the smell deriving from the production of a wealth of cash-crops – capture the combination of glut and lack that characterized the Northeast's sugar zone. As Lance La Rocque observes, Almeida "makes the hungering flesh into a main character of the novel."[69] This emphasis on the agency of hunger, in conjunction with Almeida's persistent mobilization of the paradoxical figure of the living dead, speaks to the specific dynamics of underdevelopment in the Northeast. For here the abundance of cheap labour available to the plantations when drought expelled the *sertanejos* from the backlands tended to discourage productivity-raising capital investment. The large landowners relied precisely on hunger, in tandem with the distinctive geography of the region, to perpetuate the production of surplus-value. As Mike Davis explains,

> from the 1870s onward, the Nordeste was effectively capitalized on the fluxes of labour between the backlands and the coast. Potentially explosive accumulations of poor and unemployed labourers in the littoral were diverted into the subsistence economy of the sertão, then periodically regurgitated towards the coast by drought. The sertão, in effect, provided welfare for the poor, while drought guaranteed that desperate labourers would always be available to depress wages on the coast.[70]

Almeida's emaciated yet grotesquely excessive revenants, therefore, embody the peculiar form assumed in the Northeast by capital's tendency to generate a surplus population of "wasted" labour as the very condition of expanded value production.

Trash, then, at the level of both content and imagery, registers the transformations in human and extra-human natures through which the Northeast's sugar frontier developed. But it also gestures, I want finally to suggest, to the commodity frontier's more rarefied twin: finance capital. As noted earlier, the novel's timeframe corresponds to the period of the Edwardian *belle époque*, during which the grip exerted by metropolitan finance over Brazil's economy intensified. More significantly, perhaps, the novel was written and published in the era of the Washington Luis presidency. Under Luis, the Brazilian government gave full support to the entry of foreign capital into the country (albeit with the emphasis now on US rather than British financial interests).[71] The brief "boom" this generated, in combination with the further ratcheting up of foreign domination and the strangulation of Brazilian industry, might be said to find expression in *Trash*'s formal and stylistic idiosyncrasies.

I have already drawn attention to the novel's lyrical descriptions of starving refugees. Such poeticism has been much remarked upon by critics, who highlight the unevenness of Almeida's narrative. Fred Ellison, for example, suggests that:

> there is a regrettable lack of correspondence between the observed reality of characters and actions and the language in which this reality is projected. [...] The human events upon which the novel is based are ugly and sombre, but the novelist's descriptions of them are intensely poetic, with too much imagery, too much striving for effect.[72]

This disjunctive form speaks to the uneven logic of the sugar frontier, with Almeida's images of suffering bodies emphasizing the brutal reality of exploitation in the Northeast. Yet what the author himself refers to in the novel's prologue as the narrative's "sentimental excesses" simultaneously abstract from this reality, dematerializing it through the mobilization of an affective, highly aestheticized register. Such is the intensity of Almeida's descriptions that they frequently assume a kind of phantasmagoric quality, as with his account of the *sertanejos* as "emaciated ghosts" who appear to be "carrying [their] legs" rather than being "carried by them." The narrative's flights of poetic fancy strive to evoke or capture a realm of feeling and experience that is beyond or supplementary to observable reality (in the prologue, significantly, Almeida avers that "to see clearly is not to see at all but to see what is hidden from others" [11]). Given the historical and economic context in which he was working, Almeida's striving after the unseen can be viewed as a response to a local reality in which the invisible hand of fictitious capital, emanating from distant cities (whether São Paulo or Rio de Janeiro, London or New York), periodically reshapes lives and landscapes. *Trash*'s formal disjunctions, in other words, encode a structure of feeling that corresponds to a situation in which everyday life is overdetermined by the abstract forces of finance capital, yet in which, too, such forces are peculiarly occulted by the apparent "obviousness" of the disconnection between an immediate reality of grinding rural poverty and the world of high finance.

There are a score of novels that represent the impact of finance capital in Brazil during the export boom far more explicitly than does *Trash*. Renata Wasserman notes, for example, how works

> by Lima Barreto, Julia Lopes de Almeida, and Afonso de Taunay drew, for plot and characterization, on the conditions of living in an export economy dependent on international markets [...]. In all these cases, literature was responding to financial conditions both local and international.[73]

Almeida's novel, however, provides us with a kind of phenomenology of financialization as this was experienced in the rural peripheries, away from the whirl of the stock exchange in, say, Rio de Janeiro (the setting for de Taunay's *O encilhamento*). *Trash*'s original Portuguese title, *A Bagaceira*, derives from the name of the place used to store bagasse, the fibrous matter that remains after sugarcane has been crushed and the juice extracted. It very obviously alludes to the sugar industry's devitalization of land and labour, its production of value through the systematic production of waste. But if the text thereby foregrounds the environment-making dynamics of the commodity frontier, its formal and stylistic logics bear the marks of a different kind of trash – the claims of fictitious capital which, just a year after Almeida's novel was published, would be reduced to junk by the financial crash of 1929 and the subsequent depression.

Notes

1. Marx, *Poverty of Philosophy*, 127.
2. Ibid.
3. McNally, *Monsters of the Market*, 132.
4. WReC, *Combined and Uneven Development*, 15.
5. Ibid., 20.
6. Moore, *Capitalism*, 2–3.
7. Marx, *Capital*, 375–376.
8. Marx, *Capital* Vol. 3 (1967), 745.
9. Moore, *Capitalism*, 54–55.
10. Ibid., 54.
11. Moore, "Capitalocene," 38.
12. Clover, "Autumn," 42.
13. Arrighi, *Long Twentieth Century*, 220.
14. Barraclough, *Introduction*, 44.
15. Arrighi, *Long Twentieth Century*, 177.
16. Ibid., 275.
17. Ibid., 178.
18. See, for example, the work collected at the *Discard Studies* website: http://discardstudies.com/.
19. The literature is vast, but with special reference to representations of waste in cultural production see, for example, Lincoln, *Expensive Shit*; Gamber, *Positive Pollutions*; Phillips and Sullivan, "Material Ecocriticism"; Bragard, "Introduction"; Morrison, *Literature of Waste*.
20. Bauman, *Wasted Lives*; again, the literature is vast, but for a useful summary see McIntyre and Nast, "Bio(necro)polis."
21. Denning, "Wageless Life," 96.

22. Yates, "The Huamn-as-Waste," 1687.
23. Gidwani, "Six Theses," 773.
24. Gidwani and Reddy, "The Afterlives of 'Waste'," 1626.
25. Goldstein, *Terra Economica*, 357; Porter, *Unlearning*, 56; Bauman, *Legislators and Interpreters*, 43.
26. Marx, *Capital* Vol. 3 (1981), 180.
27. Marx, *Capital*, 783, 782.
28. Ibid., 793.
29. Denning, "Wageless Life," 82.
30. Ibid.
31. Brantlinger and Higgins, "Waste and Value," 454.
32. Ibid., 460.
33. See Miller, "Sustainable Socialism."
34. Arrighi, *Long Twentieth Century*, 96.
35. Musson, "The Great Depression," 202, 225.
36. See Collins, "The Rationality."
37. Hardy, *Tess*, 329.
38. Ibid., 337, 330.
39. Ibid., 337.
40. Hardy, "On the Western Circuit," 244–245. Hereafter cited in the text.
41. Plotz, "Motion Slickness", 369.
42. Ibid., 379.
43. Ibid.
44. Ibid., 380.
45. See Triner and Wandschneider, "The Baring Crisis." Subsequent references to the novel will be cited parenthetically.
46. Baucom, *Specters*, 32.
47. Ibid., 66.
48. Ibid., 64.
49. Godden, "Labour," 419.
50. Ibid.
51. Ibid., 420.
52. Clover, "Autumn," 44–45.
53. Perry, *British Agriculture*, xiv.
54. Albuquerque, *The Invention*, 14.
55. Ibid.
56. Rogers, *Deepest Wounds*, 51.
57. Davis, *Late Victorian*, 382, 380.
58. Albuquerque, *The Invention*, 67.
59. Ibid., 68.
60. Ibid., 102.
61. Anderson, *Disaster Writing*, 93.
62. Ibid., 65.
63. The most infamous of such state interventions was the bloody campaign waged against the town of Canudos in 1897.
64. Frank, *Capitalism*, 174–175.
65. Anderson, *Disaster Writing*, 90–91.
66. Ibid., 90. Although I do not have space to pursue the point in more detail here, it is worth emphasizing how both Hardy's and Almeida's texts turn on a problematic or abortive marriage, in which anxieties over the need to "domesticate" a working-class woman speak to contemporary struggles to discipline female bodies in the quest to secure new streams of unpaid work in the context of an economic downturn.
67. Frank, *Capitalism*, 175.
68. Almeida, *Trash*, 154, 29–30. Hereafter cited in the text.
69. La Rocque, "Fields of Force," 406.

70. Davis, *Late Victorian*, 392.
71. Frank, *Capitalism*, 174.
72. Ellison, *Brazil's New Novel*, 30.
73. Wasserman, "Financial Fictions," 194.

Disclosure statement

No potential conflict of interest was reported by the author.

Bibliography

Albuquerque, Durval Muniz de. *The Invention of the Brazilian Northeast*. Durham, NC: Duke University Press, 2014.

Almeida, José Américo de Almeida. *Trash*. Translated by. R. L. Scott-Buccleuch. London: Peter Owen, 1978.

Anderson, Mark. *Disaster Writing*. Charlottesville: University of Virginia Press, 2011.

Arrighi, Giovanni. *The Long Twentieth Century*. London: Verso, 2010.

Baucom, Ian. *Spectres of the Atlantic*. Durham, NC: Duke University Press, 2005.

Bauman, Zygmunt. *Legislators and Interpreters*. Cambridge: Polity, 1987.

Bauman, Zygmunt. *Wasted Lives*. Cambridge: Polity, 2004.

Barraclough, Geoffrey. *Introduction to Contemporary History*. London: Penguin, 1967.

Bragard, Véronique. "Introduction: Languages of Waste: Matter and Form in our Garb-age." *Interdisciplinary Studies in Literature and Environment* 20, no. 3 (2013): 459–463.

Brantlinger, Patrick, and Richard Higgins. "Waste and Value: Thorstein Veblen and H. G. Wells." *Criticism* 48, no. 4 (2008): 453–475.

Clover, Joshua. "Autumn of the System: Poetry and Financial Capital." *Journal of Narrative Theory* 41, no. 1 (2011): 34–52.

Collins, E.J.T. "The Rationality of 'Surplus' Agricultural Labour." *AHR* 35 (1987): 36–46.

Davis, Mike. *Late Victorian Holocausts*. London: Verso, 2001.

Denning, Michael. "Wageless Life." *New Left Review* 66 (2010): 79–97.

Ellison, Fred. *Brazil's New Novel*. Berkeley: University of California Press, 1954.

Esty, Joshua. "Excremental Postcolonialism." *Contemporary Literature* 40, no. 1 (1999): 22–59.

Frank, Andre Gunder. *Capitalism and Underdevelopment in Latin America*. New York: Monthly Review Press, 1969.

Gamber, John Blair. *Positive Pollutions and Cultural Toxins*. Lincoln: University of Nebraska Press, 2012.

Gidwani, Vinay. "Six Theses on Waste, Value, and Commons." *Social & Cultural Geography* 14, no. 7 (2013): 773–783.

Gidwani, Vinay, and Rajyashree N. Reddy. "The Afterlives of 'Waste': Notes from India for a Minor History of Capitalist Surplus." *Antipode* 43, no. 5 (2011): 1625–1658.

Godden, Richard. "Labor, Language, and Finance Capital." *PMLA* 126, no. 2 (2011): 412–421.

Goldstein, Jesse. "Terra Economica: Waste and the Production of Enclosed Nature." *Antipode* 45, no. 2 (2013): 357–375.

Hardy, Thomas. "On the Western Circuit." In *The Distracted Preacher and Other Tales*, edited by Susan Hill, 244–268. London: Penguin, 1979.

Hardy, Thomas. *Tess of the D'Urbervilles*. London: Broadview, 2013.

La Rocque, Lance. "Fields of Force: The Claims of the Ex-Centric in Almeida's *Trash*." *Revista Hispánica Moderna* 54, no. 2 (2001): 399–412.

Lincoln, Sarah. *Expensive Shit: Aesthetic Economies of Waste in Postcolonial Africa*. Charleston, SC: Bibliobazaar, 2012.

Marx, Karl. *Capital*. Vol. 1. Translated by Ben Fowkes. London: Penguin, 1990.

Marx, Karl. *Capital*. Vol. 3. New York: International Publishers, 1967.

Marx, Karl. *Capital*. Vol. 3. Translated by David Fernbach. London: Penguin, 1981.

Marx, Karl. "The Poverty of Philosophy." In *Marx & Engels Collected Works*, Vol. 6, edited by Robert Daglish, Richard Dixon, W. L. Guttsman, Frida Knight, Margaret Mynatt, and Alick West and translated by Frida Knight, 105–212. London: Lawrence and Wishart, 2010.

McIntyre, Michael, and Heidi Nast. "Bio(Necro)Polis: Marx, Surplus Populations, and the Spatial Dialectics of Reproduction and 'Race'." *Antipode* 43, no. 5 (2011): 1465–1488.

McNally, David. *Monsters of the Market*. Leiden: Brill, 2011.

Miller, Elizabeth. "Sustainable Socialism: William Morris on Waste." *Journal of Modern Craft* 4, no. 1 (2011): 7–25.

Moore, Jason W. *Capitalism in the Web of Life*. London: Verso, 2015.

Moore, Jason W. "The Capitalocene: Part II: Abstract Social Nature and the Limits to Capital." Accessed February 16, 2016. http://www.jasonwmoore.com/uploads/The_Capitalocene___Part_II__June_2014.pdf.

Morrison, Susan. *The Literature of Waste*. New York: Palgrave, 2015.

Musson, A.E. "The Great Depression in Britain, 1873–1896: A Reappraisal." *Journal of Economic History* 19, no. 2 (1959): 199–228.

Perry, P.J. *British Agriculture, 1875–1914*. London: Methuen, 1973.

Phillips, Dana, and Heather Sullivan. "Material Ecocriticism: Dirt, Waste, Bodies, Food, and Other Matter." *Interdisciplinary Studies in Literature and Environment* 19, no. 3 (2012): 445–447.

Plotz, John. "Motion Slickness: Spectacle and Circulation in Thomas Hardy's 'On the Western Circuit'." *Studies in Short Fiction* 33, no. 3 (1996): 369–386.

Porter, Libby. *Unlearning the Colonial Cultures of Planning*. Farnham: Ashgate, 2010.

Rogers, Thomas. *The Deepest Wounds*. Chapel Hill: University of North Carolina Press, 2010.

Triner, Gail, and Kirsten Wandschneider. "The Baring Crisis and the Brazilian Encilhamento, 1889–1891: An Early Example of Contagion among Emerging Capital Markets." *Financial History Review* 12, no. 2 (2005): 199–225.

Wasserman, Renata. "Financial Fictions: Emile Zola's L'argent, Frank Norris' The Pit, and Alfredo de Taunay's O Encilhamento." *Comparative Literature Studies* 38, no. 3 (2001): 193–214.

WReC (Warwick Research Collective). *Combined and Uneven Development*. Liverpool: Liverpool University Press, 2015.

Yates, Michelle. "The Human-As-Waste, the Labor Theory of Value and Disposability in Contemporary Capitalism." *Antipode* 43, no. 5 (2011): 1679–1695.

From the *Novela de la Caña* to Junot Díaz's "cake-eater": World-literature, the world-food-system and the Dominican Republic

Kerstin Oloff ⓘ

ABSTRACT
Significant changes occurred from the 1870s onwards, which laid the foundations for today's highly uneven, globalized world-food-system. It is in this context that Dominican and Dominican-American literary aesthetics are particularly revealing, as they register the impact of the rapid integration of the Dominican Republic into the world market through the sugar industry. As I argue, while the political ecology fuelling the foundational romance *Enriquillo* by Manuel de Jesús Galván (1882) is consciously repressed in the service of producing a national fantasy, the "critical irrealist" aesthetics of Ramón Marrero Arristy's *Over* (1939) possess at least some disruptive potential. It is in this context that Junot Díaz's insistent focus on style, genre and aesthetics take on their full significance, placing *The Brief Wondrous Life of Oscar Wao* (2007) at the vanguard of thinking around the "worlding" of literary studies as well as about the role of cultural production in what Jason W. Moore calls the capitalist "world-ecology."

The contemporary world-food-system is suspended, as Raj Patel illustrates in *Stuffed and Starved* (2007), between the poles of hunger and obesity in a continuum of poverty. While starvation is readily understood as having little to do with individual choice, it needs to be stressed that obesity rates are also shaped by factors such as class, ethnicity and location, and inscribed into a highly uneven capitalist world-system of cores and peripheries. Within this context, the role of sugar was in many ways paradigmatic: as one of the original exports of the Americas, it brought wealth to the metropolitan centres and devastation to the colonies and it was from the start profoundly imbricated in the increasing mediation of food-getting via the money economy. While the *longue durée* of capitalism continues to be indispensable for an analysis of the role of sugar, significant changes occurred from the 1870s onwards, which laid the foundations for today's highly uneven, globalised world-food-system. The latter was shaped by a number of world-historical changes, including the second industrial revolution fuelled by coal and oil, the emergence of US imperialism and the corporate revolution of US capital. Related to these changes was a dramatic dietetic revolution, which increased sugar consumption in the industrial core countries, including in the USA where per capita sugar consumption "increased 211 percent in the period 1870–1930."[1] On the economic periphery of the global economy, on the other hand, the Dominican Republic was radically transformed and "modernized" by the sugar industry, which translated into the brutal exploitation of land and labour.

Sugar's relation to literary, and more broadly cultural, aesthetics is well studied.[2] For good reasons, much of this existing scholarship focuses on aesthetics in relation to colonial plantations and their lasting legacies. In this article, I want to focus on saccharine aesthetics in the age of an increasingly integrated world-food-system. Dominican, and Dominican-American, literary aesthetics – from the foundational romance *Enriquillo* by Manuel de Jesús Galván (1882), to the sugar cane novels of the first half of the twentieth century, to the migrant literature written from the US Diaspora – are particularly revealing in this context. Consider, then, the following two literary examples, both of which are centrally concerned with the political ecology of sugar as well as its cultural registrations. On the one hand, in Junot Díaz's *The Brief Wondrous Life of Oscar Wao* (2007), the tragicomic Dominican-American Oscar is an "overweight frea[k]," a "*cake eater*," whose body is shaped by a world-food-system, in which the urban majority has no access to land and lives on processed, sugar-laced foods.[3] Ramón Marrero Aristy's *Over* (first published in 1939), an archetypal *novela de la caña* [sugarcane novel], on the other hand, presents us with the starved (and mostly migrant) workers on a US-run sugar plantation in the Dominican Republic in the 1930s.[4]

Comparing these aesthetic registrations of sugar, this article situates itself within current efforts to recalibrate the field of postcolonial studies as the study of "world-literature" as championed by the Warwick Research Collective (WReC).[5] It aims to bring out what it would mean to read cultural production with a focus on the changing contexts of the production of food and its consumption in an ever more tightly globalized world in which food-getting is increasingly mediated by financial transactions and detached from locality. What do the characters eat? Who produces their food? And in what ways does the production and consumption of food in an uneven world-system relate to aesthetics? Sugar provides an ideal case study, because of its fundamental role in the rise of capitalist world-ecology, as well as the drastic transformations from the 1870s onwards. Yet, the extent to which such "registration" leads to explicit critical engagement differs drastically: while the political ecology fuelling the foundational romance *Enriquillo* is consciously repressed in the service of producing a national fantasy, the "critical irrealist" aesthetics of Arristy's *Over* possess at least some disruptive potential.[6] As I argue, Junot Díaz's insistent focus on questions of style, genre and aesthetics take on their full significance within this context, placing his text at the vanguard of thinking around the "worlding" of literary studies as well as about the role of cultural production in the capitalist "world-ecology."[7]

World-literature, saccharine aesthetics and the Dominican Republic

Changes in food-getting over the last five hundred years have been remarkable: local nutrient cycles were disrupted and increasingly linked into a globalizing capitalist world-ecology.[8] The mono-cultural production of certain crops played a central role in this world-historical process: as one of the original global export commodities of the Americas, sugar is the fruit of genocide and conquest, of the horrors of the trade of humans across the Atlantic and of their dehumanizing enslavement on the plantations. Sugar's circulation is "deeply structured by global capitalism" which enabled brutally exploitative global divisions of labour, pioneered unsustainable development by exhausting deforested Caribbean soils, and financed the industrial revolution of the European core.[9] Further, sugar was inscribed in world-historical dietetic revolutions, gradually turning into a staple food and functioning as significant energy source that lowered systemic reproduction costs, that is, food prices for the working classes. As Sidney Mintz observes, the "profound changes in dietary and consumption patterns in eighteenth- and nineteenth-century Europe were [...] the direct consequences of the same momentum that created a world economy."[10] Grasping the role of sugar within the history of capitalism and its imbrication in systemic racialization, gendering and environmental degradation necessitates a conceptualization of capitalism that goes beyond a focus on the commodification and exploitation of labour-power. "The relations necessary to accumulate abstract social labour [value] are – *necessarily* – more expansive, in scale, scope, speed, and intensity," writes environmental historian Jason W. Moore.[11] Capitalist value relations depend not only on the *exploitation* of commodified labour-time; more importantly, they depend on the *appropriation* of the unpaid (and under-paid) work and energy of human and extra-human natures.[12]

It is also important to take account of fundamental shifts that re-organized global world-ecology, such as the fossil-fuelled emergence of monopoly capitalism and of a more integrated world-food-system. Preceding the full-blown imperial expansion of the USA into the Caribbean was a corporate revolution led by the sugar refiners. Initially imitating the re-organization of the petroleum industry by forming the Sugar Trust in 1887, the sugar refiners were soon at the forefront of a "historical transformation in the structure of capitalist property,"[13] as the Sugar Trust changed into a holding company after the Sherman Antitrust Act (1890) passed congress. This was key to an unprecedented horizontal integration and also to increasing vertical integration with the "American Sugar Kingdom" after the Spanish-American War in 1898. The sugar plantations, or *centrales*, of the twentieth century were clearly different to the *ingenios* of preceding centuries, as they relied on "free" labour, increased mechanization, electrification, the use of steam and fossil fuel power, and the imperialist monopolization of lands and profits. Further, as a result of increased industrialization and urbanization (necessitating the provision of fast energy to the growing urban proletariat), sugar consolidated itself as a staple food of the emergent world-food-system.

Sugar – and saccharine aesthetics – offer an interesting way into recent debates around the "worlding" of comparative literary studies. I take my cue from WReC, who have sought to reposition the "world" in world literature as referring to the capitalist world-system: the world-literary text, in this view, would register "modernity under the sign of combined and uneven development."[14] This registration would tendentially occur in an irrealist mode, as it responds to largely invisible and hard-to-grasp forces of global capitalism and its destructive impact on local life-worlds.[15] "Saccharine-irrealism" is here particularly instructive.[16] From the perspective of consumption, the gothic topos of "blood sugar" of the 1790s, for instance, was animated by a desire to de-fetishize this commodity.[17] From the perspective of plantation societies, on the other hand, sugar's shaping of entire societies and ecologies translated, as Sylvia Wynter has noted, into "a change of such world historical magnitude, that we are all, without exception, still 'enchanted,' imprisoned, deformed and schizophrenic in its bewitched reality."[18] One does not have to search long to come across "saccharine-irrealism" of the Dominican variety. Most famously, Pedro Mir in his poem *"Hay un país en el mundo"* [There is a country in the world] from 1949 evokes a sense of "improbability" that has become a structure of feeling linked to the region's domination by export commodities: the island is situated, he writes, in an "improbable archipelago / of sugar and alcohol."[19] In this country of landless peasants, everything – from infrastructure (railroads), to the extra-human environments, to human bodies, to structures of feeling ("the boundless fury and hatred") – is property of "the company."[20] The saccharine-irrealism produced by the domination of dead labour over living labour soon turns towards monstrous and gothic imagery: his country, the narrator claims, should be called "a tomb, coffin, hole or sepulcher" and "its kiss tastes of nothing but blood."[21] These images of burial, living death, blood and implied vampirism/cannibalism, are of course all heavily over-determined. Mir's poem clearly carries denunciatory overtones vis-à-vis the brutal dictatorship of Trujillo, who, at the end of the 1940s, was in the process of extending his control over the economy to the US-dominated sugar industry. Yet, they simultaneously echo a longer history of saccharine gothic, including the US-dominated expansion of commodity relations, as well the acts of appropriation on which the latter rely. Not surprisingly, then, the lines also resound with Karl Marx's well-known description of capital as "dripping from head to toe [...] with blood and dirt." Capital, he writes, is "dead labour which, vampire-like, lives only by sucking living labour" – an apt description, even if anachronistically employed, for monopoly capitalism.[22]

The over-determination of saccharine-irrealism partly derives from sugar's histories in the Dominican Republic. While sugar cane first arrived in the Caribbean in the island of Hispaniola, brought by Christopher Columbus in 1493, by the nineteenth century, the Dominican Republic was a "society of petty commodity producers and subsistence farmers," only weakly integrated into the world-system and producing sugar only for local consumption.[23] The nineteenth-century sugar revolution rapidly transformed the country from the mid-70s onwards, powered by the technology of the steam-powered Cuban mills and financed by mostly foreign investment. These changes were welcomed by the national liberal elites and encouraged through tax exemptions, low export duties, and tariff protections. In elite discourse, sugar was associated with signs of progress and "stood for modernization, for the triumph of human ingenuity over nature, for civilization."[24] The consequences for many farming communities were devastating, as Dominican ecology – the relations between land, livestock, people and capital – was profoundly restructured. Since sugar necessitates the clearing of vast tracts of forests, entire peasant communities were displaced by the *centrales*. Yet, given that many Dominicans nevertheless continued to have access to land – to plots called *conucos* – and were hence able to produce their own food and unwilling to work under the brutal conditions of the sugar industry, foreign labourers were contracted, predominantly from the West Indies and, from the first decade of the twentieth century onwards, increasingly from Haiti, a trend consolidated by active recruitment after the beginning of the US occupation of the island.[25] Within the sugar-growing areas, local food production was disrupted, which led to increases in food prices, to the extent that "workers could barely pay for the limited foodstuffs available in the plantation stores" – a structural tendency first noticed in 1882, and gradually worsening over time.[26]

To return here to the question of saccharine aesthetics, it must be noted that the profound entanglement of Dominican literature with the history of sugar is well documented.[27] One of the texts that is seen as foundational for modern Dominican literary history is the exoticizing indigenist fantasy formulated in *Enriquillo: Leyenda Dominicana* (1882) by the liberal politician and writer Manuel Jesús de Galván. It was "almost immediately made required reading in Dominican public schools and has provided a narrative structure and cultural fixed ideas for generations of Dominican novelists to debate and reform."[28] It served to delineate an elite-driven modernizing nationalism that would exclude and marginalize the history of Africans and their descendants; it "would help readers find a common heritage shared by all Dominicans that would differentiate them ethnically, racially and culturally from the Haitians."[29] Its problematic (mis-)representation of the indigenous *cacique* Enriquillo and the social world around him excluded any traces of sugar and the social order it produced, functioning as a foundational romance that offered an "ideological synthesis" between a paternalist Hispanism and a romanticized indigenism.[30] The ecology of the romance form was thus actively repressed.

Yet, by the time of the emergence of the regionalist *novela de la caña*, the romance is no longer sustainable, as it encounters obstacles to national self-determination in the form of the domination by imperialist monopoly capitalism. Beginning in 1900, the Dominican sugar industry was being taken over by US capital, which was able to fuel a process of land concentration and take advantage of economic crises and external debt.[31] The relations between US capital and the Dominican sugar growing areas were structured by the typical centre-periphery dynamics: while a large percentage of cane and raw sugar was produced in the "American Sugar Kingdom," which offered fertile, exploitable lands and low labour costs, the more lucrative industrial process of refining was kept in the USA.[32] This uneven relation was reinforced by tariffs that would seek to keep out foreign refined sugar to protect the US refining industry. The US domination of the sugar industry was given a significant boost by military occupation (1916–1924). The military government had US economic interests at heart, shamelessly implementing policies and regulations beneficial to US investment, and enabling a phase of intense primitive accumulation and land grabbing.[33] The liberal fantasy of a world market regulating itself could not be further removed from reality, structured by a world-system that locks cores and peripheries together in increasingly unequal relations, installed and reinforced by military might. Instead, "highly organized capital came to reap the profits of colonial enterprise."[34]

"Es una fiebre, una locura": Monstrous irrealism in *Over* (1939)

Marrero Aristy's *Over*, a novel told in three parts, explicitly critiques this context. Through the narrator-protagonist Daniel Comprés, who is expelled from his father's house and can only find work as a *bodeguero* [the keeper of the company shop] on a US-owned sugar plantation, the novel offers a "metaphor for the Dominican people, who have lost their historical roots and travel alone through a hostile world, dominated by foreign economic powers and racist prejudices."[35] Set near San Pedro de Macorís, a town that had been transformed rapidly by the sugar revolution into an economic centre, *Over* depicts life in a US-dominated sugar enclave, in which all the best positions are occupied by North Americans and Europeans, while the Haitian and West Indian work-force is labouring

THE WORLD-LITERARY SYSTEM AND THE ATLANTIC   95

under de-humanizing and dangerous conditions, often fainting from lack of food. The lettered middle-class narrator is uncomfortably wedged between them, becoming complicit in a system based on structural racism, super-exploitation and deceit, and land monopolization – a system that he wants to denounce, while simultaneously displaying an unquestioned racism towards Haitians and accepting patriarchal relations as natural if disturbed by imperialism.[36] In a novel marked by various formal, stylistic and ideological tensions, neither the romance nor the *bildungsroman* form can provide adequate narrative containers and are displaced by the overbearing domination of sugar and monopoly capital. The plot therefore follows the alternating movement between zafra [harvest] and the "dead time."[37] Sugar emerges as the commodity that structures all life around its rhythms, sucking out the village's life forces.

In *Over*, the national romance has been rendered inadequate by foreign domination (while its patriarchal and racialized underpinnings are left largely intact). Its plot mechanisms are evoked rather mechanically at the beginning of part two, but then quickly discarded: his love interest – "*una indiecita*" whose father is an independent *bodeguero* – represents the hope for a national synthesis that would be grounded in a Dominican racial identity and national sovereignty through small-scale plots and commerce.[38] Ominously, the subsequent chapter starts with the suicide of another married *bodeguero* working for the *central*, and by the end part two, Daniel's wife returns from the *central*'s hospital after the death of their unborn child. As has been pointed out, Marrero Aristy's explicit critique as voiced through his character is not a radical critique of capitalism, but demonstrates support of small commerce, which is suffocated by the monopolization of food by the sugar industry.[39] Further, a much-discussed omission of the novel is its lack of any commentary on the brutal dictatorship of Rafael Leónidas Trujillo. Critical responses to *Over* are often shaped by the fact that, thanks to its publication, Marrero Aristy joined the group of intellectuals who helped to consolidate the *trujillato* through its mythification and had a very successful career until his assassination in 1959.[40] Problematically, the novel was (at least briefly) co-opted to justify the ecology of dictatorship – expanding dictatorial capitalist hoarding to the sugar industry in the name of "nationalism." One of the most pressing debates, then, has revolved around the question of whether the novel implicitly exonerates the brutal dictator (or whether it indicts him through the metaphor of the father abandoning his son).[41] While the novel's main attack is explicitly focused on US monopoly capital hence allowing for its uncomfortable co-optation, I agree with Serrata that the novel possesses critical charge. Yet, I see this as located not so much in an allegorical, covert critique of Trujillo, but rather in its style. Regardless of authorial intention and the author's political affiliations, the most subversive aspects are not related to explicit politics, but rather its employment of an at times pronounced monstrous irrealism that has subversive potential.

The novel's most obvious critique is directed at US monopoly capitalism. The one-dimensional villain, Mr Robinson, is the "symbol par excellence of Anglo-Imperialists."[42] The name is here presumably not insignificant: in Hispanic intellectual discourse on both sides of the Atlantic, Robinson Crusoe had figured as critique of the "progressive technological and economic ideals of an increasingly secularized Anglo-American empire" since the events of 1898, which were represented as an encounter between Don Quixote, symbolizing "the archaic, spiritual, moral, and civilizing ideals of the Spanish Empire," and "his Anglo-Saxon nemesis."[43] In *Over*, Defoe's Robinson Crusoe, an archetypal sovereign subject of capitalist modernity who subjugates extra-human nature to his will, is exposed as a rapacious capitalist imperialist, who in a dependent economy can extract wealth under conditions impossible in his own country. Mr Panza, as he is nicknamed, is described as enormous and obese, contrasting with the workers on the plantation, who are often reduced to the single physical sensation of hunger. Access to food, in this context, is tied to economic wealth: "his stomach grows, his bank account grows" (62). His body turns into a symbol for the core's "fattening up" at the expense of the periphery. The structural racism of this imperial world-order, a legacy of colonialism, is emphasized throughout, with an insistent emphasis on Mr Panza's blue eyes and his overtly racist attitudes. Equally, the predatory relation of US capital to Dominican environments is highlighted early on in the novel through its descriptions of the threatening presence of the "immense chimneys" of the now steam-powered sugar industry, rising to the sky as if to "stea[l] the clouds" (27).

To return to the formal tensions, the gestures towards the *bildungsroman* form are displaced by the allegorical story of the subjugation of an economically dependent society to sugar, which is also the subjugation to the law of value. At the start of the novel, Daniel, an aspiring writer, is expelled from a less firmly capitalized patriarchal village economy, and sucked up in the "vortex" of the profit-driven monopolistic sugar industry (84). Rejected by his father and by society at large, everything seems "strange," as the community ties dissolve in an atmosphere dominated "by talk of the price of sugar" (7, 17). While the Cibao – associated with smaller-sized tobacco holdings and "national character" – is briefly evoked as alternative, the dream-like houses of the company prove irresistible, evocative as they are of the "heteropatriarchal dream of domestic bliss."[44] This, then, is the story of the protagonist's proletarianization, allegorizing the region's rapid insertion into the world market. While Daniel's tale is set during a later stage – after the depression of the sugar prices on the market – he meets characters who remember, and testify to, the transformation of farmers into *"braceros* [day labourers]" (84), as well as the promise of sugar wealth at a time "when money ran down the streets" (33), when people left everything behind to "enter into this vortex" (84). The complete subjugation to value relations is symbolically and literally rendered explicit in the general absence of names, as everyone and everything, villages and people, are numbered to "save" [literally translated: "shorten/condense"] time (31). From his entry into the service of the sugar company, his labour-power is insured – monetarized – by a company overseas and Daniel is transformed into a commodity, only to be expelled at the end of the novel as waste.

While it is true that, as Sommer notes, the plot is structured by the rhythms of sugar, there is something else at work; it is a more invisible force that has re-organized ecology and thus enabled the emergence of sugar as a commodity produced on a large scale. This is what is in the novel referred to as the practice of *over*. As the narrator notes: "The *over* [in English in the original] swallowed your life [...] everything that is yours – conscience [or consciousness], body, heart – belonged to the monster that smothers men in the agony of over [or more]" (210). The over here emerges as a vampiric force, taking over his body, his affective life, and his conscience – or perhaps, more disturbingly, his consciousness (*"conciencia"* can refer to either). This monstrous description is much more disturbing than the narrator's attempts to explain "over" as a sort of surplus profit extracted through corruption, made possible by the monopolization of food, necessities and healthcare; indeed, a monopoly that allows for a whole "network of distinct forms of robbery, deceit, and illegal and racketeer administration."[45] Yet, the description of the reign of "over" as seen in the passage above goes beyond corruption, pointing towards the "monstrosity" of the imposition of value relations under the conditions of peripheral and dependent capitalism. This "over" feeds on both the *exploitation* of value-producing human labour-power and the *appropriation* of fertile soils.[46] The domination of "over" thus turns into the "reign of the absurd and the alienation of human sensibility and will."[47]

In the novel, a monstrous irrealism, which includes images of cannibalism, zombie-ism and death-in-life, most frequently emerges in relation to the exploitation of commodified labour-power (value).[48] The representation of the workers suggests that "over" (or surplus value) is produced by the labourers themselves, whose time, being, and life-force is exploited. They are thus cannibalized: "The monster swallows more men every day [...] their blood runs down the channels: it is gold, it is profit, it is over! [...] and of the men if your land there only remains bagasse" (223). This image of implied cannibalism linked to the extraction of gold has easily traceable roots in the conquest period – a link that the novel makes explicitly in relation to its description of systemic racism as well as its observations of the differential treatment of workers. Though all workers are described as "flesh" that belongs to the plantation (96), the dehumanizing treatment of Haitian workers, in particular, is reminiscent of times of slavery, as their lives are constantly put at serious risk, for instance, during their transport as "human cargo" to the Dominican Republic and their "herd[ing]" like "cattle" by the company police armed with machetes and guns (80).

Adding to these images of cannibalism/vampirism are those of zombie-ism. The workers are described as an "ill-smelling mob in rags – with a hunger that never leaves them – on the way to the harvest, like a procession of *beings without a soul*" (95, my emphasis). The descriptions here resemble Haitian tales of the zombie workers on the US sugar companies (such as HASCO), which were popularized in the USA in the late 1920s and 1930s. Just as across the border, the (often equally Haitian) workers are turned into "*mere bodies*, unthinking and exploitable collections of flesh, blood and muscle tissue."[49] As I have argued elsewhere, zombie figures are ecological in that they turn on the alienation of the proletarianized workforce from the land they inhabit.[50] As the former small-scale peasants are no longer able to grow their own food, hunger emerges as a constant feature of an integrated world-food-system, despite the equally constant claims that the industrialization of agriculture will solve food insecurities.[51] The eventual emergence of the ever-hungry zombie horde in US cinema is, from this perspective, not surprising.

Given the centrality of fossil fuels in all of this, it is striking that Marrero Aristy insistently emphasizes the unevenness of access to their benefits: fossil-fuel powered modernity individualizes some (foreign) imperialists, while transforming the majority (of Dominican, Haitian and West Indian workers) into a stratified mass of commodified labourers. Monstrous irrealist imagery thus also revolves around chimneys, locomotives and railways, which are here not coded as signs of "progress." The locomotive, which serves the *central* is described as a "monster of iron," as "a beast" that transports the masses of workers, "vomiting" them out again at their destination (82). The machine is fetishistically ascribed agency, subduing both the land that trembles and the workers who are transformed into the machine's excretions. Automobiles, on the other hand, fulfil a slightly different role: symbolic of fossil-fuelled modernization, they serve to individualize and empower the *central*'s foreign managers – including Mister Baumer, who is described as "a god who dominates the motor" (30).[52] Automobiles are not accessible to Haitian or West Indian workers, and only barely to the Dominican protagonist (who incurs debts to be driven to hospital). Throughout, they are linked to images of implied violence to land and people, as encapsulated in the image of the car carrying Daniel to his future job down a lane that is like a "scar on the stomach of the cane fields" (30).

Marrero implicitly reflects on how this affects narrative mode and form. As the narrator is transported to his bodega in the back of a car, he daydreams: "The hunger and the monotonous snoring of the machine make me fall asleep, and what I know of the big company passes through my mind like a motion film [*cinta cinematográfica*]" (28). Hunger and the car noises are here firmly tied together through the syntax and provide the context for the simile that describes his thought process. The latter is firmly inscribed in US-dominated petromodernity: film stock is itself a product of fossil fuels; and the majority of films screened at the time were imported (from the 30s onwards, usually from Hollywood).[53] The reference to film, then, does not seem coincidental – the local cinema is mentioned early on in the novel, just after Daniel overhears talk of sugar prices in the park. Within the national context, film was "not initially seen as an art for the people"[54] nor as an art *about* the people.[55] This would seem to raise questions about the role of (cinematic) realism – and yet, cinematic realism is of course itself an illusion, produced by a trick of the eye and the fast moving reel.[56] Embedded in the story of Daniel's proletarianization, then, are questions about new narrative modes, forms, and contents. To be sure, *Over* does not offer a head-on engagement with these questions, but its realist textual politics are far from simple.

Fukú Americanus, triffids, and "dreamshit"

If questions of representation, form and mode are more complex in the *novela de la caña* than sometimes acknowledged, in Díaz's novel they are at the forefront and explicitly addressed throughout. Further, the role of sugar and its relation to genre and style is central. Oscar's life is shaped by his own, and his family's, notably indirect relations to sugar. The saccharine monstrous emerges most obviously during scenes when Beli and Oscar are beaten up in the cane fields. While none of Oscar's Dominican family is involved in sugar production, they thus become victims of the profoundly patriarchal and militarized political ecology of sugar. In a scene that takes place in 1961 on the day of Trujillo's assassination, the cane stalks acquire a monstrous autonomy and seek to prevent Beli from escaping, "slash[ing] at her palms, jabb[ing] into her flanks and claw[ing] her thighs" (150) (a sexualized image that signposts the cane fields as the historic site of sexual violence and rape).[57] The violence is echoed in the scene of Oscar's death in the cane fields, taking place over three decades later, as the stalks are heard "clack-clack-clacking against each other like triffids" (320), in a reference to John Wyndham's post-apocalyptic Cold War novel, *The Day of the Triffids* (1951). The aggressive and zombie-esque triffids – which in Wyndham's text are the result of Russian science experiments and potentially profitable as a source of edible oil – are the paranoid Cold War product of anxieties around food in the context of an increasing industrialization of agriculture.

The saccharine monstrous also manifests itself at the locus of consumption through Oscar's body: "The fat! The miles of stretch marks! The tumescent horribleness of his proportions!" (29). While in *Over*, the overweight body was symbolic of monopolist hoarding, Oscar's body is invested with different meaning in a context where the lack of access to a healthy diet is compensated by a reliance on an addictive, cheap, sugar-laced diet consumed in an urbanized setting. In Yunior's narrativization, Oscar is relentlessly referred to as an "overweight frea[k]" (15), a "cake-eater," a "*gordo asceroso*" [fat disgusting person] (17), and his "monstro-ness" is emphasized (176). Of course, the "monstrous" here arises partly from Yunior's (hetero-)normalizing narrative, into which Oscar can only "fit" once he has slimmed down and lost his virginity. Yet, there is something else at work here too: while Yunior tends to blame Oscar for his lack of motivation, the novel overall takes care to situate Oscar's body within a context marked by class, race, gender, and structural as well as physical violence. Further, this is clearly situated by Díaz within a world-food-system in which American "Dunkin' Donuts," full of processed sugar, and "mind-boggling poverty" are part of the same logic and can exist side by side (277).

The appearances of the saccharine monstrous arguably invite us to adopt a broader framework to think about aesthetics, as the novel develops a complex understanding of the role of food and, more generally, capitalist world-ecology, structured around the axes of racism and sexism and shaped by the histories of colonialism and imperialism. Most importantly, it engages with the various cultural imaginaries that register the disavowed processes of the capitalist world-ecology – hence the novel's insistent engagement with the foundational romance, the genre of sci-fi, fantasy, comic books and saccharine monstrous irrealism. In interviews, Díaz has consistently highlighted the fact that modern genre narratives are the product of a world-order marked by colonialism, white supremacy and patriarchy:

> alien invasions, natives, slavery, colonies, genocide, racial system, savages, technological superiority, forerunner races and the ruins they leave behind, travel between worlds, breeding programs, superpowered whites, mechanized regimes that work humans to death, human/alien hybrids, lost worlds – all have their roots in the traumas of colonialism.[58]

As an integral part of the capitalist world-ecology, these narratives often participate in naturalizing its ideologies. However, as Díaz's novel amply demonstrates, in their style and form, they also carry subversive potential. That a combined and uneven modernity gives rise to these genre narratives is explicitly thematized in the novel, including in the following description of the cane fields in the 1960s:

> the urban dropped off, as precipitous as a beat, one second you were deep in the twentieth century (well, the twentieth century of the Third World) and the next you'd find yourself plunged 180 years into rolling fields of cane. The transition between these states was some real-time machine-type shit.[59]

The uneven development of the landscape gives rise to the subjective experience of temporal dislocations, a sci-fi-esque irrealism – a style not unrelated to marvellous realism.

Further, the novel links the consumption of food to that of women: Oscar's bullies draw on these long-standing metaphorical connections, accusing Oscar of not being able to "eat toto" (180). Yet, while Oscar may, to a certain extent, be unable to fully participate in the patriarchal order, he has certainly imbibed patriarchal narratives of courtship and assimilated the heteropatriarchal power relations on which they are based – even if perhaps to a lesser extent than Yunior. Indeed, as has been noted, Yunior is actively engaged in shaping the narrative's rather abrupt ending: "Oscar's final transformation from virgin to Dominican man is part of the foundational logic driving the novel, a consolidating impulse that aligns it with the nationalist novels of Sommer's study."[60] The diasporic Oscar is thus shoehorned into the heteronormative formal logic that is bound up with sugar-powered moderniz-ation in the Dominican Republic. Yet, unlike in *Over*, a *romance manqué* that continues to embrace the form's underlying patriarchal logic, the characters' ideological contradic-tions are continually highlighted. From Oscar's sexist statements about girls to Yunior's claims of being reformed despite seeing several women at the same time, the novel overall makes it abundantly clear that they are not always able to extricate themselves from what they partially recognize as "dreamshit" (87).

Despite the novel's often quite flamboyant self-awareness, a recent critical approach claims that it feeds "into an appetite for stories that feature a quintessential Latin American dictator, an irrational, passion-driven strongman and his violent and sexual excesses."[61] While Maja Horn offers an important analysis of cultural narratives of "tropicalization" in relation to the *trujillato*, her reading of Díaz's text is arguably off the mark. She bases her assessment in part on the exoticizing reception of the novel by US critics as voiced in newspapers and blurbs – on its consumption and consecration in the marketplace, in other words. Yet, what this reading fails to acknowledge is the specificity of the work of art as opposed to other narrative forms. Díaz, not unlike other critically aware writers who are "consumed" globally, finds "a way of registering [his] own sociological positio [n]" through his deliberate exaggeration of the tropicalization, as well as through the text's various formal and stylistic excesses; it thus manages to re-politicize "metropolitan expectations of cultural otherness."[62] Indeed, the novel self-consciously highlights the fact that the trope of the hyper-sexed Caribbean dictator is "one of those easy stories" (244).

Further, one might say that the figure of Yunior stages in exaggerated form the uneasy position of the tropicalized writer in the marketplace. Yunior, as has been pointed out by several critics, perpetuates many of the problematic gender norms enshrined in national and diasporic identities that the *trujillato* helped to reinforce.[63] Yet, Yunior also sets out to critique persistent narrative paradigms that isolate Trujillo from the larger world-historical context. In relation to the family history offered by the Leons, he notes:

> there are other beginnings certainly, better ones, to be sure – if you ask me I would have started when the Spaniards "discovered" the New World – or when the US invaded Santo Domingo in 1916 – but if this was the opening that the Leons chose for themselves, then who am I to question their historiography?[64]

However, the narrator's arrangement of the text does precisely that, since the novel overall begins with his reflections on the *fukú americanus*, which "came first from Africa, carried in the screams of the enslaved," transforming Hispaniola into its "Kilometer Zero, its port of entry" (1, 2). The trope of the *fukú* highlights the centrality of the Americas, the trans-Atlan-tic slave trade and the process of primitive accumulation to the global world order that arose out of the destruction of previous life-worlds.[65] It also immediately sets up the con-nection to the *trujillato*; as Yunior puts it, Trujillo was either "the Curse's servant or its master, its agent or its principal" (2–3), "making ill monopolies out of every slice of the national patrimony" (2). Or, as one eminent historian phrases it in a less imaginative reg-ister, he was "the personification of the accumulation of capital."[66] The history of Trujillo's ascent to power, emerging out of the ranks of the US military, was profoundly interrelated with the story of sugar, something again highlighted by Yunior in his description of Trujillo as "act[ing] like it [the country] was his own plantation" (225). While the sugar industry had initially constituted a challenge to Trujillo's absolute power over the economy, the relations between the dictator and the US-dominated sugar industry were of mutual support, as he had much to gain from the sugar industry. Thus, his economic policies, far from steering towards lessening the mono-cultural dependence on sugar, intensified it.[67] When Trujillo eventually began to extend his economic control to the sugar industry starting the late 1940s, this did not lessen the political support of the USA, who saw him as an ally in the fight against Communism. Sugar tariffs thus became a political bargaining tool of the Cold War.

It is in this context that we must read the cultural references to a long list of sci-fi, comic and genre texts produced during the Cold War. The episode "It's a good life" of *The Twilight Zone* (first aired in 1961), for instance, is referenced in relation to the description of the *trujillato*. Evoked to characterize the regime of Trujillo and its tight grip over the population, it raises questions about the type of apocalyptic scenarios and imaginative worlds produced in a Cold War context from a US perspective. In the episode, a six year-old boy isolates a small town called Peaksville from the surrounding world (making the latter disappear). He forces all inhabitants to acquiesce to his power by threatening to transform them into zombified creatures or jack-in-the-boxes, or by wishing them away into a cornfield. In Peaksville, cars – the hallmark of Fordist America – no longer work and the TV receives no outside signals. Once cut off, the village is beginning to run out of basic necessities (soap), luxury goods (whisky) and the food supply is beginning to look insecure. Thus evocative of anxieties over Communist political power and infiltration, the episode also plays with anxieties about food and resource self-sufficiency as well as, more broadly, petro-modernity. As Albritton notes,

> in the context of the cold war, self-sufficiency in food was considered a necessity, and at the same time surpluses in the form of food aid were used in some cases as an incentive to identify with the American camp.[68]

dumping the farming surpluses at low prices had a highly destructive long-term impact on the recipient countries' local food production, creating dependency and thus new markets. Díaz, then, brings out some of the inconsistencies of these Cold War fears: the cultural references most capable of conveying the brutalities of the *trujillato* are home-grown in the USA, who has long used food as a political tool. They register in displaced form its own destructive policies towards the periphery – from the dumping of surpluses as "food aid" to the propping up of dictators. The fantasy of "isolation" – also entertained by Abelard in his rumoured exposé (246) – is thus exposed as illusory and a product of Cold War politics.

Throughout the telling of the family's history Díaz continually emphasizes the world-historical character of their plight, shaped both by the *longue durée* of capitalism and the context of US imperialism and the Cold War. Thus, Abelard's arrest by the Trujillo regime coincides with the atomic bombing of Japan, while his only surviving daughter Beli is referred to as the "Child of the Apocalypse," whose back bears "a world-scar like those of the *hibakusha*" (236, 251, 257). The saccharine monstrous in the cane field episodes, evocative of course of the legacies of slavery, is also firmly inscribed in the context of US imperialism and the Cold War through its cultural references. The "Man without a Face" appears to both Beli and, decades later, to her son Oscar, as they become victims of violence associated with the political ecology of sugar. As Garland notes, the faceless man is associated both "with the hundreds of years of sugarcane slavery in Dominican history," as well as with the character of the vigilante superhero Rorschach from Alan Moore and Dave Gibbon's DC comic series *Watchmen* (1987).[69] Through Rorschach, "a radically right-wing superhero and champion of economic neoliberalism and social conservatism," Moore and Gibbon have problematized the superhero genre structured around simplistic cultural Cold War binaries.[70] Grod, another character involved in the beating in the cane fields, stems precisely from these binaries: he recalls Gorilla Grodd, the villain who possesses the mind power of brainwashing and seeks to "infiltrate American society in order to conquer it and the rest of the world, leading an army of gorillas (Marxist guerillas anyone?)."[71] Again, it is ironically a figure associated with the evils of Communism as represented in US comics that proves most apt to reflect on the persistence of the legacies of US imperialism.

While the novel places much emphasis on continuity and sugar's legacies, there are also pronounced aesthetic differences between the cane field scene in the 1960s, and the final scene of Oscar's death in the 1990s. Whereas the scene of Beli's kidnapping is close to "magical realism" in style and tone and served to highlight the political ecology of sugar underpinning the *trujillato*, in the description of the latter, this "magic" gives way to an even more intangible phantasmagoria (which is usually explained through references to Yunior's role in shaping the narrative). The scene stands out due to its remarkable brevity and a certain hollowness or weightlessness – qualities that might be related to the decline of the sugar economy in the Dominican Republic after 1976, despite the persistence of the long-term legacies of the sugar industry.[72] Thus, while the legacies of US imperialism and the Cold become visible in Yunior's narrative through the engagement with comic book and sci-fi irrealism, the more recent age of the neoliberal food regime, which manifests itself in the "monstrosity" of consumption in an urbanized setting, remains difficult to grasp. It is this cognitive difficulty that is brilliantly highlighted by Díaz through Yunior's somewhat forced attempt to offer a swift narrative and stylistic resolution. The increasing levels of monstrous irrealism register, then, not only the continuing violence of the political ecology of sugar, but also the heightening levels of fetishism masking the growing inequalities in the increasingly de-localized world-food-system.

To conclude, I would like to come back to the question of food in relation to world-literature. Food offers a way into thinking about the way in which cultures of food and capitalist world-ecology are co-constitutive. It cuts across and destabilizes Cartesian divides between "Nature" and "Culture," enabling us to think of cultural phenomena as environment-making processes. Cultures of food clearly extend beyond eating, but what about the specificity of a work of art in this context? This is where Díaz's *The Brief Wondrous Life of Oscar Wao* has much to offer. Díaz insistently poses the question of criticality in relation to the position of a given cultural text within the larger horizon of the capitalist world-ecology. Are these cultural texts co-constitutive of dominant ecologies or do they set out to engage critically with them? Can literary texts have a distancing effect and thus enable a denaturalization of, for instance, the cultural ideology of sugar?[73] Some texts – such as *Enriquillo* – aimed to reinforce the dominant ecological regime, while for the twenty-first critical reader, it renders visible the ideology of the time. If these works of art can be successful at holding a mirror to ideologies, it is in part because their "raw" materials – form and style – have sprung from historically specific ecologies.

1Lastly, another question that *The Brief Wondrous Life of Oscar Wao* poses is the question of the "time" of world-literature: the novel offers a dual, consistently over-determined, horizon for its reflections on aesthetics – the *longue durée* of capitalism and the context of US imperial intervention in the Dominican Republic. WReC, alternatively, have proposed the "two-hundred-plus years from the early nineteenth century or even the late eighteenth" as a time frame of world-literature.[74] However, if world-literature is literature that registers the capitalist world-system, would the origins of world-literature not need to be extended backwards to the sixteenth century, even if those origins would have to be thought of as uneven and occurring in spurts until reaching full "intensity" in the nineteenth century? While there are literary works from the early modern period that would rather self-evidently fit these categories – from Cervantes's *Don Quixote* (also referred to by WReC) to Shakespeare's *The Tempest* to Montaigne's "On cannibals" – such an optic also points to the need to think more expansively about the notion of literature so that it would be able to accommodate a variety of cultural texts – from the baroque, to accounts of the Spanish conquest from indigenous perspectives, to the appearance of monstrous narratives, many of which are reinvigorated during new rounds of primitive accumulation under neoliberalism.

Notes

1. Ayala, *Sugar Kingdom*, 28.
2. See Plasa, *Slaves to Sweetness*; Sandiford, *The Cultural Politics of Sugar*; Sheller, *Consuming the Caribbean*.
3. Díaz, *The Brief Wondrous Life of Oscar Wao*, 15, 17. Hereafter cited parenthetically.
4. The *novela de la caña* is a subset of the commodity novel, see Beckman *Capital Fictions*.
5. Deckard et al., *Combined and Uneven*.
6. Löwy, "Critical Irrealism," 211.
7. Moore, *Capitalism*.
8. As Moore writes, capitalism is "a way of organizing nature"; Ibid., 2.
9. Richardson, *Sugar*, 9.
10. Mintz, *Sweetness*, 158.
11. Moore, *Capitalism*, 53.
12. Ibid.
13. Ayala, *Sugar Kingdom*, 23.
14. Deckard et al., *Combined and Uneven*, 17.
15. Irrealism, in Löwy's definition, describes "the absence of realism rather than an opposition to it"; Löwy, "Critical Irrealism," 213).
16. Niblett, "Oil on Sugar," 277.
17. See Morton, *The Poetics of Spice*.
18. Wynter, "Novel," 95. Wynter implies that fictional registrations of sugar are likely to "demonstrate a structural *tendency* toward incorporating elements of the irreal"; Niblett "Oil on Sugar," 278).
19. Mir, *Countersong to Walt Whitman*, 3.
20. Ibid., 15–17.
21. Ibid., 21.
22. Marx, *Capital*, 926, 342.
23. Ayala, *Sugar Kingdom*, 193.
24. Martínez-Vergne, *Nation*, 9, 43.

25. Ibid., 93.
26. Moya Pons, *History*, 273.
27. See Sommer, *One Master*.
28. Ibid., xiv.
29. Stinchcomb, *Literary Blackness*, 27.
30. Sommer, *One Master*, 57.
31. See Ayala, *Sugar Kingdom*, 187.
32. Ibid., 63–64. See Ayala, *Sugar Kingdom*, 21 for core-periphery dynamic *within* the Dominican Republic.
33. Hall, *Sugar*, 42; Cassá, *Historia*, 223.
34. Ayala, *Sugar Kingdom*, 76.
35. Baud, "Un permanente guerrillero," 190 (my translation).
36. See McDonald, "Still a Slave."
37. Marrero, *Over*, 165. Hereafter cited in the text (my translation). See Sommer, *One Master*, 133.
38. As Reyes-Santos explains, "*indio* (Indian) and its variations (*indio claro, oscuro,* etc.) were used to indicate the racial mixture of Dominicans" (*Caribbean Kin*, 85), with the aim of differentiating Dominicans from Haitians.
39. As Baud notes, the system of vouchers and the monopoly of the sugar industry had become symbols of foreign exploitation; Baud, "Un Permanente Guerrillero," 194.
40. Serrata, "*Literatura y poder*," 109. In 1949, Marrero Aristy authored a right-wing hagiography of the dictator. Marrero Aristy associates Trujillo with progress and modernization, blaming the horrendous massacre of 1937 on the supposedly marauding Haitians.
41. Ibid., 111; Sommer, *One Master*, 125. See also Rodríguez, *Escrituras*.
42. McDonald, "Still a Slave," 38.
43. Britt, *Quixotism*, 2.
44. Martínez-Vergne, *Nation*, xiii; Reyes-Santos, *Caribbean Kin*, 88.
45. Pimentel, *Ideología*, 189 (my translation).
46. See Moore, *Capitalism*, 54.
47. Pimentel, *Ideología*, 19/4.
48. A notable blind spot is gendered housework, presented as part of the naturalized patriarchal order.
49. McNally, *Monsters*, 4.
50. Oloff, "Greening."
51. See Mir, *Historia*, 208–209.
52. The association of the plantation manager and the car is a common trope of Caribbean literature more generally. Cars were introduced in the Dominican Republic around 1909; Sáez, *Historia*, 32.
53. Ibid., 74.
54. Derby, *Dictator's Seduction*, 32. See also Sáez, *Historia*, 37.
55. quoted in Derby, *Dictator's Seduction*, 33. Pioneer filmmaker Francisco Arturo Palau was criticized for the inclusion of the working classes in his 1923 documentary, Sáez, *Historia*, 57.
56. Marcus, "Cinematic Realism," 196.
57. Symbolically, the date of 1961 also signals the beginning of a period of mass emigration (of which Oscar is the symbolic child). See Hernández, *Mobility*.
58. Taylor, "A Singular Dislocation," 101.
59. Díaz, *The Brief Wondrous Life of Oscar Wao*, 146.
60. Machado, "Dictating Desire," 526.
61. Horn, *Masculinity*, 127.
62. Mukherjee, *Environments*, 8.
63. See Horn, *Masculinity*.
64. Díaz, *The Brief Wondrous Life of Oscar Wao*, 211.
65. See Saldívar, "Conjectures on 'Americanity.'"
66. Cassá, *Historia Social*, 261.
67. Hall, *Sugar*, 19.

THE WORLD-LITERARY SYSTEM AND THE ATLANTIC 105

68. Albritton, *Let them Eat Junk*, 58–59.
69. Mahler, "Writer as Superhero," 122.
70. Ibid., 123.
71. Wright, "Through Solid Matter," 62. However, his partner, Salomon Grundy, is a DC comics zombie super-villain firmly associated with US imperial expansion into the Caribbean.
72. See Gregory, *Globalization*, 22; Hernández, *Mobility*, 63.
73. Niblett, "Oil on Sugar," 269.
74. Deckard et al., *Combined and Uneven*, 51.

Acknowledgements

I would like to thank the two anonymous reviewers for their insightful comments.

Disclosure statement

No potential conflict of interest was reported by the author.

ORCID

Kerstin Oloff ⓘ http://orcid.org/0000-0002-5324-9446

Bibliography

Albritton, Robert. *Let Them Eat Junk: How Capitalism Creates Hunger and Obesity*. London: Pluto Press, 2009.
Ayala, César J. *American Sugar Kingdom: The Plantation Economy of the Spanish Caribbean 1898–1934*. Chapel Hill: University of North Carolina Press, 1999.
Baud, Michiel. "'Un Permanente Guerrillero.' El Pensamiento Social de Ramón Marrero Aristy (1913–1959)." In *Política, Identidad y Pensamiento Social en la República Dominicana* (Siglos XIX y XX), edited by Raymundo González, Michiel Baud, Pedo L. San Miguel, and Roberto Cassá, 118–213. Madrid: Ediciones Doce Calles, Academia de Ciencias de Dominicana, 1999.
Beckman, Ericka. *Capital Fictions*. Minneapolis: University of Minnesota Press, 2013.
Britt Arredondo, Christopher. *Quixotism: The Imaginative Denial of Spain's Loss of Empire*. Albany: State University of New York, 2005.
Cassá, Roberto. *Historia Social y Economica de la República Dominicana*. Vol. II. 12th ed. Santo Domingo: Alfa & Omega, 1994.
Deckard, Sharae, Benita Parry, Graeme Macdonald, Neil Lazarus, Nicholas Lawrence, Stephen Shapiro, and Upamanyu Pablo Mukherjee. *Combined and Uneven Development: Towards a New Theory of World-Literature*. Liverpool: Liverpool University Press, 2015.
Derby, Lauren H. *The Dictator's Seduction: Politics and the Popular Imagination in the Era of Trujillo*. Durham, NC: Duke University Press, 2009.
Díaz, Junot. *The Brief Wondrous Life of Oscar Wao*. London: Faber and Faber, 2008.
Gregory, Steven. *The Devil Behind the Mirror: Globalization and Politics in the Dominican Republic*. Berkeley: University of California Press, 2007.
Hall, Michael R. *Sugar and Power in the Dominican Republic: Eisenhower, Kennedy, and the Trujillos*. Westport, CT: Greenwood Press, 2000.

Hernández, Ramona. *The Mobility of Workers under Advanced Capitalism: Dominican Migration to the United States*. New York: Columbia University Press, 2002.

Horn, Maja. *Masculinity after Trujillo: The Politics of Gender in Dominican Literature*. Gainesville: University Press of Florida, 2014.

Löwy, Michael. "The Current of Critical Irrealism: 'A Moon-Lit Enchanted Night.'" In *A Concise Companion to Realism*, edited by Matthew Beaumont, 211–224. Chichester: Wiley-Blackwell, 2010.

Machado Sáez, Elena. "Dictating Desire, Dictating Diaspora: Junot Díaz's *The Brief Wondrous Life of Oscar Wao* as Foundational Romance." *Contemporary Literature* 52, no. 3 (Fall 2011): 522–555.

Mahler, Anne Garland. "The Writer as Superhero: Fighting the Colonial Curse in Junot Díaz's *The Brief Wondrous Life of Oscar Wao*." *Journal of Latin American Cultural Studies* 19, no. 2 (August 2010): 119–140.

Marcus, Laura. "Cinematic Realism: A Recreation of the World in Its Own Image." In *A Concise Companion to Realism*, edited by Matthew Beaumont, 195–210. Chichester: Wiley-Blackwell, 2010.

Marrero Aristy, Ramón. *Over*. Santo Domingo: Ediciones de Taller, 1980.

Marrero Aristy, Ramón. *Trujillo: Sintesis de su vida y obra*. Ciudad Trujillo, Dominican Republic: Impresora Dominicana, 1949.

Martínez-Vergne, Teresita. *Nation and Citizen in the Dominican Republic, 1880–1916*. Chapel Hill: University of North Carolina Press, 2005.

Marx, Karl. *Capital*. Vol. 1. London: Penguin Classics, 1990.

McDonald, Janice-Marie. "A Slave by Any Other Name Is Still a Slave: The New Slavery as Depicted in the Novel 'Over.'" *Afro-Hispanic Review* 10, no. 3 (September 1991): 37–41.

McNally, David. *Monsters of the Market: Zombies, Vampires and Global Capitalism*. Leiden: Brill, 2011.

Mintz, Sidney W. *Sweetness and Power: The Place of Sugar in Modern History*. New York: Penguin, 1986.

Mir, Pedro. *Countersong to Walt Whitman & Other Poems*. Translated by Jonathan Cohen and Donald D. Walsh. Washington, DC: Azul Editions, 1993.

Mir, Pedro. *Historia del Hambre: Orígenes en la Historia Dominicana*. Santo Domingo: Corripio, 1987.

Moore, Jason. *Capitalism in the Web of Life: Ecology and the Accumulation of Capital*. London: Verso Books, 2015.

Morton, Timothy. *The Poetics of Spice: Romantic Consumerism and the Exotic*. Cambridge: Cambridge University Press, 2006.

Moya Pons, Frank. *History of the Caribbean*. Princeton: Markus Wiener, 2007.

Mukherjee, Upamanyu Pablo. *Postcolonial Environments: Nature, Culture and the Contemporary Indian Novel in English*. Basingstoke: Palgrave Macmillan, 2010.

Niblett, Michael. "Oil on Sugar: Commodity Frontiers and Peripheral Aesthetics." In *Global Ecologies and the Environmental Humanities*, edited by Elizabeth DeLoughrey, Jill Didur, and Anthony Carrigan, 268–285. New York: Routledge, 2015.

Oloff, Kerstin. "'Greening' the Zombie: Caribbean Gothic, World-Ecology and Socio-Ecological Degradation." *Green Letters* 16, no. 1 (October 2012): 31–45.

Patel, Raj. *Stuffed and Starved: The Hidden Battle for the World Food System*. London: Portobello, 2007.

Pimentel, Miguel. *Ideología de la Novela Criolla, 1880–1944*. Santo Domingo: Editora Universitaria, Universidad Autónoma de Santo Domingo, 1986.

Plasa, Carl. *Slaves to Sweetness: British and Caribbean Literatures of Sugar*. Liverpool: Liverpool University Press, 2009.

Reyes-Santos, Alaí. *Our Caribbean Kin: Race and Nation in the Neoliberal Antilles*. New Brunswick: Rutgers University Press, 2015.

Richardson, Ben. *Sugar*. Cambridge: Polity Press, 2015.

Rodríguez, Néstor E. *Escrituras de Desencuentro en la República Dominicana*. Mexico City: Siglo XXI, 2005.

Sáez, José Luis. *Historia de un sueño importado: ensayos sobre el Cine and Santo Domingo*. Santo Domingo: Ediciones Siboney, 1983.

Saldívar, José David. "Conjectures on 'Americanity' and Junot Díaz's '*Fukú Americanus*' in *The Brief Wondrous Life of Oscar Wao*." *The Global South* 5, no. 1 (Spring 2011): 120–136.

Sandiford, Keith A. *The Cultural Politics of Sugar: Caribbean Slavery and Narratives of Colonialism*. Cambridge: Cambridge University Press, 2004.

Serrata, Médar. "Literatura y Poder: La Invisible Presencia de Trujillo en *Over.*" *Revista Iberoamericana* 75, no. 226 (January–March 2009): 109–123.

Sheller, Mimi. *Consuming the Caribbean*. London: Routledge, 2003.

Sommer, Doris. *One Master for Another: Populism as Patriarchal Rhetoric in Dominican Novels*. Lanham, NY: University Press of America, 1983.

Stinchcomb, Dawn F. *The Development of Literary Blackness in the Dominican Republic*. Gainesville: University Press of Florida, 2004.

Taylor, Jade Taryne. "A Singular Dislocation: An Interview with Junot Díaz." *Paradoxa: SF Now* 26 (December 2015): 97–110.

Wright, Frederick A. "'I Can Pass Right Through Solid Matter!': How the Flash Upheld American Values While Breaking the Speed Limit." In *Comic Books and the Cold War, 1946–1962*, edited by Chris York and Rafiel York, 55–67. Jefferson, NC: McFarland, 2012.

Wynter, Sylvia. "Novel and History, Plot and Plantation." *Savacou* 5 (June 1971): 95–102.

Water shocks: Neoliberal hydrofiction and the crisis of "cheap water"

Sharae Deckard

ABSTRACT
This essay examines world-literary representations of neoliberal hydroculture, exploring the crisis of "cheap water." I investigate how water functions in hydrofiction as a thematic element, but also as representation and symbolic regime, product and producer of the socio-ecological relations stabilizing the neoliberal organization of water. I begin with an analysis of Latin American and Chinese hydrofictions which anticipate intensified enclosure of water commons at the moment of the neoliberal turn before moving to the analysis of twenty-first-century novels that register China's turn to "extreme water." These hydrofictions display similar tendencies towards "hydro-irrealism" that underscore the limits of the hydrological regime. I conclude with two examples of millennial "hydro cli-fi" that portray "water shock" in autumnal cores. The impulse of these Euro-American *cli-fis* is diagnostic, but also regulatory, projecting fears of a new hydrological revolution as the basis for Chinese ascendancy.

Late capitalism is mired in a crisis of "cheap nature": the loss of the frontiers in cheap labour, energy, food and resources that fuelled earlier phases of accumulation.[1] The neoliberal ecological regime is riven by mounting contradictions: the stagnation of agricultural productivity; climate volatility; geo-technical challenges to extraction of energy, minerals, and water and deposit of wastes and pollutants. Minqi Li suggests that crises of food, energy and water in China harbinger an epochal crisis of the capitalist world-economy.[2] The decline of what I call *cheap water* – the exhaustion of water frontiers, intensification of technologies of extraction and manufacture of water scarcity, combined with rising costs of appropriation – is integral to this crisis. The earth's surface is covered in 70 per cent water, but 97 per cent is saltwater unsuitable for drinking, irrigation or industry with only 1 per cent of saltwater fit for human consumption.[3] Domestic consumption of water has been commodified on an unprecedented scale, at the same time as industrial sources of "crude water" confront limits to appropriation. As climate change intensifies drought in water-poor zones and flooding in water-rich zones, capitalist cores such as the USA and industrializing states like China face water scarcity in their agricultural bread-baskets to the extent that Fred Pearce calls water "the defining crisis of the twenty-first century."[4]

Hydrological crisis is exacerbated by financialization, which institutes new socio-ecological relations between water and money, integrating the flows of finance capital with the flows of the liquid resources necessary for social reproduction. Material components of water systems and uncommodified elements of "the hydro-social cycle" are incorporated into financial networks as part of a fundamental shift in how "nature" is valued: "no longer [as] a limited stock of material inputs metabolized within the production process, but [as] an infinite series of performing assets that can be measured, evaluated, circulated and *speculated* on in financial markets."[5] Thus, investment bankers hail water as "the ultimate commodity" and "the oil of the future."[6] Richard Sandor, the inventor of carbon trading, is currently developing predictive algorithms for a US Water Futures market, exulting that "scarce resources like water and air will replace crude oil as the most important commodities of the twenty-first century."[7] Prototypes of water-financialization include the Palisades Water Index and Australian Waterfind, which purport to stabilize prices in water-strapped regions, though their growing percentage of investors are speculators, not farmers. Fredrick Kaufman warns that just as financial derivatives exacerbate global dietary instability by producing a "food bubble" of inflated prices, they will create a "water bubble" even "more catastrophic than betting on the world's food supply."[8]

The "cheap food" integral to "cheap nature" is founded not only in "cheap oil," but also in "cheap water." The Green Revolution is not only energy, but also water-intensive, silting rivers, salinating fields and desertifying water-abundant regions.[9] Just as a crop such as wheat embodies virtual oil, it also embodies "virtual water," the virtual form of 1000 tonnes needed to grow one ton of grain. Freshwater is often imagined as eternal, without limits to appropriation. Similarly, hydropower is presented as "clean" and "renewable," unlike oil reserves, which cannot be renewed once extracted, even though the energy harnessed from hydropower is constrained by the short life-spans and ecological limits of large-scale hydroelectric dams. However, as with oil, the problem is not truly one of finitude, but of how to leave what is left in the ground. The world-ecology ought to be post-oil, given atmospheric limits to carbon release, but extraction of fossil fuels persists. Graeme Macdonald calls this the regime of "extended oil, a world where petroleum, despite everything, remains undead."[10] The extent to which water is renewable faces biophysical and social limits. Virtual water ruptures the social metabolism of nature and produces a rift in the hydrological cycle. Deep "fossil" aquifers, which contain ancient water locked in the earth by geological transformations millions of years old, cannot recharge: once their water is exhausted, it is gone. "Shallow" aquifers can recharge from surface water and rain, but if drained past their refill rate, these too are easily exhausted. Surface water in lakes, rivers and reservoirs is dwindling. If the hydrological cycle of evaporation, condensation, precipitation and transpiration is disrupted – by deforestation and desertification; declining melt-fed water systems due to changes in the melt-rate of glaciers and icepacks; soil degradation; saltwater intrusion in lowland coastal areas; and increased climate volatility and variability of water – then rainfall patterns can be delayed or permanently interrupted.[11] Water is "renewable" only when the closed-circles of hydrological cycles remain complete.

Just as "extreme oil" references costly, carbon-intensive technologies of extraction, the term "extreme water" could be used to encompass the intensive technologies of aquifer pumping, hydraulic mega-projects, bore wells, oil-based deep-drilling tech, industrial desalination and cloud-seeding. Brown problematically advocates a "blue revolution" to resolve the hydrological exhaustion of the "green revolution,"[12] while the World Water Council speculates that "water productivity" can be increased by biotechnology.[13] The likelihood of a fix to maxed-out "cheap water" is dubious, however, given that technical intensification tends to accelerate crisis. Extreme energy and extreme water are destructively interrelated, with the decline of renewable sources of freshwater compounded by the huge amount of water consumed by energy and extractive regimes: in mining, fracking, smelting, semi-conductor manufacturing, in the coal, oil and nuclear industries. Even "green energy" is water-intensive: bioenergy and hydroelectricity have "water footprints" per unit of energy up to three times larger than fossil fuels or nuclear.[14]

Although I have cited critics such as Brown and Li who employ "peak" discourses, it is with a strong caveat against Green and Red Malthusian conceptions of "natural scarcity." The proliferation of neo-Malthusian ideas buttresses neoliberal forms of dispossession and the reduction of civil freedoms in the name of resource securitization.[15] Discourses of water "security" are instrumentalized to justify militarization and transform the idea of water into a "scarce" exchangeable commodity, as evidenced in the Pentagon's wargaming of extreme water impacts and strategies to colonize water reservoirs in South America.[16] Development theorists tend to over-emphasize the potential for sensational international conflicts resulting from "water wars" in contrast to the slow and incremental violence that impacts communities subjected to hydrological apartheid and hydrocolonialism. "Water scarcity" must be understood as socially manufactured, rather than naturally inevitable: the creation of capitalist hydrological regimes. Thus, "peak water" is a problematic term, since freshwater is renewable within certain socio-ecological conditions, and because peak discourses fail to recognize that water is not a static object to be extracted, but a fluid set of social relations that could be changed.

It is more useful to think in terms of cheap water, peak appropriation, exhaustion and extreme water. In his discussion of "The Four Cheaps," Moore distinguishes between "peak appropriation" and two different forms of exhaustion, "maxed out" and "wiped out." Peak appropriation signals the moment in an accumulation cycle when the least amount of capital investment can release the greatest amount of water, oil or food. Thus, my use of "cheap water" designates the period when rising volumes of water are secured and extracted through declining unit costs. By contrast, "relative exhaustion" indicates the moment when peak appropriation has been reached and exceeded, when the unit cost of a gallon of water begins to rise relative to its previous lowest cost or volume point. At this point, unpaid appropriation of water is "maxed out": a rising volume of water can no longer be appropriated without rising inputs.[17] "Wiped out," therefore, signifies the absolute exhaustion of an accumulation regime.[18] In our current conjuncture, post-peak appropriation has been succeeded by a shift towards "extreme water," a rising absolute mass of water extraction that coincides with a dynamic of rising costs. The present response to the relative exhaustion of cheap water has been to extract *more* water, not less, at rising unit costs amplified by the rising cost of energy. Such intensified extraction leads to water supply not only being "maxed out," but "wiped out." This is "extreme water," the exhaustion of historical hydrological frontiers, where intensified extraction incurs rising costs and surpasses the capacity for renewal, threatening the democratic distribution of water throughout the planet.

Vandana Shiva reminds us that the earth is a hydrosphere, and the hydrological cycle is a water democracy: "a system of distributing water for all species."[19] Water and precipitation are not distributed uniformly, which would result in homogeneity of species, but rather equitably, across agro-climatic zones. This diversity of water, promoting diversity of all forms of life, is at odds with the rationalizing logic of neoliberal capitalism. Producing asymmetries of consumption across agro-climatic zones, capitalist hydropolitics subject marginalized communities to "water shocks," acting as "an engine of destabilization."[20] Water captured by extraction schemes no longer flows freely, but rather "flows uphill, towards money."[21] "Imperial water" flows towards capitalist agribusiness, state-favoured development projects and urban centres, diverted away from riparian and traditional agrarian users.[22] Hydropolitics operate at regional, national and transnational scales along intersectional axes of class and ethnicity, as in the case of China's imperialistic attempts to monopolize Tibetan rivers or US hydropiracy in the Americas.

Hydroculture and world literature

This essay explores the cultural logic of water in the neoliberal hydrological regime – what I call neoliberal *hydroculture*, referring not to hydroponic cultivation, but rather to the cultural forms and figurations corresponding to the enclosure and appropriation of water. I examine world-literary representations of the neoliberal crisis of cheap water, beginning with a trans-hemispheric comparison of Chinese and Latin American hydrofictions that anticipate intensified enclosure of water commons in key semi-peripheries of the world-ecology at the moment of peak appropriation. American and Chinese hydrofictions are particularly ripe for comparison, given that China and the USA are empires built on "conquest of water," whose hydraulic regimes are central to their "pacification" of humans and the rest of nature.[23] Both countries have confronted post-peak appropriation by turning to extreme water. I conclude with examples of millennial "extreme water" fictions from the USA and Finland that mediate Euro-American fears of twenty-first-century water shock and hegemon crisis. Throughout these hydrofictions, I argue, water functions as a thematic element, but also as representation and symbolic regime, product and producer of the contingent socio-ecological relations stabilizing the neoliberal disposition.

My analytic framework draws on Moore's synthesis of Marxist ecology and world-systems theories. Moore uses the term "capitalist world-ecology" to designate the "patterned history of power, capital and nature, dialectically joined," arguing that capitalism does not act *on* nature, but rather emerges *through* periodic re-configurations of human and extra-human natures, alternating ecological regimes and ecological revolutions.[24] A world-ecological approach to world literature enables new forms of comparison of the structures of feeling and forms of commodity fetishism peculiar to different regimes, revealing the socio-ecological relations that stabilize hydrological, energy and agrarian regimes in different phases of capitalism. Cultural forms are historical agents in environment-making, not merely *reflective* of re-organizations of capitalist nature, but *co-productive* of them. Thus, this essay will interrogate how hydrofictions anticipate or stabilize neoliberal hydroculture, but also the ways in which they subvert the socio-ecological relations produced by dominant epistemes and technics of water.

Neoliberal hydroculture shares several key representational characteristics with *petroculture*: fluidity, hypermobility and ubiquity paradoxically conjoined with occulted visibility. The material global infrastructure of pipes, pumps and container ships is less tangible than the liquid that emerges from the tap. Like fuel reserves, the bodies of water under greatest onslaught are underground or occluded from public sight: whether groundwater despoiled by fracking, fossil aquifers pumped dry, cloud vapour captured and reseeded, feeder rivers eutrophied or oceans contaminated with petrochemicals. Significantly, as Michael Niblett has observed, in the 2008 James Bond film *Quantum of Solace*, the "non-said" of oil is seemingly reversed in the scene where the body of murdered MI6 agent Strawberry Fields appears slathered in crude.[25] This image is peculiar because the plot does not revolve around the villain's theft of oil, but rather his attempt to monopolize Bolivia's water reservoirs (an allusion to the Cochabamba water wars). This substitution of oil for water signals the way in which the hydrological regime has emerged interdependently with the petrolic regime. Whereas it is usually oil that cannot be made the direct subject of narration of the world-system because its cultural logic is that of mediation, here it is water-as-systemic-relation that eludes subjectivization, displaced by the shocking viscerality of figurative oil.

A contradictory ambivalence pervades neoliberal representations of water crisis, veiled in the fetishism through which flowing water is transformed into exchangeable, quantifiable commodities, but also charged with the sensory immediacy of the necessity of water for all life and human development. Given the interdependence of energy and water, the hydrological regime can be said, like oil, to be a relation through which capitalism articulates its structure. Oil's saturation of the world-ecology presents challenges to representation, an "imaginative block on articulation" bound up with the "certitude of its symbolic logic in the way we live now."[26] The phantasmic representation of oil has been theorized as pertaining to its seeming invisibility yet ubiquity within a mode of production wholly dependent on fossil-fuel consumption and to the fetishism of the commodity-bubbles and disparities in wealth-generation that form around its extraction. Unlike oil, however, water is visible in the form of rivers, seas and rains, and pre-capitalist imaginaries teem with metaphors of water as life, as gift, as sacred. In contrast to petroleum's ineluctable association with modernity, water has been re-imagined in symbolic regimes since the first emergence of art. Yet, as Hannah Boast observes in her pioneering study of hydrofiction, environmental literary critics have had far less to say about water than about land or energy, even though "no resource … is more fundamental than water."[27]

Rather than concentrate on non-representation, it is more productive to focus on what *can* be said about water. We may be subjects of petro-modernity, but the planet is not a petro-sphere in the same sense that it is a hydrosphere: water, not oil, spurs biodiversity. Our bodies, subjectivities and cultural formations are peculiarly fashioned by and dependent on oil, but they do not depend on oil in a biological sense for life itself. If it seems difficult to imagine modernity without oil, a world without water is simply impossible. The very urgency of the human requirement for water opens up new possibilities for political action. Whereas the "energy unconscious" of oil may be subject to erasure,[28] the politics of water are more immediate, even if critical analysis of *hydroculture* is less developed.

Water enclosure in the Americas

My first exemplary novel anticipates the neoliberal turn to water-enclosure in the Americas. In Colombian writer Gabriel García Márquez's *The Autumn of the Patriarch* (1975), an

THE WORLD-LITERARY SYSTEM AND THE ATLANTIC

ageing Central American dictator is coerced into selling the Caribbean Sea to the USA in exchange for relief from debt and a CIA-sponsored coup. As he lies dying in his beachfront mansion, his repressed guilt unfolds in a stream of consciousness whose riverine prose ironically contrasts the aridity of the seabed:

> Either the marines land or we take the sea, there's no other way, your excellency, [...] so they took away the Caribbean in April, Ambassador Ewing's nautical engineers carried it off in numbered pieces to plant it far from the hurricanes in the blood-red dawns of Arizona, they took it away with everything it had inside general sir, with the reflection of our cities, our timid drowned people [...] I granted them the right to make use of our territorial waters in the way they considered best for the interest of humanity and peace among peoples, with the understanding that said cession not only included the physical waters visible from the window of his bedroom to the horizon but everything that is understood by the sea in the broadest sense, or, the flora and fauna belonging to said waters, its system of winds, the inconstancy of its millibars, everything, but I could never have imagined that they would be capable of doing what they did to carry off the numbered locks of my old checkerboard sea with gigantic suction dredges [...] they carried off everything [...] and left behind only the deserted plain of harsh lunar dust.[29]

The eloquent flux of the first-person narration captures the rich subjectivity of the dictator's over-developed ego and centrality to the state, though interspersed with deictic shifts between the pronouns *I*, *they* and *we* that underscore the intersubjective constitution of his consciousness. Niblett observes that periodic exhaustion of commodity frontiers is frequently mediated in "irrealist" aesthetics that capture the dynamics of peripheral societies subject to price volatility and cycles of ecological regime and revolution that rapidly dissolve social unities.[30] I argue that hydrofictions like *Autumn* that imagine absolute exhaustion display similar tendencies towards *hydro-irrealism*: a preponderance of tropes of draining and dessication; plots that tend towards repetition and circularity; narration marked by the spectral or absurd; macabre and gothic atmospheres of death-in-life.

In its plot and genre, García Márquez's *novella del dictador* mediates the "neoliberal turn" during which Latin America became a laboratory for structural adjustment policies imposed by the IMF and World Bank and enforced by US-sponsored *caudillos*. These economic policies were also environmental, reorganizing Latin American societies around appropriation of ecological surpluses. The nexus between debt and hydrocolonialism in *Autumn* anticipates the rising hegemony of finance capital over accumulation from the 1970s onwards, in which asset-stripping and speculation were prioritized over productive investment. In 1975, the novel's vision may have seemed satirically apocalyptic, but it is revealing to consider alongside Roman Polanski's 1974 film, *Chinatown*, which fictionalizes the California Water Wars. The "water grab" is the structuring violence in the film noir, exceeding the individual crimes that the investigator initially sets out to track. The overarching "mystery" in need of disclosure is the sacrifice of the public good of the rural hinterland to the profit of the LA city-system.

Autumn is a dystopian mirror to *Chinatown* that projects the American west's water regime forward to imagine what happens when internal enclosures of cheap water (such as those of Owens Valley) are maxed-out. In the novel, Arizona is the anticipatory marker of water crisis in the American West. The Ogallala aquifer, one of the largest underground sources of freshwater, sprawling 170,000 square miles across eight states, is being drained faster than it can recharge. Mighty rivers like the Arkansas, the Colorado, the Rio

Grande, are disappearing or running dry. Yet states and corporations accelerate the pumping of aquifers and the importation of water, perpetuating "the Hydro-Illogic cycle," in which anxiety over scarcity is followed by amnesia about its social causes once shortages ease.[31] In *Autumn,* this hydro-illogic culminates in appropriation of the periphery's water as a temporary spatial solution to the core's hydrological crisis, an ecological fix that "wipes out" the Caribbean Sea. The impossible quantification of an entire ocean, imposing a Cartesian grid on the fluid sea, encapsulates a vision of supreme technocracy saturated with the logic of radical commensurability accompanying finance capital's attempts to rationalize the whole of reality into generic income streams. The "ocean grab" in *Autumn* is apocalyptically total, more extreme than the theft in *Chinatown.* This is underscored in the genre: there is no (anti)heroic investigator to reveal the violence immanent to the system, no prospect of legal redress within the undemocratic regime. Instead, debt-based structural adjustment and external military force combine with the weakness of the peripheral state apparatus to ensure that the water grab is experienced as a disaster without mitigation.

Today, the prospect of suction dredges to drain seas is no longer speculative. New transport corridors into the Amazon River reservoir have enabled black market traffic in crude water carried by converted oil tankers from South America to Europe, North America and the Middle East.[32] The overproduction of water-intensive food crops in capitalist cores is sustained by the extraction of hydrological resources from peripheries. The horizontal appropriation of territory for mining and agri-business by transnational corporations has been joined by *water grabs* that vertically enclose subterranean waters, projects of death that dispossess riparian communities.

In *Autumn,* the selling of the sea is a death-scheme that violently removes the basis for future socio-ecological reproduction. The patriarch develops an ecogothic horror of the "flashes of the lighthouse without a sea," a "fantastic starlike firefly that fumigated in its orbit of a spinning nightmare the fearsome outpouring of the luminous dust of the marrow of the dead" (211). This false enlightenment figures capitalism's episteme of externalized nature, which grows by eviscerating life. The US ambassador installs a wind machine that replicates "the cross currents of the tardy trade winds," but the machine's "false mistrals" reveal the hollowness of the promise of a technological fix: they cannot replenish the evaporated lifeworld, only offer simulacra (210). When US engineers dredge the sea, they take away everything it sustains: the flora and fauna, the winds and rains, the reflection of cities, even the basis for the dying patriarch's liquid narration. The autumn of the patriarch is the autumn of the "*oikeios,*" Moore's term for the dialectical interweaving of symbolic and material relations within the matrix of human and extra-human natures.[33] The text's hauntological qualities gesture to absolute exhaustion, a hydrological rupture in the social metabolism of nature that promulgates an irreversible collapse of the entire ecology.

"Great talk" of China's water

My next text captures the emergence of new social relations at the moment of China's "neoliberal turn," with a particular emphasis on the constitution of a new hydrological regime. Whereas García Márquez's *Autumn* is charged with a bitterly-resistant mediation of the ecological fix appropriating Latin American waters to resolve the hydrological

THE WORLD-LITERARY SYSTEM AND THE ATLANTIC 115

crisis of the US core, Chen Jiagong's "Number Nine Winch Alley" is energized with the inflated affects corresponding to China's ascendance. The short story was published in 1981, three years after Deng Xiaoping pronounced the "four modernizations" opening China to economic liberalization. Set in a courtyard community, the short story captures the transmutation of these modernizations into new forms of subjectivity stabilizing the emergence of the neoliberal ecological regime. The alley residents reconceive water not as the basis of communal life, but rather as a commodity to be privatized:

> One of the residents of the courtyard heard that the nation's economy was "in the red." [...] There was a vague sense that that had something to do with rising prices, and people started to get panicky. Han Delai saw the old ladies whispering together in a corner and grew angry. "Hummph! Look at all this lack of patience! In the red, in the white, what are you frightened about? I'm telling you our government has everything under control [...] Let's just talk about water for a minute. Even China's water is worth money! Haven't you heard that over in Shandong, the water of Mount Lao is worth tons of money! Fill a bottle up with water and send it overseas to the 'big noses' and fork over the money please! Hell, water – will we ever run out of it? [...] These days we've got lots of water, it's the bottles that are causing the problems. When we have more bottles, we'll be swimming in oceans of cash! Only four modernizations? ... We can do eight ... " These words put Widow Feng into a fit of ecstasy, and the "gan-qings" flowed like water, too. In fact, everyone's spirits were raised; it seemed that they were all feeling much more secure. [...] This great talk about the water of China being worth buckets of cash was Han Delai's most memorable heroic feat.[34]

In contrast to the fluid eloquence of *Autumn*'s patriarch, this third-person narration is suffused with the brash volubility of peasants-turned-entrepreneurs, focalizing a collectivity on the verge of privatization. The aesthetics are social realist, but the chatty narration radiates a certain euphoria: the creative destruction of the reimagination of Mount Lao not as sacred site but as vessel to be drained for export to capitalist cores; the heady affects of innovation and nationalist pride offered as social salves to the anxieties of price volatility and financial panic caused by integration into the world market; the illusory promise of an ecological fix to debt through the enclosure of previously uncommodified zones of life; the acquiescence to securitization under an authoritarian state. The passage sets up a striking analogy between the untrammelled expression of privatized consciousness and the crystallization of the myth of water as a flow that can be endlessly appropriated for China's modernization, as expressed in the loquacity of Han Delai and Widow Feng. Widow Feng's verbal dexterity is "blocked" when she fears the nation's economy is foundering, but is restored after Han Delai's speech, when her confident Beijing aphorisms affirming the new social reality (*gan-qing* loosely translates as "that goes without saying") "flow" once more like "water." Verbal and subjective flow are linked to the exultant endorsement of nature as a source of capital flows: the cultural fix that corresponds to Han Delai's celebration of a new hydrological frontier as part of the "ecological fix" to China's economic crisis, which accumulates new forms of value through the appropriation of externalized nature.

This process is accompanied by the financialization of everyday life. The residents enter into credit relations, reversing the Cultural Revolution's campaign to "destroy the four olds" by vigorously competing in novel forms of consumption. They purchase incongruous appliances on credit they cannot use, displaying them "ostentatiously" as evidence of social status (276). For these households, China's neoliberal reforms are "a kind of 'tease', luring them into a market economy with promises of increased autonomy while eroding all forms of collective property and security."[35] When Han Delai grows old, with the security of the "iron rice bowl" of social protections removed, he finds himself impoverished and despised by a now-atomized community, trapped in a "living death" (280).

"Number Nine's" aesthetics do not extend to dystopian prolepsis, partly because they do not register the same extremity of peripheral subordination to foreign appropriation as *Autumn* does, nor the imagination of absolute exhaustion. However, the story's narrative logic – euphoria, followed by deflation – captures the social experience of privatization, while implying the inevitable relative exhaustion of the cheap water and cheap food integral to China's modernization. The bathos of Han's decline ironically contrasts the over-inflated affect of his "great talk" of China's water, predicting the decline of the hydrological regime that he lauds. Far from being able to export its water globally, China has exceeded the carrying capacity of its hydrosphere.

Blood spurts like water

China's "water crisis" has been accelerated by three decades of compressed industrialization without environmental regulation, under the mandate of "grow first, clean up later," an ethos that Ma Jun describes as "trying to rob nature of the last drop of water to serve economic expansion."[36] China is the world's most populous country, but possesses only one quarter of the world's average per capita water resources, and faces severe challenges in the variable distribution of water.[37] The planet's largest producer of hydroelectricity, with 50,000 dams on the Yangtze alone, China has launched hydraulic super-projects such as the Three Gorges Dam and the South–North Water Transfer Project in the attempt to resolve the geographic mismatch between its northern energy reserves and southern water resources. These schemes reengineer entire ecosystems to fit abstract supply, rather than recalibrating usage in proportion to different watersheds; they have produced mass displacement of environmental refugees and undermined the Yangtze's centuries-old use as a transport-system. The compound crisis of extreme water is manifested in "the drying up of the Yellow River, devastating floods on the Yangtze, the rapid decline in northern China's water table, and the serious pollution problems of southern China's water."[38] Pan Yue, Chinese minister of the environment, recently predicted:

> This miracle will end soon because the environment can no longer keep pace. Acid rain is falling on one third of the Chinese territory, half of the water in our seven largest rivers is completely useless, while one fourth of our citizens does not have access to clean drinking water.[39]

Twenty-first-century Chinese novels like Yan Lianke's *Dream of Ding Village* (2006; translated 2011) and Ma Jian's *The Dark Road* (2012; translated 2013) are saturated with eco-gothic images of hydrological exhaustion and pollution, whose depiction of the total annihilation of riparian lifeworlds recalls *Autumn*'s apocalyptic vision. Their hydro-irrealist aesthetics sharply repudiate the extractivist logics underlying China's extreme water. *Ding Village* is posthumously narrated by a 12-year-old boy, Ding Quiang, who was poisoned by the villagers in revenge against his father, the local "blood head." Its plot revolves around the decimation of a rural village in Wei County of Henan province after the epidemic caused by unregulated blood-selling during the plasmapheresis boom.

In the mid-1990s, in response to new transnational markets for biocapital, the Chinese government transformed Henan into a leading frontier in the plasmapheresis economy, wooing foreign direct investment in bio-product enterprises and establishing paid donation stations across the province. The rural blood economy was a vertical frontier of cheap nature that delved into the arteries of life itself, treating peasants' blood as an agricultural export. Plasma obtained by the state-sponsored stations was sold to bio-pharmaceutical companies producing human blood products at extortionate markups. In Henan, the blood trade was unregulated and contaminated, driven by impatience for rapid profits, resulting in a catastrophic epidemic of AIDS that infected millions, decimating the province.[40]

In *Ding Village*, the county director urges peasants to abandon farming for blood donation as an escape from poverty: "You can travel the golden road to wealth and prosperity, or you can stay on the same dirt path and live like paupers."[41] The village elder borrows the symbolic regime of hydrological plenitude to convince the villagers to give blood:

> When Grandpa reached the riverbed, he searched around for a moist patch of sand, rubbed it between his hands and began to dig a small hole. Before long, the hole was half-filled with water. Grandpa produced a chipped ceramic bowl and began ladling the water from the hole and pouring it on to the sand. Again and again he ladled, pouring one bowl of water after another on to the sand. Just as if it seemed that the hole had gone dry, Grandpa paused. In a matter of moments, the water began to seep in, and the hole was once again full of water. [...] "Did you see that? [...] Water never runs dry. The more you take, the more it flows. [...] It's the same with blood. Blood always replenishes itself. The more you take, the more it flows." (30–31)

Here, once again, the concept of "flow" is indelibly linked to the reimagination of nature – the human body's circulatory system and the earth's groundwater – as a source of unlimited commodity flows, a fantasy of capital's circulation without barriers. The asymmetrical biocommodities trade results in the immiseration and physical enervation of the producers of blood, at the same time as it precipitates a collapse of the agrarian regime, since the weakened peasants are unable to water their fields or grow crops.[42]

The blood monoculture is inextricable from the hydrological crisis undermining the rural agrarian regime. Located in Central China's Yellow River Valley, Henan is irrigated by the mother river that has been the main artery of Chinese civilization for millennia. One of China's most populous provinces and largest producers of water-intensive crops, it has been beset since the 1990s by soaring temperatures, droughts and water shortages as a result of climate change and hydraulic engineering schemes. The overexploited Yellow River has entered a crisis of terminal dormancy, failing to reach the sea for over half the year. Upstream dry regions in northern China drain the river for agricultural and urban use, while downstream regions suffer chronic shortages in their wetlands and groundwater. The government's response is to drill deeper artesian wells and build longer diversion channels to tap fresh resources as each source is subsequently exhausted. The plasma economy, by introducing a new commodity frontier that does not require "cheap water" for agriculture, can be understood as a temporary ecological fix.

A chapter near the conclusion of *Ding Village* bleakly describes the hydrological rift. The technical fixes employed by the villagers exhaust the groundwater reserves and precipitate a rupture in the hydrological cycle that destroys not only crops, but the whole of the riparian ecology on which their lifeworld depends:

The farmers, unaware of the drought, had diverted water to their fields any way they could. They dug deep irrigation wells and used diesel engines from tractors to pump even more water from the earth. By June and July, the wheat was in ear, the cottonwoods were in bloom, and there was no moisture in the ground. With no nearby rivers to draw from, the soil was parched. [...]

When the sun burst from the eastern horizon and roared into the sky, the plants were dry, their leaves brittle under the burning sun, and their heads drooped, crumbling at the slightest touch. With each gust of wind, chalky dust rose from the scorched earth and swirled across the plain. [...]

The plain was as pale as ashes, as far as the eye could see.

The leaves on the trees withered and curled. The scholar trees, whose shallow roots couldn't absorb enough moisture from the soil, began shedding yellow leaves, as if autumn had come early. [...] The village, once green, was barren. It blended into the landscape.

Crops died in the fields. Grass withered on the plain. The soil was bleached, as far as the eye could see. (281–282)

The repetition of ashen tropes and motifs such as "as far as the eye could see" creates a sense of poetic litany, recalling *Autumn*'s lunar deathscape. The novel's structure is characterized by repetition and circularity; passages similar in language and content evoke the cyclical return of water shortages and the chronic draining of the vitality of the villagers and the land. These acquire a double significance when the extractive relations underlying blood monoculture are interlayered with those of hydrological crisis.

The narrator's grandfather is visited by monstrous dreams of the plasma economy as a vampiric infrastructure that intertwines with the pipes that drain the countryside's water resources:

For the last three nights, he'd had the same dream: the cities he'd visited [...] with their underground networks of pipe like cobwebs – running thick with blood. And from the cracks and curvatures of pipes, from the l-bends and the u-bends, blood spurts like water. A fountain of brackish rain sprays the air; a bright-red assault on the senses. And there, upon the plain, he saw the wells and rivers all turned red, rancid with the stench of blood.[43]

If Grandpa persuaded the villagers to donate blood by evoking a symbolic regime of endlessly renewable water, here the symbolic regimes of water and blood as circulatory systems are once more interlinked, but this time their idealist valence is reversed into a horror-show. The pipe is a nightmarish instrument of extraction, within which blood does not circulate perpetually, but rather "sprays" and "spurts," signalling violent rupture. This doubled figuration uses the hydrological rift caused by the draining and diversion of the Yellow River in order to articulate the asymmetries of the blood economy. The plasma infrastructure is the product of the reorganization of human labour and the wider eco-system in the wake of hydrological crisis, and thus the ways in which both regimes drain the vitality of the lifeworld must be articulated together. The extremity of ecogothic aesthetics in passages like these expresses the stark necessity of blood and water to social reproduction. By the novel's conclusion, the majority of characters are dead; those that linger on are the "stationary displaced,"[44] suspended in a form of death in life. The posthumous narration underscores the destruction of rural futurity, giving the lie to government promises that the appropriation of cheap nature would bring plenitude.

Waste and water

If *Ding Village* figures the draining of the Yellow River, my final example from Chinese fiction, Ma Jian's *The Dark Road*, mediates the hydrological crisis of China's second great river: the titular dark road of the Yangtze, black with silt and chemical waste. Whereas *Ding Village* chronicles the devaluation of the rural countryside through the perspectives of the displaced-without-moving, *Dark Road* charts the traumas of migrants and refugees. The novel represents hydrological crisis as dialectically interrelated to neoliberal frontiers of waste, pollution and hydro-energy. During 2008–2009, Ma Jian travelled extensively through Guandong, researching the experiences of boat people on China's most polluted river, discovering that "people's relationship to trash is getting closer and closer. [...] When I went to these wastelands, life was no different than death."[45] The novel narrativizes the environmental catastrophe of the Yangtze through the journey of Meili, pregnant with a forbidden second child, as she and her husband Kongzi flee the state's population control.

Leaving their upstream village, they sail south to "Heaven Township," in the Special Economic Zone of Guiyu, centre of a boom in waste-outsourcing from capitalist cores:

> As much as 70% of the world's toxic e-waste is shipped to this area of southern China, where it is processed in makeshift workshops by migrant labourers who are paid just $1.50 a day [...] In just ten years, Heaven Township, once a collection of sleepy rice villages, has become a digital-waste hell, a toxic graveyard of the world's electronic refuse. The air is thick with dioxin-laden ash; the soil saturated with lead, mercury and tin; rivers and groundwater are so polluted that drinking water has to be trucked in from neighbouring counties [...][46]

Because most men who dwell there become infertile, and many children are born with birth deformities, the official state policy of one child-one family is not enforced, making it a haven for migrants such Meili and Kongzi.

Their episodic boat journey is described in meandering aesthetics that invoke a riverine rhythm of perpetual circulation opposed to linear conceptions of modernization, while capturing their rootlessness as deracinated peasants. Their slow travel is a strategy of narrative deceleration, opposing the developmental time of the Chinese "miracle." A sense of suspended temporality pervades the first half of the novel, implying a riparian consciousness that encompasses a longer durée of civilizational-time than the neoliberal hydroculture of New China. Kongzi, who prides himself on being the "seventy-sixth generation male descendant" (5) from Confucius, proclaims that "the Yangtze is our nation's artery of life," citing classical poetry rooted in the pre-capitalist Chinese philosophy of nature (33). Meili responds by quoting Li Bai: "On both sides of the gorge, apes cry unceasingly/My light raft has already passed through ten thousand mountain folds" (33). They encounter an endangered Chinese green sturgeon with reverence for the ancient geological time it evokes, only to mourn its imminent loss: "When the dam is finished, their migration route will be completely cut off. They're doomed to extinction" (51).

For Meili, struggling against Malthusian state policies that govern her reproductive capacity and against her husband's patriarchal belief in his right to inseminate her with a male heir, the river is a feminized sphere where "she feels more free on the water than she did on the land" (52). She imagines the Yangtze as a commons whose "constant flux" repels masculinist hierarchies, in contrast to the land: "Whether it's rented or borrowed, every path of soil in this country is controlled by the state" (52). As Suya, a detainee in a camp where the state incarcerates rural migrants in an attempt to limit urbanization, tells Meili, "Grains of soil are seeds of the masculine spirit; rivers are dark roads to the eternal female" (190). Posing the river as the sacred feminine strategically equates the domination of nature and of women by the Chinese state, even if it problematically verges on biological essentialism.

The ecofeminist vision of the Yangtze is held in dialectical tension with the toxified watershed, analogizing the pollution of the river with the abuse of Meili's body and the appropriation of her unpaid labour in the sphere of social reproduction. The narrative sense of temporal remoteness from the hyper-modern metropolitan hubs of Shanghai or Beijing is constantly interrupted by industrial reminders in the form of river waste and pollution. The protagonists' subjectivities are focalized through a complex perceptual apparatus registering constantly shifting sensations of toxification: the variegated stenches of factory effluents, the colours of industrial waste, the sour and sulphurous tastes of chemicals. In Dexian, metallic rain corrodes their boat; in Guai Village, where Kongzi sells blood to a bloodhead, the riverbanks "are so darkened by dust and pollution that, compared to them, the fumes billowing from the far-away factories look clean" (142). A flood diversion area, Guai, is inundated by "yellow foamy water" from upstream factories, and its rate of birth deformities is so high that the town starts a "deformed infant trade," selling children to Shenzhen begging gangs (144).

The ironic contrast between the pastoral imagination of the river in classical poetry and its reality is sharply marked in Sanxia, a town flooded by the Three Gorges Dam, its occupants relocated against their will. Kongzi recalls Li Bai, "who sailed down this river a thousand years ago and immortalized it in his verse" (33). The affects encapsulated in Li Bai's poetic description of "the coolness at the base of the gorge, the giddiness one feels when disembarking onto the riverbanks" (42) will disappear forever once the valley is flooded. Meili is struck by the broken town's uncanny sense of folded temporality, where the residual traces of millennia-old civilization and its earlier philosophy of nature exist simultaneously with the developments that will erase them.

Meili's and Kongzi's sensation of temporal incongruity, of coming from a less capitalized region but going forward in time as they move downstream, signifies the uneven development of the rural countryside in comparison to the industrial corridor of Guandong. Everywhere they pass is pervaded by the social violence that accompanies hyper-pollution, toxification and destruction of riparian lifeworlds. The bodies of babies and women that litter the river channels draw a horrible equation between capitalism's generation of surplus value and its generation of objective waste and disposable "surplus" populations. As rural communities are reduced to humans-as-waste, they are forced into new modes of informal labour: in black markets such as the infant trade, in the blood trade or in precarious work, as when Kongzi joins dam demolition teams and Meili becomes an e-waste recycler, stripping components by hand.

Once they arrive in Heaven, the symbolic regime shifts from riverine emphasis on circulation to uterine metaphors of gestation and growth, telegraphing the frenetic energy of the recycling boom. Similar to the posthumous narration in *Ding Village, Dark Road* combines naturalistic description with an irrealist narrative device: the italicized interruptions of the spirit of Meili's unborn foetus, which is subjected to several deaths – strangulation by family-planning enforcers, miscarriage due to toxification. Eventually, it refuses to be reborn until Meili reaches a "safe" haven. The spirit embodies both her post-traumatic distress and the contradictions of her belief-system, oscillating between animism and the neoliberal rationality pervading Heaven's economic boom. As Meili confesses to the Sacred Golden Flower Mother,

> Sometimes I feel it's looking back at me from a future realm, as though my present is its past. And on some occasions, I've felt that it exists in a completely separate realm that somehow overlaps with ours. But when I try to put these feelings into words, my mind spins and time seem to go into reverse. (342)

The unborn foetus allegorizes the ecological crisis of Chinese modernity, in which economic growth is privileged over every form of life, and women's lives are disposable, considered as "cheap" as the water so thoughtlessly expended and polluted. The novel's concluding image hauntingly figures the foreclosure of social futurity: the stillbirth of the "alien-like" baby, transfigured by toxic exposure, its uncanny body glowing "as green and shiny as an apple" and its spirit-consciousness dissipating into the ether, as its mother slips lifelessly into the dead river. Like *Ding Village*, and *Autumn*, *Dark Road* ends with death, a final limit that cannot be superseded, a vision of absolute exhaustion.

Water shock

In the recent burgeoning of what Dan Bloom calls "cli-fi," a distinct genre of hydrological climate-change science fiction, or extreme water fiction, has emerged. In these, post-apocalyptic climate change scenarios are predominated by "water shock," even where oil and water remain ineluctably intertwined in figuration. In *Mad Max: Fury Road* (2015), gasoline still fuels the war-machinery of gearhead tribes as in the earlier trilogy, widely interpreted as responding to the oil shocks of the 1970s. However, the sequel's object of biopolitical control is no longer solely gas, but rather water, blood and mother's milk, an infrastructure of "four flows" associated with reproduction; the regime of extended oil is interlayered with the crisis of the hydrological frontier.[47] The gas now functions as a propellant for territorial monopoly of water, fuelling the security apparatus of vehicles that protect Immortan Joe and energizing the pumps that extract water from artesian wells deep beneath his wasteland Citadel. Here again the pump is central to the nightmare of extraction. Peak water does not replace peak oil as the object of anxiety and desire, but their symbolic regimes and technics are interknitted, enhancing each other's extremity.

I complete my trans-hemispheric triangulation of the crisis of cheap water by gesturing to two prominent cli-fi novels portraying "water shock" in autumnal cores. US writer Paolo Bacigalupi's *The Water Knife* (2015) and Finnish writer Emmi Itäranta's *Memory of Water* (2014) turn around anxieties of the decline of the USA and of the European Union as driven by post-peak water appropriation. They imagine a world dominated by a transition from American to Chinese hegemony, driven by China's innovation of new technologies that enable superior water-productivity. In *Water Knife,* Chinese-built high-rise "arcologies" in a desertified American southwest, where all remaining water sources are monopolized by robber barons, offer closed-system miniature biomes and vertical water farms where American and Chinese elites can reside in water-luxury, even as masses of dispossessed "zoners" struggle to survive outside airlocks, paying more for water than for gasoline. China flourishes from the export of hydro-technology, while the USA is bifurcated, its sovereignty severely compromised by the collapse of its western breadbaskets.

In *Memory of Water*, after an apocalyptic collapse of the EU in which rising sea waters swallow "land and freshwater" and cataclysmic resource wars are conducted over "fuel resources revealed beneath melting ice," the former social democracies of Scandinavia have been brought under the reign of the Qian empire, ruled out of "Xinjing." Imperial society is post-oil, no longer able to operate "fast-tech," reliant instead on solar, hydro and geothermal energy. This quasi-utopian energy transition is portrayed mostly in terms of privation and authoritarian control (an anxious correlative, perhaps, to the neoliberal austerity regimes that have dismantled European welfare states since 2008). The Qian Empire is founded in hydrological monopoly, sending water patrols across the hemisphere to police the metered consumption and rediversion of freshwater to Asia. The water-impoverished denizens of former Europe are driven to drinking salt-water and committing forms of "water theft" punishable by death. The young protagonist – a tea master who protects a secret spring in a cave-system and learns of a source of freshwater in a hidden glacier – is condemned to starvation by Qian interrogators after she refuses to surrender the water to imperial control.

The Chinese hydrofictions I explored primarily treat water crisis as an expression of the internal contradictions threatening the current regime's survival, articulated from the perspectives of the peasants who bear their costs. By contrast, in these Euro-American *cli-fis*, the crisis of the neoliberal hydrological regime is articulated through outward-looking discourses of China as simultaneously technotopian and hydrocolonialist, focalized through middle-class protagonists. Their impulse is diagnostic, seeking to anticipate the future of the world-ecology after climate change and the end of "cheap water," but also regulatory, projecting Euro-American fears of the emergence of a new hydrological revolution as the basis for Chinese ascendancy. In contrast to the consciousness of slow violence that predominates in the two Chinese texts, these cli-fis are energized with more thriller-like plots and speculative imaginaries of sensational resource violence. Written in conjuncture with America's "Asian pivot" in foreign policy, which seeks to contain Chinese expansion by blocking access to vital resources, these novels are exercises in hegemon crisis culture, which anticipate the transfer of power from the US world empire, its hegemony foundering with the erosion of its frontiers in cheap nature, to a Chinese empire imagined as hegemonic as a result of its production of new ecological fixes.

If texts like these anticipate hegemon crisis, they can also contribute to imagination of more emancipatory forms of environment-making. Vandana Shiva, descrying the "ecology of terror" pervading neoliberal geopolitics, calls for alternative visions of nature-society in which water rights are no longer the object of private ownership or state control, but rather a common good for humans and the rest of nature: "We can work with the water cycle to reclaim water abundance. We can work together to create water democracies."[48] The hydrofictions I have examined are haunted by apocalyptic or gothic imaginaries of water crisis as permanent disaster and death-in-life. The novels conclude with the deaths of their main protagonists and with the total desiccation or toxification of environments, underscoring the exhaustion of "cheap water." Yet, alongside these deathly imaginaries, there are intimations of alternative conceptions of water that refuse the instrumentalist epistemes of sink, commodity, input and object that have precipitated hydrological exhaustion. These are rooted in residual and indigenous philosophies, as in Meili's ecofeminist conception of water as sacred mother; or in the imagination of technics that transcend the hydraulic regimes of America and China's empires of water, as in

Bacigalupi's arcologies, which if liberated from the elite, could enable equitable use by the many; or in restorations of earlier modes of water use, as in the tea master's memory of usufructuary irrigation. The very title of *Memory of Water* signals its impulse to restore to consciousness conceptions of water as dignity and reciprocity. If these fictions are dominated by aesthetics of hydro-irrealism and water shock that correspond to their critique of the hydro-illogic of the neoliberal regime of water, they are also shot through with the dialectical tension of their struggle to summon not-yet-possible alternatives into consciousness. The question they pose, therefore, is how to think beyond hydrological catastrophe to a world that is post-capitalist, rather than post-water.

Notes

1. Moore, *Capitalism*, 291.
2. Li, *The Rise of China*, 15.
3. McWhinney, "Water," online.
4. Pearce, *When the Rivers*, 1.
5. Bresnihan, "Neoliberalization," online.
6. McWhinney, "Water," online.
7. Ren, "Sandor Predicts," online.
8. Kaufman, "Futures Market," 469.
9. Brown argues that "peak water" poses a greater challenge than "peak oil," because of the volume of water used in agriculture (Brown, "Real Threat," online). See Pearce, *When the Rivers*, 81.
10. Macdonald, "Improbability Drives," online.
11. Moore, "Climate Change," 26.
12. Brown, "Real Threat," online.
13. World Water Council, *World Water*, 24.
14. Hoekstra, "Switching," online.
15. Ross, *Chicago Gangster*, 12.
16. Maceda, "Pentagon Preps," online.
17. Moore, *Capitalism*, 225.
18. Ibid.
19. Shiva, "Resisting," 2.
20. Parenti, *Tropic of Chaos*, 99.
21. Shiva, *Water Wars*, 28.
22. Worster, "Water," 13.
23. Ibid., 6.
24. Moore, *Capitalism*, 8.
25. Niblett, "Oil on Sugar," 1–3.
26. Hitchcock, "Oil," 86.
27. Boast, *Hydrofictions*, 1.
28. Yaeger, "Editor's Column," 309.
29. García Márquez, *Autumn*, 208–210. Hereafter cited parenthetically.
30. Niblett, "Oil on Sugar," 8.
31. DeBuys, "Age of Thirst," online.
32. McDougall, "Caribbean Water," 191.
33. Moore, *Capitalism*, 35.
34. Chen, "Number Nine," 275–276. Hereafter cited parenthetically.
35. Anagnost, "Strange Circulations," 510.
36. Jun, *China's Water*, vii.
37. Ibid., 26.
38. Ibid.

39. Lorenz, "The Chinese Miracle," online.
40. Anagnost, "Strange Circulations," 517.
41. Yan Lianke, *Ding Village*, 31. Hereafter cited parenthetically.
42. See Anagnost, "Strange Circulations," 510.
43. Ibid., 8.
44. Nixon, *Slow Violence*, 42.
45. Ma Jian, "Questions and Answers," online.
46. Ma Jian, *Dark Road*, 280–281. Hereafter cited parenthetically.
47. Wark, "Fury Road," online.
48. Shiva, *Water Wars*, xiv, xv.

Acknowledgements

Many thanks to Graeme Macdonald and Jason W. Moore, the Left Ecology Network, Nicholas Lawrence and Hannah Boast for feedback and suggestions.

Disclosure statement

No potential conflict of interest was reported by the author.

Bibliography

Anagnost, Ann S. "Strange Circulations: The Blood Economy in Rural China." *Economy and Society* 35, no. 4 (2006): 509–529.

Bacigalupi, Paolo. *The Water Knife*. Kindle ed.London: Orbit, 2015.

Boast, Hannah. "Hydrofictions: Water, Power and Politics in Israeli and Palestinian Literature." PhD diss., University of York, 2015. Accessed 1 November 2017. http://etheses.whiterose.ac.uk/12508/.

Bresnihan, Patrick. "The Neoliberalization of Vital Services." *ENTITLE: A Collaborative Writing Project on Political Ecology*, 27 August 2015. Accessed 1 November 2017. http://entitleblog.org/2015/08/27/the-neoliberalization-of-vital-services-the-bio-financialization-of-irish-water/.

Brown, Lester. "The Real Threat to Our Future Is Peak Water." *The Guardian*, 6 July 2013. Accessed 1 November 2017. http://www.theguardian.com/global-development/2013/jul/06/water-supplies-shrinking-threat-to-food.

DeBuys, William. "The Age of Thirst in the American West." *TomDispatch*, 4 December 2011. Accessed 1 November 2017. http://www.tomdispatch.com/blog/175475/.

García Márquez, Gabriel. *Autumn of the Patriarch*. Translated by Gregory Rabassa. London: Penguin, 1996.

Hitchcock, Peter. "Oil in an American Imaginary." *New Formations* 69 (Spring 2010): 81–97.

Hoekstra, Arjen Y. "Switching to Biofuels Would Place Unsustainable Demands on Water Use." *The Guardian*, 28 May 2015. Accessed 1 November 2017. http://www.theguardian.com/sustainable-business/2015/may/28/switching-to-biofuels-would-place-unsustainable-demands-on-water-use.

Itäranta, Emmi. *Memory of Water*. Kindle ed.New York: Harper Voyager, 2014.

Jian, Ma. *The Dark Road*. Translated by Flora Drew. London: Vintage, 2014.

Jian, Ma. "Questions and Answers." *Foyles*. Translated by Flora Drew. Accessed 10 February 2016. http://www.foyles.co.uk/ma-jian.

Jiangong, Chen. "Number Nine Winch Alley." In *Worlds of Modern Chinese Fiction*, Kindle ed., edited by Michael Day, translated by Michael S. Duke. London: Routledge, 1991.

Jun, Ma. *China's Water Crisis*. Translated by Nancy Yang Liu and Lawrence R. Sullivan. Norwalk: Eastbridge, 2004.

Kaufman, Frederick. "Futures Market: Wall Street's Thirst for Water." *Nature* 490 (2012): 469–471.

Li, Minqi. *The Rise of China and the Demise of the Capitalist World Economy*. London: Pluto, 2008.

Lorenz, Andreas. "The Chinese Miracle Will End Soon." *Der Spiegel*, 7 March 2005. Translated by Patrick Kessler. Accessed 1 November 2017. http://www.spiegel.de/international/spiegel/spiegel-interview-with-china-s-deputy-minister-of-the-environment-the-chinese-miracle-will-end-soon-a-345694.html.

Macdonald, Graeme. "Improbability Drives: The Energy of SF." *Strange Horizons*, 16 February 2016. Accessed 1 November 2017. http://strangehorizons.com/non-fiction/articles/improbability-drives-the-energy-of-sf/.

Maceda, Jim. "Pentagon Preps for Conflicts Sparked by Climate Change." *Global Policy Forum*, 16 December 2009. Accessed 1 November 2017. https://www.globalpolicy.org/security-council/dark-side-of-natural-resources/water-in-conflict/48559.html.

Mad Max: Fury Road. Directed by George Miller. 2015.

McDougall, Russell. "Caribbean Water and Hydro-Piracy." *Kunapipi* 34, no. 2 (2012): 191–199.

McWhinney, James E. "Water: The Ultimate Commodity." *Investopedia*. 24 May 2013. Accessed 1 November 2017. http://www.investopedia.com/articles/06/water.asp#ixzz3dFAPuPNS.

Moore, Scott. "Climate Change, Water and China's National Interest." *China Security* 5, no. 3 (2009): 925–939.

Moore, Jason W. *Capitalism in the Web of Life: Ecology and the Accumulation of Capital*. London: Verso, 2015.

Niblett, Michael. "Oil on Sugar: Commodity Frontiers and Peripheral Aesthetics." Paper presented at "Imperialism, Narrative and the Environment," Rachel Carson Center for Environment and Society, Munich, Germany, 11–12 October 2012.

Nixon, Rob. *Slow Violence and the Environmentalism of the Poor*. Cambridge, MA: Harvard University Press, 2011.

Parenti, Christian. *Tropic of Chaos: Climate Change and the New Geography of Violence*. New York: Nation Books, 2011.

Pearce, Fred. *When the River Runs Dry: Water – The Defining Crisis of the 21st Century*. London: Eden Project Books, 2007.

Quantum of Solace. Directed by Marc Forster. 2008.

Ren, Lucy. "Sandor Predicts a U.S. Water Futures Market." *Medill Reports Chicago*. 3 June 2015. Accessed 1 November 2017. http://news.medill.northwestern.edu/chicago/sandor-predicts-a-u-s-water-futures-market.

Shiva, Vandana. "Resisting Water Privatisation, Building Water Democracy." Paper presented at the *World Water Forum*, Mexico, March 2006, 1–22. Accessed 1 November 2017. http://www.globalternative.org/downloads/shiva-water.pdf.

Shiva, Vandana. *Water Wars: Privatization, Pollution, Profit*. Cambridge, MA: South End Press, 2002.

Wark, McKenzie. "Fury Road." *Public Seminar*, 22 May 2015. Accessed 1 November 2017. http://www.publicseminar.org/2015/05/fury-road/.

World Water Council. *World Water Vision: Making Water Everyone's Business*. London: Earthscan, 2000.

Worster, Donald. "Water in the Age of Imperialism – and Beyond." In *The World of Water, Vol. III*, edited by Terje Tvedt and Terje Oestigaard, 5–17. London: I.B. Tauris, 2006.

Yaeger, Patricia. "Editor's Column: Literature in the Ages of Wood, Tallow, Coal, Whale-Oil, Gasoline, Atomic Power and Other Energy Sources." *PMLA* 126, no. 2 (2011): 305–310.

From fishery limits to limits to capital: Gendered appropriation and spectres of North Atlantic fishery collapse in *The Silver Darlings* and *Sylvanus Now*

Michael Paye

ABSTRACT

This article uncovers a North Atlantic narrative pertaining to the longue-durée crisis of overfishing through Neil Gunn's novel of the nineteenth-century Scottish herring boom, *The Silver Darlings* (1941), and Donna Morrissey's representation of the mid-twentieth century Newfoundland cod boom, *Sylvanus Now* (2005). Comparing these two novels within a world-ecological framework reveals how aesthetic and plot developments come from the novels' needs to mediate the dialectical interchange between the uneven modernity of the capitalist world-system and the local relations of the inshore fishery. Through aesthetics and motifs synonymous with silver mining in Gunn's novel and oil culture in Morrissey's, the narratives form a cultural critique of capitalist fishery practices, from the local to the global level, over the last 200 years.

Literary critics adapting world-systems and world-ecology approaches towards environmental criticism have recently argued for comparative reading of the aesthetic registration of commodities in different geographical settings. Sharae Deckard has highlighted "structural homologies and similarities of concern" in depictions of commodity monocultures, while Michael Niblett has suggested that "it is the contours of the world-system as world-ecology that provide the ultimate interpretative horizon for world literature".[1] Following these interventions, I argue that literary depictions of fishery frontiers speak to more than just an overfishing crisis, but a general consciousness of capitalism's inherent contradictions.

These contradictions can be read productively through the cultural depiction of commodities that have been essential to the reproduction and expansion of the capitalist world-ecology during particular hegemonic periods. The capitalist world-ecology is "a patterned history of power, capital, and nature, dialectically joined" and "grounded in the *technics* of capitalist power and the conditions for the expanded reproduction of capital".[2] The "appropriation" of silver and oil has been essential to its reproduction, part of the "ecological surplus" contributing to "large volumes of unpaid work/energy".[3] The plunder of bullion from India balanced Britain's books in preparation for its hegemonic dominance over the long-nineteenth century, while oil is also imbricated in global violence, yet central to the cheap energy that powered America's hegemony over the long-twentieth century.[4] In the fishery novels to be analysed here, silver and oil's textual presence unveils the underlying contradictions of the fisheries in their larger world-ecological contexts, while also contributing to the ideals of independence and self-sufficiency synonymous with, in the context of trawler-based fishery exhaustion, traditional fishery culture. Oil and silver have associations with boom and prosperity, volatility and environmental degradation across the world, while herring and cod, major sources of cheap protein during both of these periods,[5] are associated with physical labour and community in Scottish and Canadian culture.

Neil Gunn's 1941 novel of the early nineteenth-century Scottish herring boom, *The Silver Darlings*, mediates the relationship between fishery and imperial bullion in Scotland's case, and Donna Morrissey's 2005 novel of the mid-twentieth-century Canadian cod fishery, *Sylvanus Now*, mediates the relationship between fishery and oil in Newfoundland's. I have chosen these two novels because they demonstrate an intensity of aesthetics, forms and affects around regional fishery culture and its place in the world-system. *The Silver Darlings* begins in the aftermath of the Highland Clearances, which saw thousands of clan members displaced towards industrial centres and new fishing villages.[6] The narrative follows a young protagonist, Finn, who becomes the greatest fisherman of his generation, while also registering the imperial channels through which the fishery operated. *Sylvanus Now* follows Sylvanus and his wife, Adelaide, during the trawler boom of the 1950s and 1960s. Sylvanus continues a tradition of (now motorized) small boat fishing passed on over the generations while other fishermen join trawlers and sell direct to the factories, as a frozen fish complex overtakes the traditional salt cod fishery.

World-ecology theory enables me to determine how the aesthetics of silver and oil – ignored in other critiques of these works – are in tension with the ethics and practices of the respective inshore fishing communities. Jennifer Wenzel's theorization of the lower level of alienation associated with locally sourced commodities in the context of Nigerian literature illustrates this fish–silver and fish–oil dialectic. She asks, 'is it possible that the rise of petroleum makes palm [oil] seem more "local", less alienated and alienating, that petro-violence makes palm seem peaceful by comparison?'[7] Following Wenzel, I argue that the identification of silver and oil with global capitalist plunder and alienation co-constitutes the symbolic association of herring and cod with regional, communal networks in these novels. The clan's tragedy cedes to fishery *Bildung* in Gunn's novel, punctuated by images of pastoral's demise when the weight of capitalist imperialism becomes too great for the *Bildungsroman* genre to sublate or map. Morrissey's idyllic, pastoral narrative of the inshore cod fishery is spatiotemporally separate from the realist, positivist politics of fishery development in Canada, leading to formal and narrative dissonance. Through liberalist optimism, clanship fuses with the fishery's capitalist development in Gunn's narrative, while Morrissey's matrifocal pastoral collapses as the static protagonist cannot evolve at the same speed as the trawler fishery, its development a precursor to neoliberal structuration.

My world-ecology methodology takes inspiration from Adrian Ivakhiv's approach to understanding the global totality through formal and material discrepancies, a "Freudian uncanny [...] that invades the representational frame" of texts, symbolizing capitalism's contradictions, yet "remaining outside those relations [of daily life] and in some way fundamentally inassimilable to them".[8] Silver "invades" the narrative of *The Silver Darlings*, its beauty and plenty a metaphor of fishery success and the capitalist potential of the sea, but also the brutality of imperialism. In *Sylvanus Now*, the novel's often sexualized depiction of fisherman–sea relations is infiltrated by oil culture through factory ships, aestheticized through sudden, sexually violent images of bloody ecocide and nylon nets, which, lost to the sea, independently lurk its depths, appropriating myriad animals and objects into a zombie-like coagulation of plastics and organisms. Petroleum's promise of comforts and conveniences offsets these horrors but is not independent of them. As such, while Ivakhiv's generally irrealist interruptions might be random, Gunn's and Morrissey's respective silver and oil invasions are here considered specific to the appropriable natures that cheapen(ed) capitalist exploitation during the British and American hegemonic periods, respectively. Furthermore, the contradictions unearthed through silver and oil speak to the concerns of each writer around fishery production and its future in their respective contemporary moments.

The world-ecology lens therefore offers a new way of reading these putatively regional novels within the context of the North Atlantic fisheries' literary depiction. Equally, it allows an interpretation of "capitalism's innate tendency to abstract in order to extract" through a gendered lens.[9] Critics of Gunn's work often "adopt his terminology rather than clarifying its implications", failing to question his masculinist vision of the Highlands,[10] while Morrissey's critics have under-theorized the implications of the matrifocal, sexualized relationship between Sylvanus and the sea in *Sylvanus Now*. A world-ecological reading of the novels unveils that these genderings emerge from what Jason Moore terms the "nature/society abstraction". For Moore, "The emergence of nature as a violent, but real, abstraction was fundamental to the cascading symbolic-material transformations of primitive accumulation in the rise of capitalism", and this "epistemic rift" normalizes pre-existing patriarchal codes, racism and chauvinism. The work of women, animals, slaves and the sea itself are therefore part of "Nature" and, as such, free for appropriation.[11] Gunn's novel genders the new relations of the fishery as masculinist in an attempt to fuse clan and capital, while Morrissey's pastoral matrifocalism represents a critique of capitalist patriarchy beyond Gunn's masculinist, semi-proletarian *Bildungsroman*.

Having outlined how world-ecology offers a new mode for understanding these two novels in their world-historical contexts, I will now demonstrate how Gunn's tragic and Morrissey's pastoral opening chapters are symbolic representations of pre-capitalist social relations. In Part I, through Mikhail Bakhtin's theorizations of pastoral and idyll, I will show how Gunn's fraternal and Morrissey's matrifocal sense of communalism critique the abstractions of capital despite the symbolically conservative gendering of masculine labour and female (appropriable) Nature in both texts. Part II will demonstrate how the threat of fishery collapse emerges through a lexicon obsessed with development and appropriation, associated with silver in Gunn's novel and (unconsciously) oil in Morrissey's. The formal and tonal clashes materialize in moments of disaster and brutality, whereby silver and oil bring out the darker underside of capitalist development through sudden ecocidal spectacles of fish destruction and masculine violence. Equally, the press-ganging of a minor character named Ronnie in the opening chapter of Gunn's text speaks to the long-term effects of capitalist appropriation and exploitation, while nylon (petroleum-based) gill nets in Morrissey's novel equally suggest capitalism's ongoing violence. Man and net therefore gesture towards an aesthetic rendering of "slow violence [...] that occurs gradually and out of sight".[12] The narratives thereby habituate readers to the

THE WORLD-LITERARY SYSTEM AND THE ATLANTIC

spectre of collapse across Atlantic fisheries as not limited to exhaustion independent of the mode of production, but tied to larger *ongoing* processes of capitalist extractivism.

Masculine bonds and matrifocal mythos: Stability at the inshore fishery

Textual moments of spatiotemporal stability conflict with the respective texts' developmental narratives, as symbolic responses to alienated labour. Bakhtin has argued that pastoral and idyllic chronotopes formally break down in the face of new social relations and developing modes of class stratification, resulting in "a pastoral-idyllic chronotope riddled with decay, its compact isolation and self-imposed limits destroyed, surrounded on all sides by an alien world and itself already half-alien".[13] Bakhtin considers the collapse of pastoral and idyll as a formal response to new rounds of primitive accumulation, Marx's term for "the historical process of divorcing the producer from the means of production", a procedure that Marx himself considered "anything but idyllic".[14] While Gunn's fishermen develop in tandem with this "alien" world and retain the bonds of the clan, Morrissey's characters suffer a conclusive loss in the face of the "alien" trawler regime, mitigated by the novel's imagination of reciprocity between man and mother ocean. As will now be shown, the tragedy of Finn's father sets the scene for a new mode of production to take over in *The Silver Darlings*.

At the start of *The Silver Darlings*, Tormad, father of the unborn protagonist, Finn, sets out on a fishing voyage, leaving his pregnant wife, Catrine, at home. Following several allusions to impending tragedy compacted into a few pages – the constant reminder of the violence of the Highland Clearances, Catrine's sense of foreboding and the death of Catrine's uncle by drowning – Tormad is murdered during an impressment, allowing the novel to switch to a coming of age narrative that focuses on Finn. Recently dispossessed of his home by Scottish lairds turned British capitalists, Tormad embarks on his community's first journey to sea, with "Napoleon safely on St. Helena".[15] After the trauma of enclosure on land, Tormad looks beyond his loss, calming his crew when they spot an unidentified vessel, telling them, "the sea, at least, is free" (*Silver* 27). While clearly a reference to the cultural conception of the sea as a free space,[16] Tormad's sentiment reveals the double-edged sword of liberalized productive relations and imperialist violence, as the approaching vessel turns out to be an impressment ship, demonstrating that the free gifts of the sea are not for men on the boat but the system of capitalist imperialism that put them there. Tormad is fatally wounded in the ensuing struggle, as the masculine cooperation on the open boat finds its uncanny counterpart in masculine violence in relation to impressment. Tormad's remaining presence in the narrative, which he "haunts" as lost manhood and the spirit of the people,[17] is representative of the communalism associated with the clan on the one hand, and the far-reaching imperialist system on the other.

This imperialist system threatens previous cultural forms and their emergence across new generations. Tormad's boat is a recycled piece of equipment, bought from a man in Golspie who had used it 50 years previously when white fishing represented a principal enterprise for coastal communities. This man also presented Tormad with a buoy, while the crew use a second buoy made from a set of bagpipes that belonged to a piper who "cursed" the "sasenach" husband of his landlord, dying soon afterwards. The narrator optimistically suggests that this might "mar[k] not an end but a beginning!" (*Silver* 24). This shared knowledge of dispossession and rejuvenation through means of production is both anti-imperial and generationally communal, as the piper's rage against the Clearances foregrounds both the bodily violence of the coming impressment and the clanship that finds a new zone on the herring boat, where there is no "real class distinction", just like the foregone land agreements between laird and tenant, as Gunn would have it.[18] Such idealism is violently obliterated, however, as "The sea glittered from Berridale Head to Loth, vacant in all that space save for one small derelict boat" (Silver 30).[19] The boat, so central to the men's brotherhood and sense of excitement, has instantly been evacuated of its previous identity, of all hopes, aspirations and communal feeling. It represents what Niblett has referred to in another context as "the imprint of the environmental trauma [...] detectable only indirectly through a particular constellation of images".[20] Basing much of his imagery on Peter Anson's work on derelict fisheries, dereliction and death are commons motifs that signify the loss of the Scottish fishing industry for Gunn, as "The fishings were dwindling, boat hulks lay rotting at their haulage", while a "pervasive sense of decay" haunts previous boom towns.[21]

The traumatic opening therefore sets up the conflicting stories of success and failure at the herring fishery. The day after the impressment, "Coopers, gutters, and packers were busy as they liked to be, and life went on in this new exciting game of catching prosperity as it swam past" (Silver 33). Gunn's narrative tonally symbolizes the boom–bust dynamics of capitalism, 'irreducibly bi-polar, periodically lurching between hyped-up mania (the irrational exuberance of "bubble thinking") and depressive come-down'.[22] The new fisheries' general hyperactivity bespeaks this unpredictability, as the narrative creates a sense of drive from which "there could be no relief now [...] except in death. Whatever was pursuing them, it was after them with bare teeth" (Silver 34). The sometimes metaphorically monstrous narration therefore prefigures the tensions between capitalist imperialism and clanship. Gunn's opening tragedy thereby cedes to Bildung as the clan system must evolve in step with the "alien" world, part of a new "ecological regime" that "establish[es] norms through which labour-power is organized, food is grown [and fished] and exchanged, resources extracted, and knowledge developed".[23]

Like Gunn's opening tragedy, Sylvanus Now's pastoral opening emphasizes the erasure of pre-existing stability through capitalist revolution. Most of the dominant members of Sylvanus' outport community and in Sylvanus' life are female: Eva (his mother), Adelaide and the sea itself, nurturing mothers and proud lovers, radiating a "lulling" calm but also a "siren's song".[24] Sylvanus' respect for this orientation is explicit as he captures a "mother-fish" full of roe at the beginning of the novel. The fish stands as synecdoche for "The ocean's bounty, [...] and woe to he who desecrated the mother's womb" (Sylvanus Now 4). Jennifer Bowering Delisle, as well as a number of literary reviewers, have criticized the unevenness of this moment, its "elevated language" and imagery.[25] However, this "elevation" arguably represents a formal response to global inequality by manifesting stability at the frontier through a heightened rhetoric. This pastoral image is oppositional to capitalist ecological development, a form of "moral protest [...] based on a temporary stability".[26] As he fishes with his handline, a more discerning implement than the trawl net, Sylvanus thinks, "It was this, the immediacy of it, which fulfilled him [...] tallying his own worth – unlike the hours spent over school books, studying letters and figures that made no sense" (2). Reading this moment through Bakhtin's concept of "historical inversion", the cod pastoral can be said to represent a "state of nature", an idealization of the past or present that "dissects and bleeds" the future of its "materiality".[27] This "trans-position" towards an idealized "Golden Age" gestures towards an alternative future, opposing the positivism of capitalist development through a formal rejection of the logic of resource extraction, but equally infers the hopelessness of a stable future due to the pastoralist idealization of the present – the novel was written after the 1992 cod moratorium, which shut down the cod fishery and left tens of thousands of people without work indefinitely, so this moment should be read in the context of larger fishery exhaustion. Sylvanus himself might therefore be considered the peak-cod idealiz-ation of the past, following the near-extermination of North Atlantic stocks. Morrissey therefore gestures towards a horizontal, reciprocal environmental consciousness through Sylvanus, who is immediately rewarded for releasing the mother-fish as he hooks a "twenty pounder" (4). What Herb Wyile identifies as "anti-modern" in the novel might be more productively read as the friction between such pastoral moments and the "capitalist realism" of "no alternative" that predominates in the text,[28] formally regis-tering at an early stage the cultural desire for reciprocal labour based on communal knowl-edge and kinship.

Morrissey's depiction thereby replicates the usual gendered divisions of labour and the symbolic associations of fishing communities, which often emphasize male agency over a passive female presence.[29] Yet her emphasis on reciprocity between woman–nature and man–worker, though problematic in its gendered essentialism, arguably corresponds to the cultural conception of the frontier's destruction as the work of greedy, uncaring male elites. *Sylvanus Now* represents an evolution from Gunn's work, tying environmental violence and violence against women explicitly together in a way that Gunn's narrative cannot. This shift corresponds to a larger mid-twentieth century cultural identification of resource extraction and toxicity as not only popularly paired with masculine violence, but inherently embedded in capitalist patriarchy.[30] Yet ultimately, neither novel chal-lenges the dualisms of capitalism, rather working through them to critique its violence.

In the next section, I will demonstrate how both texts figure the modernization and indus-trialization of fishing frontiers through a lexicon based around development and individual-ism that threatens the inshore fishery. Capitalism energizes Gunn's clanship but also undermines the clan's traditional makeup, while it stymies Morrissey's desire for stability through matrifocal reciprocity. Monstrous incidences and moments foreshadow or rep-resent sudden violence in the novels, corresponding to capitalism's boom–bust cycles. In *The Silver Darlings*, silver acts as a fetish of herring fishery success, but also dialectically cor-responds to the violence of imperialism through the character of Ronnie, whose lost youth signifies the temporal disjunctions and violent appropriative processes of the capitalist world-ecology. In Morrissey's novel, sexualized violence against feminine Nature erupts as the inshore is fished out. Oil aesthetics and affects seep into the fishery in *Sylvanus Now* through the factory trawler regime, violating the matrifocalism of the opening pastoral, already under pressure from Adelaide's uncertainty about her own desires.

The catastrophic "world-ecology": Monstrous prefiguration, modernization rhetoric and cyclical violence

Commodity fetishism occurs when relations between people are subsumed within the system of commodity exchange, thereby normalizing the capitalist mode of production.

As Michael Taussig writes in the context of peasants entering proletarian relations in South America, devil beliefs and fetishes can be interpreted as historically specific modes of critiquing the alienation of capitalism, "what it means to lose control over the means of production and to be controlled by them".[31] In *The Silver Darlings*, this loss of control is communicated through the fetish of silver, as the herring's benevolent status as "silver darlings" corresponds uncomfortably to the history of violence around silver extraction. In order to articulate this fish–silver dialectic, I will now analyse how Gunn connects a dogfish attack and fight between Finn and Roddie to the gambles of fish curers and markets in the Caribbean. I will then articulate the shock of capitalist violence through a reading of a dream Catrine has near the beginning of the novel, and conclude that Ronnie's return from the Indies, with a silver plate in his skull, demonstrates the horrors of the extractive regime of British imperialism. Taken together, these moments undermine Gunn's optimistic conjunction of capitalism and clanship through the fetish of silver, questioning the novel's cultural idealism around fishing for "silver darlings", a popular term for herring across the Atlantic.

In a lecture he gave to the Highland Society in the late 1780s, philanthropist and advisor John Knox opined that the herring would bring to "the native country an annual flux of wealth, superior, in many respects, to that which Spain receives, in cargoes of gold and silver, from Peru and Mexico".[32] The language of positivist imperialism draws a correlation between different parts of the empire, as frontier commodities are abstracted into financial referents, in this case, gold and silver. The explicit identification of the fishery with peripheralized nations for which Spain historically acted as "conveyor belt" underlines the peripheralization of the Scottish east coast and Highlands as a resource mine of military manpower and fish.[33] The curers and merchants in *The Silver Darlings* maintain a sense of control over the fishery via this rhetoric and epistemology, and it is predicted that "the creels of silver herring will turn into creels of silver crowns", representing a veritable "gold mine" and "silver mine" (*Silver* 72, 75, 80–81, 101, 120, 354, 421). Such attention to the bullion(ish) status of herring is similar to how imperialist explorers projected the "material demands of the emerging capitalist economies" of Europe onto the environment itself, perceiving "mineral wealth" in the colonies' soils.[34] In Gunn's novel, this self-fulfilling increase in commodity production symbolizes the dialectic of capitalist development, whereby the quantitative herring catch qualitatively changes into silver and gold currency. The technics of mining connects the work of the capitalist curer to that of the imperialist explorer, propping up the British Empire through the appropriation of fish and bullion from different peripheries.

Gunn's novel maintains a long-running narrative around Finn's journey of formation, which eventually sees him take part in kelp production and in a ceilidh in North Uist, where he gains an understanding of the immanence of kinship to the continuing health of the community.[35] Throughout the novel, the "silver darlings" are "welcomed", and are often described as "dancing" into the boat, in an imminent, ceilidh-like bonding that lessens, in the moment of welcome, the collaboration and victimization of Scottish peasants and proletarians in British imperialism (*Silver* 416, 435, 577). Yet the novel features several moments that undercut the optimism around the fishery, making explicit the herring fishery's immersion in the imperialist system of appropriation from peripheries. Following a week of poor fishing at Stornoway Harbour, Finn spots silver glints in the water and gulls overhead. Roddie's crew finally fill their herring nets with "silver darlings".

As they haul, Rob, a crew member, responds to the "first-comers" with a welcoming "Come in, my darlings!" only to witness their massacre:

> one was bitten clean away from the head. Others were slashed. [...] Finn looked over the side and saw the dark swirls, the dark-swirling bodies of dogfish. The sea by the nets was alive with them, alive, and evil, and abominable. (349)

Here, a "Gothic lexicon" of capitalist takeover again rears its head in the narrative, similar to the "bared teeth" and bipolar tone that follow Tormad's impressment.[36] This moment is not simply an example of the misfortunes that might face herring fishermen, but, in its "abominable" description, uncovers the tensions underlying Gunn's combination of clan-ship and capitalism.

Indeed, while repairing their nets following the dogfish attack, the fishermen overhear curers talking about the market. Duncan, fish curer, warns his fellow curers against specu-lation "in this business o' the German market [...] [as] there never yet was speculation but in the long run, in the long run, it meant smash" (353). Duncan recognizes the cyclical nature of capitalist boom and bust, pointing to the collapse of the West Indies trade fol-lowing emancipation in Jamaica as a warning against unrestrained development and com-petition (353). The majority of this trade was in "spent fish" with 60,000 barrels per year going to Jamaica alone. Duncan tells his fellow curers, "This is playing wi' the foreign market as the dogs played wi' the herring this morning – an' if it gaes on, the market will get torn like the nets" (350), thereby connecting speculation, the destruction of means of production and the market. Furthermore, such destruction threatens the balance that the open boat represents. Finn himself feels an "occasional dogfish swirl" as Gunn uses the image of dogfish to link Finn's unconscious anger to the mysteries of the market (395), and Roddie and Finn get into a fist-fight due in no small part to the stress of new capitalist relations. Whyte has argued that "The novel does nothing to con-textualize or distance this outburst of male violence", suggesting that such outbursts con-stitute the gender binary of masculine power and female passiveness predominant in the novel.[37] However, a world-ecological reading sees this binary on two levels. On the level of the capitalist world-ecology, the binary mediates the relationship between appropriable, passive female Nature and exploitable masculine labour, which erupts suddenly in mascu-line aggression and dogfish attack. At the regional level, the violence symbolizes the pre-existing entropy of the disavowed clan system, as the fishermen's allegiance to their curer contributes to confusion and anger towards each other, while the market remains shrouded in mystery, outside of their knowledge networks. While Roddie's growing attrac-tion to Finn's mother further contributes to the drama in the novel, the gambles of capi-talists and curers are much bigger threats to Gunn's imagining of a clan-based capitalist fishery, even though such gambles allow the bonds between fishermen to grow. The mon-strosity of the dogfish attack therefore underlines how the vagaries of the market and speculation undercut the fishery itself.

However, the dogfish are not the only creatures that foreshadow capitalism's bust moments in the novel. Prior to Tormad's murder, Catrine dreams that he is stolen by a kelpie, a mythical waterhorse. David McNally points out that the contemporary term, "monster", comes from the Latin verb *monere*, to warn. He continues, "Amongst other things, monsters are warnings – not only of what may happen but also of what is already happening."[38] Catrine's temporary "second sight" metaphorizes the materialization of boom–bust cycles through the monstrous, as her prediction of Tormad's death "prefigur[es] [events] of the present"[39] in the same way as the derelict boat prefigures the "environmental trauma" of fishery collapse.[40] The kelpie, suddenly stealing Tormad away, represents the monster of British imperialism through the regional mythology of a water demon, as Tormad becomes another victim of a system that appropriates human subjects, disappearing them into a globally dispersed system of exploitation and appropriation.

As such, the sudden traumas of dogfish attack and kelpie kidnapping can be understood as *capitalist* traumas through the slower, more geographically dispersed sense of the violence of capital, "incremental and accretive, its calamitous repercussions playing out across a range of temporal scales".[41] This dynamic is further captured through the return of Ronnie from "The Indies", allowing an exploration of imperial violence beyond the curers' references to the Caribbean trade. After 20 years in the colonies, he tells Finn of "our world", symbolizing the peacefulness of "the world before the clearances, in its pastoral ways" (450). This romanticized pastoral is a common feature in the literary depiction of post-plantation and extraction peripheries,[42] and unlike the sudden erasure of Tormad and the shock of the dogfish attack, Ronnie's pensiveness allows a more meditative consideration of imperialist brutality. While the "silver darlings" combine silver mining and herring fishing through the communalism of ceilidh, Ronnie reveals the unseen barbarity of the imperialist system through "a little silver clasp in his skull" (*Silver* 452). As a victim and participant in imperialist violence, Ronnie cuts through the positivism of capitalist and narrative development, telling Finn that ideas of "great adventure" are "a delusion", where a man's nature can only change "for the worse" as part of the machine of British imperialism (450–451). Instead, he encourages Finn to "justify your father" and remain at home. Capitalist development therefore profoundly disrupts the narrative of fraternal clanship while it simultaneously provides the markets, rhetoric and labour relations necessary for the fishery's success. Pastoral man (in this case, Ronnie, but also Tormad and Sylvanus) cannot survive in this new world. Catrine rejects Ronnie's eventual marriage proposal as he remains out of joint from the rest of the world, temporally dislocated by the violence of capitalist imperialism, a victim of its development and its associated genre, *Bildungsroman*, which depicts a "world that seeks its meaning in the future rather than the past".[43] As the imperial nexus and clan combine to make fishing for herring possible, Ronnie and Tormad are its tragic sacrifices, and their demise corresponds to capitalism's expansion, a dynamic through which Finn grows.

In both novels, therefore, pastoral is under threat, a distant past in Gunn's novel and unsustainable present in *Sylvanus Now*, hence the latter novel's "capitalist realist" formal limit. Having traced the levels of violence, slow and sudden, through which capitalism and clanship clash, and the ways in which silver fetishizes fishery success but also undermines the communalism of the success story of *The Silver Darlings*, I will now demonstrate how factory ship ecocide represents the shock of new rounds of accumulation in *Sylvanus Now*. Finally, in counterpoint to the comforts of oil culture, I will show how free-floating fishermen's gill nets make palpable the "invisibility" of the long-term and expanding violence of capitalist development,[44] not unlike the silver clasp Ronnie must carry with him for the rest of his days.

In *Sylvanus Now*, government officials placate concerned fishermen with promises of easier lifestyles in the trawlers and factories, echoing the optimism of the curers in *The Silver Darlings*. While trawlers destroy "billions" of fish, along with the mother-fish "whose bellies were swollen with pounds of roe not yet spawned" (*Sylvanus Now* 14),

THE WORLD-LITERARY SYSTEM AND THE ATLANTIC   135

these officials play the role of "rational man" taking control of feminine Nature: "worry ye not about the ocean's floor when a good trawling is necessary for thinning her beds and thickening her growth" (122),[45] the same specious conclusions of various fishing and trawling commissions of the nineteenth century.[46] They encourage the fishermen to join the "sixty-foot liners" that sell direct to "fish plants and freezers" for American consumers "and their nice modern housewives and their want for nice recipes and fish sticks made out of fresh fish" (44). Such hegemonic idealism is reminiscent of what Matthew Huber calls post-war "petro-privatism [...] centred on single-family homeownership, automobility, and the nuclear family".[47] As the end of the Jamaican trade necessitates a higher quality grade of fish and expansion into the Baltic for Gunn's curers, a similar standardization in quality is necessary for the new North American middle-class consumer for whom the fish plants process commodities. As oil mentality seeps into the fishery, and a new boom combining technological, oil-fuelled revolution combines with consumerism, Sylvanus sees the negative effects of the decreased time-scale of work that accompanies new desires for "new stuff – the new markets, and them big, pretty boats" (*Sylvanus Now* 265). With the pressures on the inshore from midshore skiffs and offshore factory ships, Sylvanus works extra hours to reach his own quota, "always racing the tide to get back out for the evening catch, and then racing against the falling light, now that fall was taking on, to get back to shore" (218). While Sylvanus traditionally "worked till his fish was done", a schizoid logic manifests as simplified Fordist tasks on trawler and in the factory replace processes of jigging, gutting and drying cod on the flakes,[48] which Sylvanus sees as symptomatic of "men who had once worked their own lives [...] now paid to work *overtime* on another's" (201).

Along with this sense of temporal displacement, the chauvinism of Sylvanus' mother ocean narrative, his desire to "tether" Adelaide to their home (*Sylvanus Now* 103), evolves into overt misogyny as the factory ships and trawlers continue their pillage, "degrad[ing]" Nature in sexually violent ways, which represents a symbolic correlative to capital's need to cheapen Nature in general.[49] Following a fight with his brothers who try to give him fish to see him through winter, Sylvanus is particularly embittered, and feels "the mother's nervousness" as he jigs for cod. She is "reluctant to yield" (note the sexual vocabulary) to the jiggers, as cod half the size of the previous year swim "wearily" along (*Sylvanus Now* 253). He notices a massive factory ship appearing out of nowhere, the "mammoth beast" encroaching near his space. The net winch begins turning, and "The ocean beneath started broiling, foaming white as the net breached" (254). The 1000-foot net looms large before him, pulsating and monstrously alive through the marine life it holds, "bulbous [...] and vibrating with its thousands of fish all crushed together and bulging". The net splits, leaving a "ruptured sore upon the face of the sea", while the massacred fish surround him, "their eyes bulging out of their sockets":

> The sea of red broke, Sylvanus clutched his side sickeningly as he took in the spread of the creamy white pods now floating before him. Mother-fish. Thousands of them. A great, speckled gull perched atop one of the pods nearest him, jabbing at her belly, weakening it, rupturing it, till the mother's roe trickled out like spilt milk. (*Sylvanus Now* 255)

The swelling of pride Sylvanus feels in terms of the earlier release of the mother-fish, rewarded by the reciprocal bounty of the ocean, turns to horror in the face of the brutal penetration of the sea bed, momentarily fusing sexual violence and ecological degradation. The sense of "maximum motility and liveness" that accompanies oil, its "charisma", evident in the forefathers' earlier advice to allow "a good trawling" of the feminine sea, finds its corresponding "petromelancholia" in images of violent extraction and exhaustion,[50] evocative, in this case, of sexual violence. This is a vicious assault on the mothering, nurturing ocean, the "forever fertile" mother (*Sylvanus Now* 203–204), who takes Sylvanus to "her breasts, fanning his face whilst he straddled her belly, plumbing her depths, his hips swaying to her heaving and ebbing beneath him" (250–251). The Madonna–sexual partner erotic of the mother ocean narrative hereby fuses monstrously with oil's affects and aesthetics, the uncanny invasion of oil at the fishery. The monsters necessary to Gunn's work to mediate "metabolic shift"[51] are no longer needed, as the unreal becomes reality through the new technologies and machines unleashed on the Atlantic Ocean (and other oceans as well) with the third trawler revolution,[52] powered by petrol and petrochemicals.

Yet not all violence is sudden. A more pervasive, invisible violence is represented by the nylon gill nets, known as "ghost nets" by fishermen, freely given to them to compete with the trawlers (*Sylvanus Now* 212). They are "low in instant spectacle but high in long-term effects", in Rob Nixon's terms.[53] Their longevity represents an ongoing assault on the ocean floor in which the fishermen are complicit, but, in Morrissey's novel, also represents an imaginary of capitalism's long-term horrors, thereby complimenting the more obvious degradation of factory trawlers with a slower meditation on environmental damage. This is where the aesthetics of the novel might be suggestive of the contemporary economic contradictions that have manifested in the inability of capital to renew itself materially through a new regime of appropriation.[54] Like the "walking dead" scouring the landscape of graphic novels and television, so too will the nets of *Sylvanus Now* (and real life) drift forever in the ocean, zombified and spectral. The nets are made from

> nylon [a petroleum polymer], and never rotted – which was a good thing, except that they were always breaking from their moorings and then floating about for years in the sea, filling up with fish till their weight sank them to the bottom, and how, when all the fish rotted or were eaten by other fish they rose again, fishing themselves full, till their weight sank them again, and again, fishing and rotting, fishing and rotting, and entangling other things like sharks and seals, and becoming a floating larder for other fish to feed on as they drifted by with their fresh and rotting carcases. (*Sylvanus Now* 190)

In comparison to the elevation of language in the opening of the novel, which aestheticized a place-conscious, arguably matriarchal, sensibility, the conjunction-heavy sentence signifies the accumulation regime's unstoppable greed. The ideal of unlimited resource accumulation finds its dystopic correlative in the monstrousness of factory ships and nylon nets immune to the ravages of time, not unlike the fetish of infinite herring accumulation that finds expression on Ronnie's mutilated body in Gunn's *The Silver Darlings*. These oil-made nets turn ecocidal and cannibalistic, gobbling up fish, detritus and other animals, while fishermen scavenge these half-rotten nets as they wash up onshore, picking out the recently caught fish and putting them into barrels, continuing a cannibal economy of human and non-human life. This constitutes a materialization of "dead labour"[55] through environmental destruction, registering the wider impacts of neoliberalism and the "zombified afterlife of petroleum" in a world-ecology that lacks the cheap inputs (including cheap fish and oil) that are required for material expansion.[56] As such, oil haunts the oceans in more ways than the violence of sudden spill and toxification to which news reports have accustomed us, but permeates the fishery through trawlers, nets and lifestyle changes.

Conclusion: The impasse of peak-fishery

When Finn's crew "raise the neid-fire" over his new craft to appease "the dark ones" late in *The Silver Darlings*, there is a fusion between folk belief, masculine ritual and fishery success, causing "an inflow of comradeship and confidence" (527). This symbolic fix through ritual connects boat, worker and fish through clannish bonds, covering over the sporadic outbreaks of masculine rage in the novel, as well as the violence of the imperial mission that the narrative consciously articulates. As such, considering the historical moment in which the novel was released, one in which a form of socially democratic Keynesianism was becoming the dominant system of capitalism, Gunn infers that a softer form of capitalism can benefit all if old ties remain, an ideal undercut by silver's multiple inscriptions in the novel. Morrissey's novel critiques the masculinist, militaristic posturing exemplified by Canadian fisheries minister Brian Tobin during the "cod wars", in an industry predominately governed by white male elites,[57] unveiling the toxicity of masculinism through the unconscious emergence of oil affects. With neoliberalism's anti-democratic, anti-labour practices firmly established when Morrissey wrote this novel, it is unsurprising that she looks back to utopian ideals of the cod fishery before the factory trawler boom. With capitalist realism overtaking the pastoral fishery, Sylvanus suffers a heart-attack at the opening of the sequel novel, *What They Wanted*, as "anchors left behind by the uncles [...] now bleeding red onto the rocks" along with the "ribbed skeleton of a boat" are all that remain.[58] Taking the two novels together, it appears that while the tragedy of the derelict boat at the beginning of Gunn's narrative cedes to the optimism of development, in Morrissey's world, the boat returns to its original meaning in *The Silver Darlings*: a symbol of capitalism's horrors.

As such, the development in form, aesthetics and character of literary depictions of fisheries at the regional level narrate world-historical concerns. Combining novels like *The Silver Darlings* and *Sylvanus Now* allows us to trace an overall dissatisfaction with fishery management and a development in attitudes, forms and styles through which the fisheries are narrated. World-ecological comparativism reveals that the novels rely on dualisms that limit inshore fishery culture to conservative social relations. The narratives thereby suggest little in terms of possible cultural evolutions for a revitalized fishery, but, through silver and oil, mediate the sense of impending violence that awaits communities at the frontier.

Notes

1. Deckard, "Editorial," 5–14; Niblett, "Oil on Sugar," 282.
2. Moore, *Capitalism in the Web*, 8, 204.
3. Ibid., 73–106.
4. On hegemonic periodization, see Arrighi, *The Long Twentieth Century*, 30–31, 219–246; on bullion and British hegemony, 55, 191–193; on oil and US hegemony, see LeMenager, *Living Oil*, 3–19.
5. Moore, "Ecology and the Rise," 182–186; Harris, *Lament for an Ocean*, 54–63.
6. On Clearances, see Nadel-Klein, *Fishing for Heritage*, 33.
7. Wenzel, "Petro-magic Realism," 453; see also LeMenager, *Living Oil*, 66–101.

8. Ivakhiv, "Stirring the Geopolitical Unconscious," 102.
9. Nixon, *Slow Violence*, 41.
10. Whyte, "Fishy Masculinities," 49–68. Another related mode of Gunn critique is the positivist critical method, whereby Gunn's earlier works are seen as formal failures or experiments. Gunn's highest accomplishments are therefore represented by the later works (like *The Silver Darlings*) that successfully evoke his circular philosophy, as in McCullough, *The Novels*, 9, 27; and Burns, *A Celebration of the Light*, 1. Subsequent (and some previous) realist readings of Gunn's work have been principally informed by Gunn's constitution of national identity, Highland politics and his formal response to the pre-Scottish Renaissance tradition. Representative – though not exhaustive – examples include Caird, "Neil M. Gunn," 49; Inness, "They Must Worship," 133–149; and McCleery, "The Sources," 177–196. Contemporary political and separatist debates have influenced more recent studies, relating Gunn's work to the wider context of Scottish nationalism, internationalism, resource control and colonization (see, for example, McCleery's 2013 edited collection, *Nation and Nationalism*).
11. Moore, *Capitalism in the Web*, 9, 48, 76.
12. Nixon, *Slow Violence*, 2.
13. Bakhtin, "Forms of Time," 103.
14. Marx, *Capital*, 874–875.
15. Gunn, *The Silver Darlings*, 12. Subsequent references to the novel will be cited parenthetically as *Silver*.
16. See Brannigan, *Archipelagic Modernism*, 13; Nadel-Klein, *Fishing for Heritage*, 24.
17. Campbell, "True Imagination," 145.
18. Gunn, "The Scottish Clans," 1–26.
19. Sherrie Inness sees the impressment as symbolic of English economic control, indicating "the conflict between the Scots and the English that is a dominant theme throughout the text" ("They Must Worship,"141). Yet textual analysis reveals an antagonism between the folk and capitalist imperialism, and very few English characters actively take part in the novel itself.
20. Niblett, "When You Take," 240.
21. Anson, *Fishing Boats*, 122; Gunn, *The Grey Coast*, 38–39, 174.
22. Fisher, *Capitalist Realism*, 35.
23. Moore, *Capitalism in the Web*, 113.
24. Morrissey, *Sylvanus Now*, 21, 9. Subsequent references to the novel will be cited parenthetically.
25. Bowering Delisle, "The Newfoundland Diaspora," 63.
26. Williams, *The Country and the City*, 44. As Williams points out, such idealization might conceal complex class struggles and the contradictions of pre-capitalist formations (44–45), the latter submerged within the mother-fish pastoral of *Sylvanus Now*.
27. Bakhtin, "Forms of Time," 147–149; 225.
28. Wyile, *Anne of Tim Hortons*, 34–40; on the sense of "no alternative," see Fisher, *Capitalist Realism*, 1–12.
29. Nadel-Klein and Davis, "Introduction: Gender in the Maritime Arena," 7.
30. Plumwood, *Feminism and the Mastery of Nature*, 1–18; Merchant, *The Death of Nature*, xv–41.
31. Taussig, *The Devil and Commodity Fetishism in South America*, 17.
32. Knox, *Observations on the Northern Fisheries*, 108.
33. Moore, "Amsterdam," I: 44–46.
34. Niblett, "When You Take," 238.
35. The Oxford English Dictionary defines a ceilidh as "(a) an evening visit, a friendly social call; (b) a session of traditional music, storytelling, or dancing" ("ceilidh, n").
36. Shapiro, "Transvaal, Transylvania," 30.
37. Whyte, "Fishy Masculinities," 61.
38. McNally, *Monsters of the Market*, 9.
39. Cowan, "The Discovery of the Future," 6–7.
40. Niblett, "When You Take," 240.
41. Nixon, *Slow Violence*, 2.

THE WORLD-LITERARY SYSTEM AND THE ATLANTIC 139

42. DeLoughrey, Didur, and Carrigan, "Introduction," 1–7.
43. Moretti, *The Way of the World*, 5.
44. Nixon, *Slow Violence*, 4.
45. Plumwood, *Feminism and the Mastery of Nature*, 7.
46. Roberts, *The Unnatural History of the Sea*, 137–157.
47. Huber, "Refined Politics," 302–306.
48. The jig is a fishing lure, and flakes are outdoor platforms for drying cod.
49. Moore, "Introduction: Anthropocene or Capitalocene?" 2–3.
50. LeMenager, *Living Oil*, 103–141.
51. Moore, *Capitalism in the Web*, 75–83.
52. Roberts, *The Unnatural History of the Sea*, 133.
53. Nixon, *Slow Violence*, 10.
54. Moore, *Capitalism in the Web*, 228–235.
55. Cartographies of the Absolute, "Landscapes of Capital."
56. Macdonald, "Research Note," 13.
57. Harris, *Lament for an Ocean*, 19–22.
58. Morrissey, *What They Wanted*, 69.

Acknowledgements

Thank you to Sharae Deckard for her support and advice and to Anne Cormican for her feedback during the drafting process. A special thank you to Sorcha Gunne for her tireless efforts during the publishing process and support for this article.

Funding

This publication has been made possible by the support of the Irish Research Council for the Humanities and Social Sciences (2013–2015 [grant number GOIPG/2013/94]) and a Dobbin Scholarship from the "Ireland Canada University Foundation" (2015–2016).

References

Anson, Peter. *Fishing Boats and Fisher Folk on the East Coast of Scotland*. Dent: Fisheries, 1930.
Arrighi, Giovanni. *The Long Twentieth Century: Money, Power and the Origins of Our Times*. London: Verso, 2010.
Bakhtin, Mikhail. "Forms of Times and the Chronotope in the Novel." In *The Dialogic Imagination: Four Essays*, edited by Michael Holquist and translated by Caryl Emerson and Michael Holquist, 84–258. Austin: Texas University Press, 1981.
Bowering Delisle, Jennifer. "The Newfoundland Diaspora." PhD diss., University of British Columbia, 2008. Accessed January 31, 2016. https://circle.ubc.ca/bitstream/id/3224/ubc_2008_fall_delisle_jennifer.pdf.
Brannigan, John. *Archipelagic Modernism: Literature in the Irish and British Isles, 1890–1970*. Edinburgh: Edinburgh University Press, 2015.
Burns, John. *A Celebration of Light: Zen in the Novels of Neil Gunn*. Edinburgh: Canongate, 1988.

Caird, J. B. "Neil M Gunn: Novelist of the North." In *Essays on Neil M. Gunn*, edited by David Morrison, 41–51. Thurso: Caithness Books, 1971.

Campbell, Donald. "True Imagination: The Silver Darlings." In *Neil M. Gunn: The Man and the Writer*, edited by Alexander Scott and Douglas Gifford, 141–156. Edinburgh: Edinburgh University Press, 1973.

Cartographies of the Absolute. "Landscapes of Capital." Accessed April 20, 2016. https://cartographiesoftheabsolute.wordpress.com/2015/03/02/landscapes-of-capital.

"ceilidh, n." OED Online. Accessed December 1, 2016. Oxford University Press. http://www.oed.com/view/Entry/29391?redirectedFrom=ceilidh.

Cowan, Edward. "The Discovery of the Future: Prophecy and Second Sight in Scottish History." In *Fantastical Imaginations: The Supernatural in Scottish History and Culture*, edited by Lizanne Henderson, 1–28. Edinburgh: John Donald, 2009.

Deckard, Sharae. "Editorial: Reading the World-Ecology." *Green Letters: Studies in Ecocriticism* 16, no. 1 (2012): 1–14.

DeLoughrey, Elizabeth, Jill Didur, and Anthony Carrigan. "Introduction: A Postcolonial Environmental Humanities." In *Global Ecologies and the Environmental Humanities: Postcolonial Approaches*, edited by Elizabeth DeLoughrey, Jill Didur, and Anthony Carrigan, 1–32. New York: Routledge, 2015.

Fisher, Mark. *Capitalist Realism: Is There No Alternative?* Winchester: Zero Books, 2009.

Gunn, Neil. *The Grey Coast*. London: Souvenir Press, 1976.

Gunn, Neil. "The Scottish Clans." Neil Gunn Archive, National Library of Scotland, n.d. TS 209/9/141.

Gunn, Neil. *The Silver Darlings*. London: Faber and Faber, 1941.

Harris, Michael. *Lament for an Ocean: The Collapse of the Atlantic Cod Fishery – A True Crime Story*. Toronto: McClelland and Stewart, 1998.

Huber, Matthew. "Refined Politics: Petroleum Products, Neoliberalism, and the Ecology of Entrepreneurial Life." *Journal of American Studies* 46, no. 2 (2012): 295–312.

Inness, Sherrie. "'They Must Worship Industry or Starve.' Scottish Resistance to British Imperialism in Gunn's *The Silver Darlings*." *Studies in Scottish Literature* 28, no. 1 (1993): 133–149.

Ivakhiv, Adrian. "Stirring the Geopolitical Unconscious: Towards a Jamesonian Ecocriticism." *New Formations* 64 (2008): 98–109.

Knox, John. *Observations on the Northern Fisheries. With a Discourse on the Expediency of Establishing Fishing Stations or Small Towns in the Highlands of Scotland, and the Hebride Islands*. Charring Cross: J. Walter, 1786.

LeMenager, Stephanie. *Living Oil: Petroleum Culture in the American Century*. New York: Oxford University Press, 2014.

Macdonald, Graeme. "Research Note: The Resources of Fiction." *Reviews in Cultural Theory* 4, no. 2 (2013): 1–24.

Marx, Karl. *Capital: A Critique of Political Economy*. Volume I. Translated by Ben Fowkes. Middlesex: Penguin Books, 1976.

McCleery, Alistair, ed. *Nation and Nationalism*. Caithness: Whittles, 2013.

McCleery, Alistair. "The Sources of *The Silver Darlings*." *Studies in Scottish Literature* 20, no. 1 (1985): 177–196.

McNally, David. *Monsters of the Market: Zombies, Vampires and Global Capitalism*. Leiden: Brill, 2011.

Merchant, Carolyn. *The Death of Nature: Women, Ecology, and the Scientific Revolution*. San Francisco: HarperCollins, 1990.

Moore, Jason. "'Amsterdam Is Standing on Norway.' Part I: The Alchemy of Capital, Empire and Nature in the Diaspora of Silver, 1545–1648." *Journal of Agrarian Change* 10, no. 1 (2010): 33–68.

Moore, Jason. *Capitalism in the Web of Life: Ecology and the Accumulation of Capital*. London: Verso, 2015.

Moore, Jason. "Ecology and the Rise of Capitalism." PhD diss., University of California, Berkeley, 2007. Accessed February 2, 2014. http://www.jasonwmoore.com/uploads/Moore__Ecology_and_the_Rize_of_Capitalism__PhD__2007_.pdf.

Moore, Jason. "Introduction: Anthropocene or Capitalocene? Nature, History, and the Crisis of Capitalism." In *Anthropocene or Capitalocene? Nature, History, and the Crisis of Capitalism*, edited by Jason W. Moore, 1–13. Oakland: PM Press, 2016.

Moretti, Franco. *The Way of the World: The Bildungsroman in European Culture*. Translated by Albert Sbragia. London: Verso, 2000.

Morrissey, Donna. *Sylvanus Now*. London: Sceptre, 2005.

Morrissey, Donna. *What They Wanted*. Ontario: Penguin, 2008.

Nadel-Klein, Jane. *Fishing for Heritage: Modernity and Loss along the Scottish Coast*. Oxford: Berg, 2003.

Nadel-Klein, Jane, and Donna Lee Davis. "Introduction: Gender in the Maritime Arena." In *To Work and to Weep: Women in Fishing Economies*, edited by Jane Nadel-Klein and Donna Lee Davis, 1–17. Newfoundland: Institute of Social and Economic Research, 1988.

Niblett, Michael. "Oil on Sugar: Commodity Frontiers and Peripheral Aesthetics." In *Global Ecologies and the Environmental Humanities: Postcolonial Approaches*, edited by Elizabeth DeLoughrey, Jill Didur, and Anthony Carrigan, 268–285. New York: Routledge, 2015.

Niblett, Michael. "'When You Take Thing Out the Earth and You En't Put Nothing Back': Nature, Form and the Metabolic Rift in Jan Carew's Black Midas." *Journal of Commonwealth Literature* 46, no. 2 (2011): 237–255.

Nixon, Rob. *Slow Violence and the Environmentalism of the Poor*. Cambridge, MA: Harvard University Press, 2011.

Palmer McCullough, Margery. *The Novels of Neil M. Gunn: A Critical Study*. Edinburgh: Scottish Academic Press, 1987.

Plumwood, Valerie. *Feminism and the Mastery of Nature*. London: Routledge, 1993.

Roberts, Callum. *The Unnatural History of the Sea*. Washington, DC: Island Press, 2007.

Shapiro, Stephen. "Transvaal, Transylvania: Dracula's World-System and Gothic Periodicity." *Gothic Studies* 10, no. 1 (2008): 29–47.

Taussig, Michael. *The Devil and Commodity Fetishism in South America*. Thirtieth Anniversary ed. Chapel Hill: The University of North Carolina Press, 2010.

Wenzel, Jennifer. "Petro-magic Realism: Towards a Political-Ecology of Nigerian Literature." *Postcolonial Studies* 9, no. 4 (2006): 449–464.

Whyte, Christopher. "Fishy Masculinities: Neil Gunn's *The Silver Darlings*." In *Gendering the Nation: Studies in Modern Scottish Literature*, edited by Christophe Whyte, 49–68. Edinburgh: Edinburgh University Press, 1995.

Williams, Raymond. *The Country and the City*. New York: Oxford University Press, 1973.

Wyile, Herb. *Anne of Tim Hortons: Globalization and the Reshaping of Atlantic-Canadian Literature*. Waterloo, ON: Wilfrid Laurier University Press, 2011.

Feminist politics and semiperipheral poetics: Eavan Boland and Aislinn Hunter

Sorcha Gunne

ABSTRACT

Putting world-systems and materialist feminist schools in conversation with work about the Celtic Tiger, this article engages with critical conversations about capitalist modernity in Ireland, contending that it cannot be delinked from gender and sexual politics. I examine how anxieties about capitalist development in Ireland are gendered in the literary aesthetics of Seamus Heaney and Eavan Boland, albeit very differently. My subsequent discussion of Aislinn Hunter's novel, *Stay* (2002), shows how it draws on Irish literary inheritance to illustrate the tension between perceived traditional values, on the one hand, and modernity on the other. I suggest that tradition is a part of rather than opposite to modernity: I argue for the simultaneity of tradition and modernity. In both its form and content, Hunter's novel considers how capitalist modernity is always already specifically gendered.

[I]t has become time for women in their individual disciplines in Ireland to look at the present and find a credible narrative of the past to hand on to their daughters and their granddaughters. So much silence. So much oppression. How did it happen?[1] (Eavan Boland)

I begin this article about literature and modernity in Ireland with a quotation from the acclaimed Irish poet Eavan Boland. Boland has long been critical of both the social and the literary treatment of women in Ireland and, in "The Minds and Voices of Modern Irish Women," calls for a collective challenging of gender politics in Ireland; one that is inclusive to women beyond their historical role as "icons and objects."[2] This exhortation is addressed by Canadian writer Aislinn Hunter in her 2002 novel, *Stay*, in which she examines how modernity in Ireland is inflected by development and historical trauma. Published prior to the economic crash of 2008, the novel notes the accelerated change brought about by the economic boom of the 1990s and early 2000s, particularly in terms of tourism in the west of Ireland, where suddenly it seemed "every second house is a bed and breakfast, a craft shop opened last year and now there are rumours of a second hotel."[3] Furthermore, like Boland's poetry, the novel's feminist politics index the tense co-existence of the traditional and the modern in the unique environment of Ireland's Atlantic seaboard in a way that engenders a semiperipheral aesthetic where "tradition" is not opposite to, but the coeval of modernity. Hunter's novel depicts a feminist reimagining of classic tropes of Irish literary tradition – such as the body in the bog –

not only to engage with Boland, but also to suggest that capitalist modernity cannot be delinked from gender and sexual politics.

Putting world-systems and materialist feminist schools in conversation with work about the Celtic Tiger, I engage in critical conversations about capitalist development in Ireland. I analyse how anxieties about development in Ireland are constellated in gendered terms, both socially and in literary aesthetics, for example, in poetry by Seamus Heaney and Eavan Boland, albeit very differently. This contextualizes the subsequent discussion of Hunter's novel which examines how it draws on Irish literary inheritance to illustrate the tension between perceived traditional values on the one hand and modernity on the other. My reading of Hunter's novel suggests that tradition is a part of rather than opposite to modernity: I argue for the simultaneity of tradition and modernity. Hunter situates her novel in an Irish literary landscape by drawing on recurring tropes – such as excavation and bodies in bogs – and inflecting a seemingly realist narrative with fantastic, supernatural and modernist elements characteristic of Irish writers. Her feminist politics is thus articulated through a semiperipheral aesthetic that responds to the simultaneity of the traditional and the modern in the west of Ireland. As a Canadian writer and poet who has lived in Ireland and as an academic, Hunter offers the unusual perspective of being both insider and outsider when considering how the structure of feeling of capitalist modernity is gendered, a perspective that presents a more complex portrait in contrast to the celebratory tones of much of the commentary on Celtic Tiger Ireland.

In the 1990s, Ireland's historical narrative – long marred by colonization and conflict, poverty and emigration – was reimagined as the country became the proud poster child for economic development in the age of multinational neoliberal capitalism, a process that Denis O'Hearn refers to as the transformation "from green donkey to Celtic tiger."[4] The Celtic Tiger brought with it a reimagining of Ireland's social narrative as a new, modern, confident, and globalized nation. "Ireland's contemporary culture," contend Peadar Kirby, Luke Gibbons and Michael Cronin in the introduction to *Reinventing Ireland* (2002), "is seen as an eloquent expression of new-found confidence where the liberalisation of internal markets is matched by the celebration of individual rights and liberties."[5] This new and confident Ireland appeared to be casting off the shackles of its colonial legacy and emerging from the shadows of famine, civil war, religious oppression, and economic depression to flourish on the capitalist world-stage.

A key element of this "reinventing" pertained to the role of women in Irish society. In the early twentieth century, the emergent free state had established regressive gender politics, including Article 41.2 in the 1937 constitution, which declares:

> [T]he State recognises that by her life within the home, woman gives to the State a support without which the common good cannot be achieved. [...] The State shall, therefore, endeavour to ensure that mothers shall not be obliged by economic necessity to engage in labour to the neglect of their duties in the home.[6]

With this article, the Constitution of Ireland formalized the social role of women in Ireland as limited to the domestic sphere, equating womanhood with motherhood and, since then, gender politics in Ireland has been manifestly regressive. After the dissolution of the marriage bar in 1973 and the election of Mary Robinson as Irish President in 1990, however, more and more women in Ireland joined the work force coinciding with an economic boom.[7] The Celtic Tiger continued to gather momentum into the first decade of the new century, seemingly signalling that Ireland had finally arrived to take its rightful place amongst the world leaders of globalization and development, evidenced not only by the growing numbers of women in paid employment, but also by the fact that for the first time in history rates of immigration exceeded those of emigration. This celebratory narrative circulated in the social imagination and was reflected in much of the mainstream literature and journalistic coverage at the time.

In what turned out to be a somewhat prophetic study, however, Peadar Kirby's *The Celtic Tiger in Distress* (2002), highlights the misguidedness of the triumphalism abounding in the commentary about the Celtic Tiger and, I would add, gender equality too. Kirby's scepticism at this celebratory assessment of the model of development in operation in Ireland is astute and his contrapuntal argument is useful because it identifies a serious problem with the relative lack of critical thinking and reflection during (and since) the boom years, a lack of critical analysis that is as applicable to the gendering of Irish society as it is to discussions of the economy. "The mainstream reading of Ireland's transformation," he writes,

> fails to acknowledge sufficiently this ambiguity at the heart of the Celtic Tiger, preferring to concentrate on aggregate increases in living standards and employment rather than on how these things are distributed. It therefore rests on a view of successful development which gives priority to economic growth over social equity and quality of life, though any discussion of what development might or should mean is remarkably absent from the mainstream literature.[8]

Kirby is not only correct to identify the lack of analysis of what modernity "might or should" be in Ireland, he is also accurate in his assessment that growing social inequality is a characteristic of development clearly evident in Ireland. Inequality is, after all, a consequence of capitalism, where the logic of accumulation dictates that the driving force is profit not people. Furthermore, the instability of the type of growth encouraged is evinced, as Coakley notes, by the fact that immediately after the 2008 crash, the financial press, in contrast to earlier lauding, re-categorized Ireland "as one of the EU's 'peripheral states.'"[9]

Since 2002, Kirby and others have produced thought-provoking work problematizing the Celtic Tiger, the subsequent crash, and the effects of neoliberalism on the Irish economy, culture and society. There are many strengths to these works, not least that they establish a much needed critique of global capitalism and its manifestation in the Irish context – chiefly, the analysis of the role of commodity fetishism in consumer culture and the inequality inherent in capitalist development; as Kirby, Gibbons and Cronin declare "Romantic Ireland may be dead and gone but that has not prevented it re-emerging in commodity form."[10] Some of the commentaries, however, tends towards reading the Celtic Tiger (and subsequent crash) as a consequence of globalization in the contemporary moment rather than as a symptom of capitalism's *longue durée*. Take, for instance, Tom Inglis's *Global Ireland* (2008). First published shortly after the dramatic demise of the Celtic Tiger, *Global Ireland* offers compelling insights into the specific manifestation of "globalization" in Ireland. Inglis's analysis covers the combination of culture and capitalism in Ireland on a range of topics including the role of the Catholic Church and how neoliberalism begets inequality precisely because it is "about exploitation, greed and selfishness."[11] He notes that those who believe in capitalism subscribe to the notion that everyone can get rich, and richer, and richer, and that "liberal-individualism is the way the rich justify being rich. It is the symbolic domination that lies behind economic domination."[12] Along with Maurice Coakley's *Ireland in the World Order* (2012) and Joe Cleary's *Outrageous Fortune* (2007), Inglis's *Global Ireland* goes some way to remedying the uncritical narrative identified by Kirby of the Celtic Tiger as a wholly positive phenomenon. There is no doubt, in this respect, that his work makes an important and valuable contribution to understanding how multinational capital operates at a local level and the accompanying structures of feeling in contemporary Ireland, particularly as he speaks of a world capitalist system in order to highlight the social consequences for a model of economic growth that is characterized by inequality, arguing that "[t]he world capitalist system has changed the conditions in which we realize our sameness and difference. It has changed the nature of our social bonds."[13] He continues by contending that since the 1950s there has been "a mixture of the old and the new, of traditional Irish ways of being becoming mixed with new global cultural elements."[14] Though the idea the old and the new combining in modern Ireland is insightful and one of the strengths of Inglis's study, the argument is held back because of the restrictive timeframe deployed. Inglis considers globalization in Ireland to belong to the latter half of the twentieth century. He puts it thus:

> In the last 50 years, Ireland has changed from being an isolated, insular, Catholic rural society revolving around agriculture, to a more open, liberal-individualist, secular urban society revolving around business, commerce and high-tech, transnational corporations. In the last 15 years, the pace of change became more dramatic and Ireland is now identified as one of the most globalized societies in the world.[15]

There has undoubtedly been dramatic social change in Ireland over recent decades, as evidenced by the economy, which has become increasingly reliant on multinational corporations on the one hand, and on the other, increasing secularization. There has also been some change for women with the repeal of the marriage bar. In that respect, Inglis is correct. However, this is a characterization that seems to support an assessment of economic development in Ireland based on the logic of modernization and dependency theories which read Ireland as merely "catching up" to modernity.[16] Following critics such as O'Hearn, Coakley, and Cleary, however, I want to suggest that Ireland has long been a participant in the world-system and that inequality, regressive gender politics, religion and so on are constituent of globalizing processes. The Celtic Tiger, in other words, is just the latest phase in this larger process. To consider globalization as a product of the late twentieth century is to misunderstand the structural formation of semiperipheral modernity. As Coakley insists: "Ireland's historical trajectory can only be grasped if we take into account both 'internal' and 'external' factors and how they interact. This was the case in the late Middle Ages and it remains so today."[17] Therefore, what Inglis identifies as contemporary globalization should instead be understood in terms of the *longue durée* of the capitalist world-system and as features of semiperipheral modernity rather than isolation and insularity subsequently followed by belated global engagement resulting in prolific economic growth. For example, though Inglis links Catholicism to capitalism in Ireland, positing that Catholicism made capitalism different in Ireland, he aligns Catholicism with tradition and secularism with capitalist modernity, contending that there is "a traditional Irish Catholic habitus" that can be combined with "a modern cosmopolitan global habitus."[18] This dualism makes a degree of sense in the context of the late twentieth century. However, it unravels when considering the *longue durée* of capitalist world-history. Perhaps Ireland's catholicization is instead symptomatic of the longer process of globalization, of Ireland's participation in the world-system. Perhaps capitalism in Ireland has always been interconnected with Catholicism and vice versa. Furthermore, to understand Ireland as long being participant in a world-system is to understand the gains in wealth referred to as the Celtic Tiger as evidence of Ireland's enduring semiperipheral status rather than its belated emergence on a global stage.[19] As Wallerstein suggests, economic boom is the "major concern" of semiperipheral states: "to keep themselves from slipping into the periphery and to do what they can to advance themselves towards the core."[20] Ireland's continuing economic reliance on multinational corporate finance incentivized by a low rate of corporate taxation seems only to confirm this hypothesis. The Celtic Tiger – and the subsequent collapse thereof – was then the most recent phase of its positioning in the capitalist world-system.

Ireland's location in the world-system is also inseparable from colonization. In other words, Ireland's history of colonization highlights the particularity of its semiperipherality. As Lionel Pilkington puts it, Ireland's "colonial history makes the experience of modernity seem always tantalizingly just out of arm's reach," as was the case with many nations world-wide.[21] Colonization, therefore, did not simply have an effect on Irish cultural identity, but, as Cleary contends,

> From its inception, the colonial process was never simply a matter of the subjugation of this or that territory. It was, rather, an *international* process through which different parts of the globe were differentially integrated into an emergent world capitalist system.[22]

The crucial point here is that Ireland's history of colonization makes clear that it has not been insular for a very long time.[23] Or, more precisely, that Ireland only comes into existence through the world-system, as prior to that there was no understanding of "Ireland." Cleary goes on to elaborate on how Ireland, like the Americas and the West Indies, was among the colonial sites that were

> commercially oriented towards the emerging Atlantic economy, but imperial mercantilist policy was designed to prevent the colonies from developing independent trading links with each other. Instead, trade had to be channelled through the British and Spanish imperial centres, inhibiting independent economic development and diversification within the colonies over the longer term and thereby establishing the structures that would condition future economic dependence.[24]

Though Cleary is at times hesitant to subscribe wholesale to a world-systems approach, his argument is nonetheless suggestive in that regard and, because he is cognizant of the historical complexities of capitalism's *longue durée*, his analysis of modernity in Ireland is particularly insightful. For example, he notes that the Celtic Tiger was not the first period of rapid renovation to Ireland's economy. As the seventeenth century began, Ireland was ostensibly undeveloped and pastoral. By the close of the century, however, it had undergone a considerable transformation: "[a]s it was commercially reoriented to service the expanding English mercantile state [...] Ireland underwent 'the most rapid transformation in any European seventeenth century economy, society and culture.'"[25] Recognizing that Ireland has been integrated into the capitalist world-system for centuries rather than a few decades means that Inglis's argument about the belated dismantling of Ireland's insularity in the 1950s should be reconsidered. Cleary's analysis involves an acknowledgement of the *longue durée* of capitalism, which is necessary in order to engender an understanding of the capitalist world-system, more broadly, and what might at first seem to be the perplexing particularities of modernity in Ireland, more specifically.

In identifying the limits of modernization in relation to enduring social inequalities Cleary posits that,

> Based on a crude dichotomy between "traditional" and "modern" societies, modernization theories sought to explore the institutional arrangements, cultural values and other social variables that might allow traditional societies to become modern as quickly and effectively as possible. From this perspective, the problems [...] [that plagued Irish society] were understood to mean that Ireland remained a dysfunctional traditional society that had still to make the necessary transition to a properly modern social order.[26]

Following the rationale of modernization theories, then, the Celtic Tiger might have been expected to finally force this transition in Ireland, causing tradition to be abandoned in favour of a universal modernity. This has, however, not been the case. Instead, there exists an uncomfortable simultaneity of traditional and modern where gender discrimination remains prevalent in a variety of facets of Irish life – legislatively, socially, and culturally. Thus Article 41.2 of the Irish Constitution, for instance, which declares a woman's rightful place to be in the home. Recognizing that Ireland has long been a part of the world-system is highly significant, however, because it radically changes how gender politics and gender discrimination in Ireland must be understood. In answer to Boland's question that began this article – "So much silence. So much oppression. How did it happen?" – the treatment of women in Irish society, and the registration thereof in literature, is not a result of a "dysfunctional traditional society." It is, rather, a consequence of the capitalist world-system. In other words, the treatment of women as "objects and icons" is not a symptom of an insular, catholic, or rural nation that will end with globalization or secularization, with modernity.[27] Discrimination against women in Irish society – including as a consequence of religion and other perceived traditional forms – is, rather, a symptom of the capitalist world-system. Masculine domination endures in various combinations and permutations, albeit in distinct forms, precisely because capitalism is inherently patriarchal.

In *Patriarchy and Accumulation on a World* Scale, Maria Mies contends that

> the development of the capitalist world economy was based not only on a particular international division of labour ... but also on a particular manipulation of the sexual division of labour. The logic governing both divisions is the contradictory relationship between the progress of one pole and the retrogression of the other.[28]

World-system theorist Immanuel Wallerstein makes a similar contention in his article "The Ideological Tensions of Capitalism." Wallerstein analyses how both racism and sexism are fundamental to, and act as a safety valve for, the mechanisms of capitalism. For capitalism to operate at its most efficient (creating maximum profit) there must be the right dose of universalism and the right dose of racism-sexism which then

> allows one to expand or contract the numbers available in any particular space-time zone for the lowest paid, least rewarding economic roles, according to current needs. It gives rise to and constantly re-creates social communities that actually socialize children into playing the appropriate roles [...] And it provides a nonmeritocratic basis to justify inequality [...] It allows a far lower reward to a major segment of the work force than could ever be justified on the basis of merit.[29]

Like Mies, Wallerstein goes on to argue that, with regards to gender, the capitalist solution is to invent the tradition of the "'housewife' and assert that she is not 'working,' merely 'keeping house.'"[30] Silvia Federici also makes these connections. Moreover, she goes on to assert that there is a link between capitalist socio-economics and socially conservative policies on the family. She states that

> capitalist production relies on the production of a particular type of worker – and therefore a particular type of family, sexuality, procreation … . In this context, policies forbidding abortion could be decoded as devices for the regulation of the labor supply, the collapse of the birth rate and increase in the number of divorces could be read as instances of resistance to the capitalist discipline of work. The personal became political and capital and the state were found to have subsumed our lives and reproduction down to the bedroom.[31]

These arguments are important in understanding Ireland's problematic gendered and sexual politics – currently evidenced by Article 41.2 and the 8th Amendment of the Irish Constitution, expensive privatized childcare, a maximum of two weeks paternity leave with no option to transfer maternity leave, and historically by the ban on married women working in the civil service until 1973, the ban on divorce until 1996, the outright ban on contraceptives until 1980, with restricted availability until 1993. Such policies and laws are not only a consequence of conservative Catholic policies, but, following Mies, Wallerstein and Federici, are intricately bound up with the particularity of capitalist development in Ireland. The history and trajectory of women's role and status in Irish society, therefore, clearly demonstrates a tense co-existence or simultaneity of traditional and modern – what Mies calls progress and retrogression – that is characteristic of capitalist modernity.[32]

Conceptualizing traditional and modern, progress and retrogression, as being experienced simultaneously rather than as geographical binary opposites or as temporally chronological calls to mind the Blochian concept of the "simultaneity of the non-simultaneous" or that tradition is a constituent part of modernity, rather than, for example, a parody of itself for the purposes of tourism.[33] In other words, Ireland is both traditional and not, *and*, at the same time, is both modern and not. The description of layered modes of production – expressed by Marx in *Capital* and Fredric Jameson in *The Political Unconscious* – has a continuing relevance in this regard. There is an "overlay" of several modes of production and they can coexist simultaneously and, as Jameson posits, there can be

> vestiges and survivals of older modes of production, now relegated to structurally dependent positions within the new, as well as anticipatory tendencies which are potentially inconsistent with the existing system but have not yet generated an autonomous space of their own.[34]

Jameson, here, it seems to me, is legislating, or making space, for this paradoxical co-habitation of the traditional with modernity. He argues that to speak of the "coexistence of *several* modes of production" is "not synchronic in this sense, but to open to history in a dialectical way" and he continues by contending that "texts emerge in a space in which we may expect them to be crisscrossed and intersected by a variety of impulses from contradictory modes of cultural production all at once."[35] The idea of texts emerging in a space that is "crisscrossed and intersected" between, or "overlaid" with, different modes of production is well represented in Irish literary tradition by the imagery of earth and bog, two notable examples of which are provided by the poets Seamus

Heaney and Eavan Boland. More importantly, however, it highlights the feminist politics that inform the plot devices and literary strategies at work in the novel.

In "Digging," Heaney famously describes his grandfather cutting turf and his father digging potatoes. He connects his father and grandfather's relationships with the land and Irish heritage to his project as a poet, declaring that he will follow his father and grandfather by using his pen to dig instead of a spade. Heaney's poem evokes a sense of evolving patrilineal tradition articulated through earth and turf as the sibilance of phrases such as "the squelch and slap of soggy peat" are not only onomatopoeic, but resonate with the body politic. This is further evoked in the subsequent line as "living roots awaken" in the speaker's head.[36] As the poem unfolds back in time from speaker to father to grandfather; from writing poetry, to digging potatoes, to cutting turf; and then back again, there is a correspondence between the "overlay" of generations depicted in the poem with layers of earth that is suggestive of what the Warwick Research Collective have termed "the simultaneity of material and immaterial."[37]

In his 1975 collection, *North*, Heaney delves deeper into this fascination with earth and bog deploying a poetics that draws on the fantastic and grotesque in the series known as the "Bog Poems." They are well known as political poems written for "The Troubles" in Northern Ireland. What is striking about them, however, is how the embodied land is imagined. "Bog Queen," "The Grauballe Man," "The Tollund Man," and "Punishment" are just some examples of where Heaney evokes history by deploying the trope of the bog as the body. For example, in "Bog Queen" there is a stanza that illustrates how Heaney's metaphorical bog body operates: "My diadem grew carious, / gemstones dropped / in the peat floe / like the bearings of history."[38] The decaying headband of the speaker, presumably the eponymous Bog Queen, not only emphasizes the body politic, but melts into the bog just as history melts into memory – material and immaterial become a *mille-feuille*. Furthermore, what is notable here, as in all these poems, is that bog and body are "braille" or allegories for violence and violation. There is a long tradition of linking land and nation with women's bodies, more broadly in postcolonial writing, but also specifically in Irish writing – one only has to recall the *Aislings* or even Yeats and Lady Gregory's *Cáitlín Ní Houlihan*, for instance.[39] This trope continues in Heaney's "Bog Poems" where there is a tendency to overemphasize the metaphor of bodies, particularly women's bodies, as violated territory. Such a move is potentially reductivist as it restricts women's experience to that of allegory, something that is perhaps reflected in the Bog Queen's decaying diadem which speaks to a loss of sovereignty and, furthermore, by evoking a sense of nostalgia privileges the traditional over the modern.[40] This allegorical tendency reflects the broader social treatment of women in Ireland as object and icon that has been so normalized that it goes almost unnoticed.

As I began this article by noting, Boland has long been a critic of this limited space for women in Irish society and literature. Consequently, her poetry offers an alternative perspective on imagining history and culture as layered materially and immaterially in the earth, a perspective that asks questions about the treatment of women. In her poem "Wisdom" from *Domestic Violence* (2007) there is a distinct connection between past and present made through the land. When "metal touched clay" and the "digging" began, it was not only earth and stone that was excavated, exposed and extracted, but "an era, a city, my life."[41] Though Yeats's influence on Boland is more frequently cited, the reference to digging and land echoes Heaney's poetic legacy.[42] Furthermore, the combination of era, city, and life is significant as time and space are linked not only to each other, but to the speaker's personal narrative. Memory resides in the earth, not only recalling Heaney's poems, but evoking the simultaneity of material and immaterial. This is reinforced as the poem unfolds and the speaker rejects the notion that archaeology is merely scientific, actual, or material. Instead, materiality is twinned with symbolism (immateriality) as the project of digging reveals "an art of memory" and brings together the earthy with the literary. The speaker claims that this "is how / legends have been, and will always be, edited – / not by saying them, but by unsettling / one layer of meaning from another and / another."[43] Jameson's hypothesis of overlayering evidently resonates as the secrets are revealed layer by layer and the legends are not written, but "edited," like an earthy palimpsest. The subsequent revelation that the artefact unearthed is a mundane plate is arresting, contrasting the "eerie and expectant" atmosphere of the preceding lines (maybe particularly so for those familiar with Heaney's earlier work).

The manufactured nature of the plate is incongruous with the common yield of the earth (perhaps even juxtaposing the potatoes in Heaney's poem "Digging"), however, the everydayness of the plate in this context evokes the eponymous violence of domesticity addressed by the collection as a whole. This is Boland's poetic project: to register the everyday affect, or structure of feeling, of contemporary Ireland and she does so in a way that suggests a deep-seated anxiety with the gendered politics of both traditional imaginings and capitalist modernity. By uncovering a domestic plate, Boland is making a statement against the allegory of woman and nation, as she refuses the literary inheritance of woman as nation, of icon and object, of "Mother Ireland."[44] The striking interplay or tension between organic and manufactured objects: the metal and the clay; cigarettes and lilac; machines and wits; the plate and the mythic salmon of knowledge reinforces the point as these pairings further suggest the interconnectedness or layering of past and present, traditional and modern without fetishizing women's bodies. This is powerfully echoed in another poem "Windfall."

> We say *Mother Nature* when all we intend is
> A woman was let die, out of sight, in a fever ward
>
> Look. In the distance you can see the estuary.
> Feel under your feet October's rotten fruit.
>
> Now say *Mother Ireland* when all that you mean is
> There is no need to record this death in history.[45]

The poem recalls Heaney in its earthy, autumnal resonance (not only the bog poems, but also "Blackberry-Picking" where he speaks of fermenting fruit) and other Irish poets, such as Thomas Kinsella in "Another September." Boland, though, is critical of making woman's material body a symbolic (immaterial) national allegory and protests against how, despite, or even because of, the circulation of maternal metaphors – *Mother Nature* and *Mother Ireland* – women themselves are written out of material history. Her poetry, thus, both belongs to and challenges Irish literary legacy even as it registers the recombination and coexistence of tradition and modernity, progression and retrogression, in Ireland.

Set on Ireland's Atlantic seaboard, Hunter's novel *Stay* follows in Boland's footsteps. Though Hunter, a poet, turns to the novel form here, her narrative draws on Irish poetic traditions in articulating its feminist politics. The main focus is 26-year-old Abbey, a young Canadian woman who has come to Ireland in an effort to escape from her haunted past – an alcoholic father, who has recently passed away, and a mother who long ago deserted the family. Throughout the novel, Abbey moves between Dublin where she occasionally works as a waitress and Spiddal, a small *Gaeltacht* – or Irish speaking – village in Connemara in the west of Ireland where she stays with her older lover, Dermot. Like Abbey, Dermot is haunted by demons from the past. He had been a medieval historian by trade, but after a sex scandal – or more precisely and significantly, given Ireland's history on the topic, an abortion scandal – involving a student, he was fired and has subsequently been unable to secure academic employment, and has thus retreated to Connemara. To read Abbey as the peripatetic protagonist frames this novel as a variant of the *bildungsroman*. However, the narrative is broadened by the addition of a motley crew of village characters brought together to capture the structure of feeling of the west. Hunter's narrative inflects their stories with Irish literary inheritance and recurrent tropes, such as bodies in bogs, in order to depict the peculiar gendered combination of traditional and modern that characterizes the semiperipherality of the west of Ireland.

The novel speaks to the continuities and the changing realities for women brought about by the new wealth of the Celtic Tiger – Abbey's arrival in Ireland itself indexes this. Hunter, moreover, picks up and redeploys the trope of the body in the bog that is so readily identifiable in Heaney's "Bog poems." She does so, however, in a way that suggests her project has more in common with Boland's feminist politics. Boland writes of unearthing a plate in "Wisdom" and of the burying of an anonymous woman in "Windfall." Hunter, however, writes of unearthing an anonymous woman from the bog. The discovery and subsequent unearthing of the body in the bog is the central event in the narrative and the importance of history told through the land is explicitly pondered when, in a chapter titled "Dialectics," Dermot muses on the development of the bog and the corresponding attempt at conservation. He notes that discoveries of artefacts are "[t]he ground giving history back. Something returned to you, long after it had been forgotten" (158). The bog and the discovery of the body in it are not only symbolic, but are material embodiments of the proximity of that past. This literary trope is activated in an effort "to peer back into the past, by way of recovering both the specific history of the present and the alternative histories that might have been."[46]

The bog is a site of rich cultural tradition and heritage, a wealth of historical preservation, something that Michael – the English archaeologist who is a friend of Dermot's – notes in the novel when he contrasts Ireland with England: "In Ireland it's about making history, wrenching history from the ground" (129). It is, however, also implicated in capitalist industry because peat turf has become industrialized. Instead of cutting the turf in traditional ways (like Heaney's grandfather), machines are used in mass harvesting for maximum profit. The bog, then, is a wealth of socio-historical and ecological riches as well as a source of natural resources to be mined in the service of the capitalist world-system. In the novel, the "*Bord na Mona* men," in many ways, embody the tradition/modernity *mille-feuille* because they are, at the same time, the nostalgic men of the land and also the modern wage labourer alienated from it emphasized by the "pay by results" system they endure.[47] It is the *Bord na Móna* men who trigger the events in the narrative when they happen across a thin strap of leather in the bog which pre-empts the discovery of the body of a woman and the subsequent archaeological excavation led by Michael. The dig soon becomes the narrative focus – Dermot helps, and the entire town shows up to witness the spectacle, the local baker even sells cookies at the excavation site. By prominently featuring the excavation of the bog as a collective event, Hunter's novel seems to suggest that the present is infused with the past, and that the past is experienced in the present. It is "both modern and traditional, both 'ahead of' and yet 'behind the times' [...] [as if] multiple histories were being lived in one and the same space."[48] In short, the preserved body in the bog embodies the feeling of a peculiar simultaneity of tradition and modernity that, in its peculiarity, resonates with the collective experience of the west of Ireland. Like the revealing of the plate in Boland's "Wisdom," Hunter's narrative adopts similar connections with history, memory, and structures of feeling and like the body in the bog deployed by Heaney, Hunter's body in the bog is also historically significant.

Chiming with Boland's feminist politics, however, Hunter's bog body reimagines rather than repeats Heaney. The descriptions of the woman in the bog recall Heaney's as Dermot and Michael dig the woman out: "The woman's eyes squeezed shut, thin traces of roots woven over them like a thin veil. The fine arc of her eyebrows above" (265). The description, however, focuses on her face and a conspicuously absent description of the body suggests a refusal of the facile allegory of woman and land that Heaney's poetry succumbs to, an allegory that has dominated the Irish body politic. Instead, the men rebury the woman for conservation and, again, the description focuses only on how her facial features have meshed with the bog: "A medieval woman in a bath of peat, roots growing out her ears, out of the hole that was her nose [...] Putting a layer over her for safekeeping and then another [...] Layer after layer until she's gone again" (266). Hunter reimagines Heaney's bog bodies, but does not expose the female body, does not fetishize it or make it vulnerable, as in "Punishment." Instead, it is reburied to conserve it until it is properly excavated, and the details of the face appear to give the anonymous body an identity or at least a sense of personhood. Moreover, the narrative emphasizes the structure of feeling of the uncovering of the body, depicting it as a community event that is embodied by the layers in the bog.

The thematic combinations of tradition and modernity evidenced here and elsewhere in the novel – for example, the Irish language television station *Tele Gael*'s arrival in Spiddal – are further reflected in Hunter's narrative form which draws on a range of techniques, from supernatural experiences and numinous environments to modernist devices, that work to disrupt any straightforwardly realist reading. In her article "Realism and the Irish Immigrant," Clair Wills notes that 1960s Irish realism was concerned with "both traditional and modern within Irish society."[49] I would add, however, that this concern with traditional and modern extends well beyond 1960s realism and is in fact evidenced in a wide range of literature from and about Ireland from the nineteenth century to the present day and in a variety of literary forms from the gothic to dark comedy.[50] Moreover, what is evidenced in this literature is characteristic of a disrupted realism rather than realism proper: Hunter draws on these conventions and combines realism with a touch of romance, comedy, and a distinctive numinosity that, in another article, Wills notes has long been characteristic of Irish women writers. These elements of the novel are numerous and obviously signal non-realist – maybe even irrealist – tendencies, including an exorcism, the dilapidated and rotting Church of Saint Éinde, a teenager's drug-induced hallucinations, and the slippage between the world of the living and the world of the dead that is particularly evident in Abbey's experience of the ghost of her father, Frank. It is never really clear whether this ghost is just a "feeling" derived from past emotional trauma or whether in the world of the novel, Frank is actually haunting her. The ambiguity is vividly and viscerally brought to life when Abbey is choked by her co-worker Dan, but she suspects Frank is behind the attack (165–7). This episode resonates with Dermot's earlier contention that he "no longer trusts his own delusions [...] 'Real / seems real / entirely fabricated'" (53).[51] What is most striking, however, is how Hunter's novel taps into what Wills refers to as "popular religion and the bonds of the community" evidenced particularly in writing by Irish women.[52]

Wills, in her article "Women Writers and the Death of Rural Ireland," focuses on Maura Laverty and Mary Lavin and there are echoes of their styles across the pages of Hunter's novel. But it is not only the techniques Hunter selects, but how she deploys them that associate her prose writing, whether consciously or not, with writers like Laverty and Lavin in addition to Boland, and therefore with a semiperipheral modernity that insists on a feminist politics, an insistence that is all the more necessary given the continuing mistreatment of women in Ireland. Writing about 1940s Ireland, Wills observes that

> the use of surreal, expressionist, and satirical techniques in the literature of the period may have had less to do with the fact that the realism associated with the novel was not suited to Irish society, as recent critics have argued, than that a moralized "documentary" of rural Irish life was all too well knitted into the state's "neutral-minded" propaganda.[53]

In addition to allusions to Heaney and Boland, Hunter's feminist politics is evident when she brings together the heady mix of pregnancy, death, religion, and community. The most notable instance of this is the episode in which Deirdre McGilloway, temporarily returned from Dublin, where she works, to bury her mother, goes into labour at the wake. The chapter called "The Space Between" in Part II, "Excavations," begins: "The moment Deirdre McGilloway reaches down and touches her dead mother's face, she feels her first serious contraction" (92). The village of Spiddal has attended the wake and so is there to witness Deirdre in the throes of labour lying beside the corpse of her mother:

> [Deirdre] looks over at her dead mother then back at the crowd on either side of the oak dresser, then at a statue of the Madonna on the side table. She goes to put her hand between her leg again, goes to stand up, the mattress lifting up as she comes away from it, her mother's body rolling in the opposite direction. The crowd gasps as the dead woman's lilies tumble loose; her hand still cleaved around a few stalks. Deirdre sits down again [...] The weight makes her mother loll close once more, her head tilting, the right arm coming off her chest and hitting Deirdre in the thigh. Deirdre emits a high-pitched whine. Dermot, thinking it's labour pains, lays the girl down on her back [...] Deirdre is lying next to her mother, Eileen's slightly swollen face tilted towards her daughter, her hand next to Deirdre's hip. The family resemblance is striking. (94)

At a thematic level, echoing work by Laverty and Lavin, births and deaths are recurrent throughout the novel. Here, they are twinned in spectacularly exaggerated, if not slightly inappropriate, terms. The religious imagery – notably the halo made by the lamp light and the statue of the Madonna on the side table – is not accidental. Juxtaposed with Deirdre herself – not an icon, but a real-life woman, pregnant and, significantly, unmarried – this image resonates with a modernity that is inflected by (not opposite to) Catholicism. Moreover, it signifies how tradition is perceived to be aligned with Catholicism, which masks the gendered structural inequality inherent in capitalist modernity as described by Mies, Federici and Wallerstein. Wills's evaluation of Laverty and Lavin is helpful in analyzing this particular passage. She notes that in Laverty's writing, "The clichés, the gossipy tone, the exclamation mark all signal a benevolent, if earthy, story of communal affairs."[54] Similarly, here, the clichés, the gossipy tone and the gasps from the crowd all highlight the communal aspect of both birth and death. The absurdity of the episode is underscored by the description of both bodies lolling and flailing around on the bed, punctuated by the observation that the "family resemblance was striking." The absurdity also operates in an analogous fashion to what Wills describes as Lavin's "causticness." Wills praises Lavin for

> her ability to use the language of sentiment and nostalgia against itself to subtly puncture the alliance between nostalgia and consensus-forming realism common to the popular literature of the period. The result is a series of stories that Frank O'Connor deemed "caustic."[55]

For Wills, it is this causticity that injects Lavin's writing with a powerful social critique, particularly with regard to domestic violence. For Hunter, the caustic social critique is evoked through communal events in the novel – such as the excavation and the wake – which, like Boland's collection *Domestic Violence*, highlight the everyday violence done to women in Ireland.

By putting world-systems and materialist feminist schools of thought into conversation with critical commentary on economic, social and cultural development, this article has suggested not only that Ireland's semiperipheral modernity is structured by inequality and unevenness, but also that this condition is always already gendered. The consequences of such systemic gendered inequality are material – as evidenced by laws and policies – and immaterial – as evidenced by the prescribed role of icon and object in literature and culture more broadly. Hunter's novel addresses these concerns in both its form and content. She draws on the poetic legacies of both Heaney and Boland – reimagining Heaney's body in the bog trope in a way that suggests Boland's feminist politics – in order to articulate the specificity of semiperipheral modernity that indexes progression and retrogression simultaneously. Her semiperipheral aesthetic, like Boland's poetry, expresses a feminist politics that challenges the sexism inherent in the capitalist world-system; a sexism that manifests itself in Irish literary tropes such as the body in the bog or religion and absurdity and is contested in Hunter's novel. Articulated through semiperipheral poetics, therefore, both Boland's poetry and Hunter's novel critique capitalist modernity by reimagining classic tropes in ways that begin to make a credible space for a feminist politics beyond "icons and objects."

Notes

1. Boland, "The Minds and Voices of Modern Irish Women," 7.
2. Ibid.
3. Hunter, *Stay*, 112. Hereafter cited parenthetically.
4. O'Hearn, *Atlantic*, 2001.
5. Kirby, Gibbons, and Cronin, *Reinventing Ireland*, 7.
6. Bunreacht na hÉireann/Constitution of Ireland, 162.
7. See Kennedy, "Irish Women" and Ferriter, "Women and Political Change."
8. Kirby, *Celtic Tiger*.
9. Coakley, *Ireland in the World* (Chapter 4). Coakley goes on to critique Ireland's continued dependency on investment from multinational corporations after 2008, arguing that "subordinating Ireland to North Atlantic capital has hugely increased the country's vulnerability to shocks" (Chapter 4, kindle edition).

10. Kirby, *Celtic Tiger*, 10.
11. Inglis, *Global Ireland*, 47.
12. Ibid., 47.
13. Ibid., 7–9.
14. Ibid.
15. Inglis, *Global Difference*, 7.
16. Wallerstein, *World-Systems*, 12.
17. Coakley, *Ireland in the World*, Chapter 4.
18. Inglis, *Global Difference*, 250.
19. O'Hearn discusses Ireland's current "semiperipherality" in an interview with Beatty, Coakley, and Deckard.
20. Wallerstein, *World-Systems*, 29.
21. Pilkington, "Pitfalls," 538.
22. Cleary, *Outrageous Fortune*, 45.
23. See also Coakley, *Ireland in the World* and O'Hearn, *The Atlantic*.
24. Cleary, *Outrageous Fortune*, 33.
25. Ibid., 34.
26. Ibid., 17.
27. See Barnard and Shapiro, *Pentecostal Modernism*.
28. Mies, *Patriarchy*, 112.
29. Wallerstein, "Ideological Tensions," 350.
30. Ibid.
31. Federici, *Revolution*, 97.
32. See Kennedy, "Irish Women."
33. See Ernst Bloch, *Heritage of Our Times*.
34. Jameson, *Political Unconscious*, 95.
35. Ibid., 81. See also the discussion of "syntime" in De Loughry, "Imagining the World," 140–7.
36. Heaney, "Digging," *Death of a Naturalist*, 3–4.
37. Deckard et al., *Combined and Uneven*, 70.
38. Heaney, "Bog Queen," *North*, 25–27.
39. *Aisling* refers to a genre of vision poems from the seventeenth and eighteenth centuries where Ireland appears in the form of a woman to the dreaming poet.
40. See Gunne and Thompson, "Feminism Without Borders."
41. Boland, *Domestic Violence*, 23. Permission for this and subsequent citations granted by Eavan Boland.
42. See Burns, "Beautiful Labors."
43. Boland, "Wisdom," *Domestic Violence*, 23.
44. A sentiment powerfully stated in her poem "Mise Eire."
45. Boland, "Windfall," *Domestic Violence*, 42, original italics.
46. Deckard et al., *Combined and Uneven*, 72.
47. *Bord na Mona* is the national body responsible for bogs and peat turf.
48. Larsen, *Determinations*, 140.
49. Wills, "Realism and the Irish Immigrant," 374. See Cleary, "Realism after Modernism."
50. From Bram Stoker to Seamus Deane, for example, or from Flann O'Brien to Frank O'Connor, or W.B. Yeats to Boland and Heaney.
51. Deckard et al., *Combined and Uneven*, 101.
52. Wills, "Women Writers and the Death of Rural Ireland," 207.
53. Ibid., 198.
54. Ibid., 211.
55. Ibid., 212.

Disclosure statement

No potential conflict of interest was reported by the author.

Bibliography

Barnard, Philip, and Stephen Shapiro. *About Pentecostal Modernism: Lovecraft, Los Angeles, and World-Systems Culture*. London: Bloomsbury, 2017.

Beatty, Aidan, Maurice Coakley, and Sharae Deckard. "Interview with Denis O'Hearn." *Journal of World-Systems Research* 22, no. 1 (2016): 202–213.

Bloch, Ernst. *Heritage of Our Times*. Translated by Neville Plaice and Stephen Plaice. Cambridge: Polity, 1991.

Boland, Eavan. *Domestic Violence*. New York: W.W. Norton, 2007.

Boland, Eavan. "The Minds and Voices of Modern Irish Women." *Journal of Women's History* 6, no. 4 (1995), 7, no. 1 (Winter/Spring): 6–8.

Bunreacht na hÉireann/Constitution of Ireland. Accessed 6 April 2012. https://www.constitution.ie/Documents/Bhunreacht_na_hEireann_web.pdf.

Burns, Christy. "Beautiful Labors: Lyricism and Feminist Revisions in Eavan Boland's Poetry." *Tulsa Studies in Women's Literature* 20, no. 2 (2001): 217–236.

Cleary, Joe. *Outrageous Fortune: Capital and Culture in Modern Ireland*. Dublin: Field Day, 2007.

Cleary, Joe. "Realism after Modernism and the Literary World-System." *Modern Language Quarterly* 73, no. 3 (2012): 255–268.

Coakley, Maurice. *Ireland in the World Order: A History of Uneven Development*. London: Pluto, 2012. Kindle.

Dalla Costa, Mariarosa, and Giovanna F. Dalla Costa, eds. *Women, Development and Labor of Reproduction: Struggles and Movements*. Asmara, Eritrea: Africa World Press, 1999.

Deckard, Sharae, Benita Parry, Graeme Macdonald, Neil Lazarus, Nicholas Lawrence, Stephen Shapiro, and Upamanyu Pablo Mukherjee. *Combined and Uneven Development: Towards a New Theory of World-Literature*. Liverpool: Liverpool University Press, 2015.

De Loughry, Treasa. "Imagining the World: The Global Novel and Capitalism-in-Crisis." PhD diss., University College Dublin, 2016.

Federici, Silvia. *Revolution at Point Zero: Housework, Reproduction and Feminist Struggle*. Oakland, CA: PM Press, 2012.

Ferriter, Diarmaid. "Women and Political Change in Ireland since 1960." *Éire-Ireland* 43, no. 1&2 (2008): 179–204.

Gunne, Sorcha, and Zoë Brigley Thompson. "Feminism Without Borders: The Potentials and Pitfalls of Re-theorizing Rape." In *Feminism, Literature and Rape Narratives: Violence and Violation*, edited by Sorcha Gunne and Zoë Brigley Thompson, 1–20. New York: Routledge, 2010.

Heaney, Seamus. *Death of a Naturalist*. London: Faber, [1966] 1991.

Heaney, Seamus. *North*. London: Faber, 1975.

Hunter, Aislinn. *Stay*. Vancouver: Raincoast Books, 2002.

Inglis, Tom. *Global Ireland: Same Difference*. New York: Routledge, 2008.

Jameson, Fredric. *The Political Unconscious: Narrative as a Socially Symbolic Act*. Ithaca, NY: Cornell University Press, 1981.

Kennedy, Sineád. "Irish Women and the Celtic Tiger Economy." In *The End of Irish History? Critical Reflections on the Celtic Tiger*, edited by Colin Coulter and Steve Coleman, 95–109. Manchester: Manchester University Press, 2003.

Kirby, Peadar. *The Celtic Tiger in Distress*. Basingstoke: Palgrave Macmillan, 2001.

Kirby, Peadar, Luke Gibbons, and Michael Cronin, eds. *Reinventing Ireland: Culture, Society and the Global Economy*. London: Pluto, 2002.

Larsen, Neil. *Determinations: Essays on Theory, Narrative and Nation in the Americas*. London: Verso, 2001.

Lazarus, Neil. "Cosmopolitanism and the Specificity of the Local in World Literature." *The Journal of Commonwealth Literature* 46, no. 1 (2011): 119–137.

Mies, Maria. *Patriarchy and Accumulation on a World Scale: Women in the International Division of Labour*. London: Zed Books, 2014.

O'Hearn, Denis. *The Atlantic Economy: Britain, the US and Ireland*. Manchester: Manchester University Press, 2001.

Pilkington, Lionel. "The Pitfalls of Theatrical Consciousness." *Kritika Kultura* 21/22 (2013/2014): 533–542.

Wallerstein, Immanuel. "The Ideological Tensions of Capitalism: Universalism Versus Racism and Sexism." In *The Essential Wallerstein*, 344–352. New York: The New Press, 2000.

Wallerstein, Immanuel. *World-Systems Analysis: An Introduction*. Durham, NC: Duke University Press, 2004.

Wills, Clair. "Realism and the Irish Immigrant." *Modern Language Quarterly* 73, no. 3 (2012): 373–394.

Wills, Clair. "Women Writers and the Death of Rural Ireland." *Éire-Ireland* 41, no. 1 (2006): 192–212.

Index

actor-network theory 17
Affect Studies 17
Afro-futurism 14–15
Afrocentrism 59, 60
Alberti, Leon Battista 32
Albritton, Robert 101
Albuquerque, Durval Muniz de 81
Alexander, Michelle 64–65
Almeida, José Américo de 4, 73, 74, 75, 81–86
Amazon (company) 16
Amazon (River) 114
Ambedkar, Bhimrao Ramji 59, 63, 64
"American," definition of 1, 7, 8
American Studies 1–2, 4, 7–8, 9, 11–12, 13–14, 16, 65–66
Anderson, Mark 83
Anson, Peter 130
anthropocentric turn 25
Apple (company) 11
Aptheker, Herbert 63
The Autumn of the Patriarch (García Márquez) 112–115, 116, 118, 121

Bacigalupi, Paolo 121, 122–123
Bacon, Francis 31
Bakhtin, Mikhail 128, 129, 130–131
Ball, Charles 40, 41
Bandung 54, 55
Bangladesh 56
Barbados Code of 1661 41
Baring crisis of 1890 78
Barnard, Philip 15
Barrett, Ross 14
Baucom, Ian 79
Bauman, Zygmunt 75
Beckert, Sven 14
Behaim, Martin 23
belle époque (1896–1914) 75, 85
Bender, Thomas 21, 24
Bengal 55, 56
Bessarion, Cardinal 23
Best, Stephen 17
biocapital 117
Birmingham School of Cultural Studies 15, 54
Black Reconstruction (Du Bois) 54, 65

blood economy in Henan province 116–117, 118
Bloom, Dan 121
Blyden, Edward Wilmot 60
Boast, Hannah 112
Boelhower, William 4, 21–37
"Bog Poems" (Heaney) 149, 151
Boggs, Colleen G. 3
Boland, Eavan 4, 142–143, 147, 148–150, 152, 153, 154
Border Studies 14
Bould, Mark 14
Brantlinger, Patrick 76
Brazil 32, 73, 75, 81–86
The Brief Wondrous Life of Oscar Wao (Díaz) 91, 102, 103
Brown, John 4, 38–53
Brown, Lester 110
Buck-Morss, Susan 12
Buell, Lawrence 7

Cabot, Sebastian 26, 30, 32
Cabral, Pedro Álvares 22, 28
Cacho, Lisa Marie 14
Cadamosto, Alvise 27–28
Campanella, Tommaso 31
Canavan, Gerry 14
cannibalism 97, 103
Capital (Marx) 13, 18, 148
capitalism 10, 12–13, 15–16, 17, 72–73, 74–76, 80, 111, 126, 127, 144–145, 147; capitalist modernity 4–5, 73, 95–96, 142–153; and early modern travel 26, 28–29, 32; in Ireland 4–5, 142–154; *longue durée* of 90, 101, 103, 144, 145, 146–147; monopoly capitalism 92, 93, 94, 95–96; nautical 14; and racism/imperialism 59, 60, 111, 127, 147; and sexism 99, 147–148, 154; and slavery 12, 50–51; and waste 119, 120; and water supplies 108, 110, 111, 112, 114, 115; *see also* finance capital; fishing industry; sugar industry
Carboni, Stefani 22
Cartier, Jacques 26
caste and race 54–68
Catholicism 144, 145, 146, 148, 153

Celtic Tiger 4–5, 142–154
Cervantes, Miguel de 103
Chamerovzow, Louis 42, 47
Chaplin, Joyce 26
Chatterjee, Partha 57
China 4, 11, 14, 23, 27, 57, 63, 108; and
    hydroculture 111, 114–122
Chinatown (film) 113
Cleary, Joe 145, 146–147
climate change 108, 117, 121
Clover, Joshua 74, 81
Coakley, Maurice. 144, 145
Coca-Cola 11
Cold War 9, 11, 98, 101–102
colonialism 2, 58, 64, 96, 99, 113;
    hydrocolonialism 110, 113; *see also* cores;
    peripheries
Columbus, Christopher 23, 28, 29, 30, 31, 32, 93
combined and uneven development 3, 7–18, 92
Combined and Uneven Development (WReC) 1
commodities: commodity chain history 14;
    commodity fetishism 92, 111, 112, 131–132,
    144; commodity frontiers 3, 4, 14, 73, 74,
    75, 81, 85, 86, 113, 132; and early modern
    travel 27, 28, 29; *see also* hydroculture; sugar
    industry
communism 8–9, 60, 101, 102
Comparative Literature (Comp. Lit) 8–9, 21
conspicuous consumption 76
Contarini, Gasparo 31, 32
cores 11, 13, 16, 17, 24, 146; and water supplies
    108, 114–115, 121; and world-food-system
    90–91, 92, 94, 96; *see also* peripheries
Cosmographia (*Geography*) (Ptolemy) 24, 25, 28
cotton 14, 38, 39, 40, 49–50, 81
Cox, Oliver Cromwell 65
The Crisis: A Record of Darker Races (NAACP)
    54, 56
Cronin, Michael 143, 144
Crummell, Alexander 60
Crusoe, Robinson 95–96
The Cultural Front (Denning) 7–8
*The Culture and Commerce of the Early American
    Novel* (Shapiro) 15, 16
Cushman, Gregory 14

da Gama, Vasco 24
Dalits in India 59, 60, 63, 64, 66
Dark Princess (Tagore) 54, 55, 57, 59
The Dark Road (Jian) 116, 119–121
Davies, Martin 23
Davis, Mark 85
Dawn Institute (Canada) 39, 40, 48–49
de Taunay, Alfonso 86
Deckard, Sharae 4, 14, 108–125, 126
Defoe, Daniel 95–96
Delle Navigationi et Viaggi project (Ramusio) 25,
    26, 27–28, 29, 32
Denning, Michael 1, 4, 7–8, 75, 76

Díaz, Junot 4, 91, 98–103
Digital Humanities 17–18
Dillon, Elizabeth Maddock 12
Domestic Violence (Boland) 149, 154
Dominican Republic 4, 90–107
Dorfman, Ariel 11
Douglass, Frederick 40, 41, 43, 48, 49
Dream of Ding Village (Lianke) 116, 117–118,
    119, 120, 121
Drexler, Michael J. 4, 12, 38–53
Du Bois, W. E. B. 4, 54–68

e-waste 119–121
Egypt 22, 58, 60
Eliot, T. S. 8
Ellison, Fred 85
Ellison, Ralph 64
enclosure: of common wastes 76; of water
    commons 111, 112–114
English Literature Studies (Eng. Lit.) 8, 9
Enriquillo (Galván) 91, 94, 102
Erasmus of Rotterdam 23, 27, 30, 31
exceptionalism 1–2, 4, 7, 9–11, 12, 55, 57, 64–66

The Family of Man (exhibition) 11
Federici, Silvia 148, 153
feminism 4–5, 142–157
Ferraro, Joanne 22
Fiering, Norman 12
finance capital 4, 72–89, 109, 113
financialization 10, 74, 75, 78, 81, 86, 108–109,
    115
fishing industry 4, 126–141
fossil fuels 92, 97–98, 109, 111–112, 121, 126–
    127; *see also* oil
Fracastoro, Girolamo 28
Freyre, Gilberto 82
fukú americanus 100

Galván, Manuel de Jesús 91, 94
Gandhi, Mahatma 59, 60, 63
García Márquez, Gabriel 112–113
Gastaldi, Giacomo 25, 28
Geggus, David 12
gender 100; in Ireland 4–5, 142–157; and North
    Atlantic fisheries 126–139
geography, early modern 23, 24–25, 28
Georgia 4, 38–52
Ghose, Aurobindo 63
Gibbon, Dave 102
Gibbons, Luke 143, 144
Gidwani, Vinay 75, 76
"gig" economy 16
Gilmore, Ruth 14
Gilroy, Paul 9
Glasgow, John 42–43, 48, 49
globalization 3, 14, 21, 24, 25, 26, 29, 75, 91; and
    Ireland 143, 144–146, 147
Globes (Sloterdijk) 26

globus 24–27, 30
Godden, Richard 80, 81, 84
Godechot, Jacques Leon 9, 12
Google 16
Gora (Tagore) 55, 57
Goyal, Yogita 3–4, 54–71
Gramsci, Antonio 9
Grant, Madison 60
Grocyn, William 23
Guandong province 119
Guiyu Special Economic Zone 119
Gunn, Geoffrey 21
Gunn, Neil 127, 128, 129, 130, 131, 132, 134, 136, 137
Gunne, Sorcha 1–6, 142–157

Haiti: Haitian revolution 12, 13; labourers in Dominican sugar industry 93, 94–95, 97
Hakluyt, Richard 32, 33
Hall, Stuart 15
Hardy, Thomas 4, 73, 74, 76–81
Harvey, David 14
Heaney, Seamus 143, 148–149, 150, 151, 153
Heidegger, Martin 24–25, 26
Henan province 116, 117
Henson, Josiah 38–39, 40, 41, 48–49
Higgins, Richard 76
Hinduism 62, 63–64
The Home and the World (Tagore) 55, 57
Horn, Maja 100
Huber, Matthew 14, 135
Huckleberry Finn (Twain) 8, 44
humanism 23, 24, 25, 26, 28, 29, 31, 56, 57, 63–64
Humboldt, Alexander von 10
Hunter, Aislinn 4, 142, 143, 150–153, 154
hybridity 13
hydroculture 4, 108–125

imperialism 54, 59, 60, 75, 81, 90, 94, 97, 99, 101–102, 103, 111, 131, 132, 134; and the fishing industry 127–128, 129–130, 132; and the sugar industry 90, 92, 94, 95–96, 101–102; *see also* cores; peripheries
India 4, 10, 28, 39, 54–68, 126–127
Indian Ocean 21, 22, 24, 28, 29
inequality 13, 17–18, 59, 65, 130, 144–145, 147, 153, 154
Inglis, Tom 144, 145, 146
internal colony thesis 58
internationalism 9, 11, 56, 57, 66
Ireland 4–5, 142–157
irrealism 3, 4, 91, 92–93, 94–98, 99, 102, 113, 116, 120, 128, 152
Italy 8, 21–33
Itäranta, Emmi 121, 122, 123
Ivakhiv, Adrian 127, 128

Jameson, Fredric 2, 14, 16, 55, 148
Japan 11, 57, 59, 63, 101
Jay, Paul 3
Jiagong, Chen 114–116
Jian, Ma 116, 119–121

Kaisary, Philip 12
Kaufman, Fredrick 109
Kelmscott Press 76
King, Anthony 15
Kinsella, Thomas 150
Kirby, Peadar 143, 144, 145
Knox, John 132
Kouru (French Guiana) 32
Kuhn, Thomas 16

La Rocque, Lance 84
labour 4, 11, 14, 54, 61, 72–89; *see also* slavery
Las Casas, Bartolomé de 27, 32
Latin America 4, 31–32, 81, 111, 112–113, 114–115; *see also individual countries*
Laverty, Maura 153–154
Lavin, Mary 153–154
Lazarus, Neil 1–6, 7–20
Le Menager, Stephanie 14
Li Bai 119, 120
Li, Minqi 108, 110
Lianke, Yan 116
Liberia 63
Linacre, Thomas 23
Luis, Washington 85

Macdonald, Graeme 109
Mad Max: Fury Road 121
Magellan, Ferdinand 23, 26, 29, 31
Mahler, Anne Garland 102
Malthus, Thomas Robert 110, 119
Manutius, Aldus 23, 24
maps 23, 24, 25, 27, 28; *see also globus; mundus*
Marcus, Sharon 17
Marrero Aristy, Ramón 91, 94–98
Marx, Leo 8
Marxism/Karl Marx 8–9, 11, 12–13, 17, 40, 58, 59–60, 72, 73, 76, 93, 111, 129, 145–148
Marzo Magno, Alessandro 23
matrifocalism 127, 128, 129–131
Mattelart, Armand 142–154
McNally, David 72
Medici, Lorenzo di Pierfrancesco de 31–32
Memory of Water (Itäranta) 121, 122, 123
microhistorical approach 4, 21–37
Mies, Maria 147, 153
Miéville, China 14
Mintz, Sidney 92
Mir, Pedro 93
monopoly capitalism 92, 93, 94, 95–96
Monroe Doctrine 14
Montaigne, Michel de 103

Montalboddo, Fracanzio da 25, 26, 27, 28, 31, 32
Moore, Jason W. 14, 73, 74, 92, 102, 110, 111, 114, 128
More, Thomas 27, 31, 32
Moretti, Franco 16
Morris, Aldon 54
Morris, William 76
Morrissey, Donna 127, 128, 129, 131, 136, 137
Moses, Wilson 59
Mullen, Bill 60
mundus 24–27, 29
Mundus Novus (Vespucci) 27, 32
Myrdal, Gunnar 65
"myth and symbol" school of literary criticism 16–17

nation-states 2, 7, 9, 11
nationalism 9, 56, 57, 58, 59, 63, 66, 94, 95
naufragium genre 4, 21, 25, 26, 29–31
The Negro (Du Bois) 54, 63–64
neoliberalism 10, 18, 55, 102, 103; and the fishing industry 127, 136, 137; and hydroculture 4, 108–125; in Ireland 143, 144
network theory 17–18
Niblett, Michael 4, 14, 72–89, 112, 113, 126, 130
Nietzsche, Friedrich 76
Nigeria 127
Nixon, Rob 136
Northup, Solomon 41
"Number Nine Winch Alley" (Jiagong) 114–116
Nuñez Cabeza de Vaca, Alvar 30, 31
Nussbaum, Martha 57

O'Connor, Frank 154
Ogallala aquifer 113
O'Hearn, Denis 143, 145
oil 4, 14, 74–75, 90, 109–110, 112, 126–127, 128, 131, 134, 135–137
Oloff, Kerstin 4, 14, 90–107
"On the Western Circuit" (Hardy) 4, 73
Osterhammel, Jürgen 14
Over (Marrero Aristy) 91, 94–98, 99, 100
Oviedo, Gonzalo Fernández de 26, 30

Palmer, R. R. 9, 12
Park, Robert 65
Pasqualigo, Pietro 22
pastoralism 120, 127, 128, 129, 130–131, 134
Patel, Raj 90
patriarchy 32, 82, 83, 95, 96, 98, 99, 119, 128, 131, 147
Patterson, Anita 3
Paye, Michael 4
Pearce, Fred 108
Pentecostal Modernism: Lovecraft, Los Angeles, and World-Systems Culture (Shapiro and Barnard) 15
periodization 4, 8

peripheries 11, 13, 15, 16, 17, 21, 29, 113, 134, 144, 146; in Brazil 73, 75, 86; and water supplies 111, 114; and world-food-system 90, 91, 94, 96, 97, 101, 132; *see also* cores; semi-peripheries
petroculture 14, 111–112; *see also* fossil fuels
Pigafetta, Antonio 23, 24, 26, 29, 30, 31
Pilkington, Lionel 146
Plotz, John 78
Polanski, Roman 113
Polo, Marco 23, 27
Pordenone, Odorico da 27
Portuguese exploration 21, 22, 24, 27–28, 31, 32
Posnock, Ross 57
Postone, Moishe 80
printing 22–24, 27, 32
prison abolitionism 12, 13–14
Priuli, Girolamo 22
Ptolemy 24, 25, 28
Purchas, Samuel 31

Quantum of Solace (James Bond film) 112
Quesnay, François 17
Quiroga, Vasco de 27, 32

racism 99, 128, 147; and sugar industry in Dominican Republic 94, 95, 96, 97; in the USA 8, 54–68
Ram, Harsha 2–3
Ramusio, Giovanni Giambattista 25, 26, 27, 28, 29, 30–31, 32, 33
Reséndez, Andrés 14
Robinson, Kim Stanley 14
Robinson, Mary 143
Rogin, Michael Paul 9
Ruskin, John 22, 76
Russia 58, 59; *see also* Soviet Union

Said, Edward 22
Sandor, Richard 109
Sansovino, Francesco 27, 31
Scherer, Stephanie 4, 38–53
semi-peripheries 3, 16, 17, 24, 73, 111, 142–157
Serrata, Médar 95
sexism 99, 100, 147, 154; *see also* gender; patriarchy
Shakespeare, William 103
Shapiro, Stephen 4, 5n2, 7–20
Sherman Antitrust Act (1890) 92
shipwrecks 25, 27, 28–29, 30, 33; *see also* naufragium genre
Shiva, Vandana 111, 122
Silicon Valley 16
The Silver Darlings (Gunn) 4, 127–130, 131, 132–134, 136, 137
silver mining 4, 126–128, 131
Sinha, Manisha 12
Slave Life in Georgia (Brown) 4, 38–53

162   INDEX

slavery 4, 8, 12, 13–14, 18, 38–53, 61, 62, 63, 65, 66, 91–92, 97, 100, 101–102
Sloterdijk, Peter 26
Smith, Neil 14
"soft power" 11
Sommer, Doris. 96
Sony 11
The Souls of Black Folk (Du Bois) 54, 55–56, 57
Soviet Union 8, 9; *see also* Russia
Spanish exploration 21, 22, 24, 26, 29, 31, 32, 103
"spheropoiesis" 26, 28
Spillers, Hortense J. 45
spiragmatic approach 16
Stay (Hunter) 142, 150–153
Stephen, Edward 11
Steven, Craig 12
Stoddard, Lothrop 60
Stowe, Harriet Beecher 38, 39–40, 41, 46, 48, 49
sugar industry 4, 73, 75, 81–86, 90–103
surplus-value 76, 84–85, 97, 120
Sylvanus Now (Morrissey) 4, 127, 128, 130–131, 134–136, 137
Szasz, Thomas 17

Tagore, Rabindranath 4, 54–68
Taussig, Michael 132
Tess of the D'Urbervilles (Hardy) 77
Third Worldism 54, 66
Three Gorges Dam 120
Tibet 111
Tobin, Brian 137
translation 11, 21, 23–24, 66
transnationalism 3–4, 54–68
Trash (Almeida) 4, 73, 75, 81–86
travel collections 4, 21–33
Trotsky, Leon 15, 17
Trujillo, Rafael Leónidas 93, 95, 98, 100–101
Truth Stranger than Fiction: Father Henson's Story of His Own Life (Henson) 39–40, 41
Twain, Mark 8, 44
The Twilight Zone (American TV series) 101

Uncle Tom's Cabin (Stowe) 39–40, 41, 46–47
United Nations 64
universalism 10, 28, 50, 55, 56–57, 58, 147
university system 10; and slavery 12, 13
Utopia (More) 31, 32
utopia, the 4, 21, 25–26, 27, 31–33

Vaca, Cabeza de 30–31
Vargas, Getúlio 83
Veblen, Thorstein 76, 78
Venice 21–33

Vespucci, Amerigo 24, 27, 28, 30, 31–32
Victoria, Queen of England 39, 40
Vivekananda, Swami 63

Waldseemüller, Martin 32
Wallerstein, Immanuel 2, 3, 9, 15, 16, 24, 146, 147–148, 153
Warwick Research Collective (WReC) 1, 7, 73, 91, 92, 103, 149
Washington, Booker T. 60–61
Wasserman, Renata 86
waste 4, 72–89, 96, 119–121
Watchmen (DC comic series) 102
water 4, 108–125
Watson, Cathryn 60
Weber, Max 10
Weinstein, Donald 22
Well, H. G. 76
Wenzel, Jennifer 127
West Indies 49, 50, 58, 93, 94–95
white supremacy 40, 56, 58, 99
Whyte, Christopher 133
Williams, Raymond 10, 15, 16, 17, 18
Wills, Clair 152–154
"Windfall" (Boland) 150, 151
"Wisdom" (Boland) 149, 151
Wolff, Janet 15, 16
Womack, Ytasha 14–15
Wong, Edlie 42
Woodward, C. Vann 65
Worden, Daniel 14
The World and Africa (Du Bois) 54, 59
world-ecology 3, 4, 72–89, 91, 92, 99, 102, 109, 111, 112, 122, 126–128, 131–137
world-food-system 4, 90–107
world literature 1, 4, 11, 17–18, 57, 73, 90–107, 126; and hydroculture 111–112; microhistorical approach to 21–37
world-systems approaches 1–3, 9, 12–13, 14, 15–16, 17, 21, 73, 92, 126; and Ireland 4–5, 143, 146–147, 154
Wyile, Herb 131
Wyndham, John 98
Wynter, Sylvia 92–93

Xiaoping, Deng 115

Yangtze River 116, 119–120
Yates, Michelle 75
Yeats, William Butler 56, 149
Yellow River (China) 116, 117, 118, 119
Yue, Pan 116

zombie-ism 97, 101